My Samsung
Galaxy Tab™

Eric Butow
Lonzell Watson

800 East 96th Street,
Indianapolis, Indiana 46240 USA

My Samsung Galaxy Tab™

Copyright © 2012 by Pearson Education, Inc.

ISBN-13: 978-0-7897-4797-6
ISBN-10: 0-7897-4797-9

Library of Congress Cataloging-in-Publication data is on file.

Printed in the United States of America

First Printing: December 2011

Trademarks

All terms mentioned in this book that are known to be trademarks or service marks have been appropriately capitalized. Que Publishing cannot attest to the accuracy of this information. Use of a term in this book should not be regarded as affecting the validity of any trademark or service mark.

Warning and Disclaimer

Every effort has been made to make this book as complete and as accurate as possible, but no warranty or fitness is implied. The information provided is on an "as is" basis. The authors and the publisher shall have neither liability nor responsibility to any person or entity with respect to any loss or damages arising from the information contained in this book.

Bulk Sales

Que Publishing offers excellent discounts on this book when ordered in quantity for bulk purchases or special sales. For more information, please contact

U.S. Corporate and Government Sales

1-800-382-3419

corpsales@pearsontechgroup.com

For sales outside the United States, please contact

International Sales

international@pearson.com

EDITOR-IN-CHIEF
Greg Wiegand

ACQUISITIONS EDITOR
Michelle Newcomb

DEVELOPMENT EDITOR
TheWordsmithery, LLC

MANAGING EDITOR
Sandra Schroeder

SENIOR PROJECT EDITOR
Tonya Simpson

COPY EDITOR
Barbara Hacha

INDEXER
Lisa Stumpf

PROOFREADER
Sheri Cain

TECHNICAL EDITOR
Christian Kenyeres

PUBLISHING COORDINATOR
Cindy Teeters

BOOK DESIGNER
Anne Jones

COMPOSITOR
Bronkella Publishing

Contents at a Glance

Table of Contents

About the Authors

Eric Butow began writing books in 2000 when he wrote *Master Visually Windows 2000 Server*. Since then, Eric has authored or coauthored 15 other books. Those books include several chapters in Que Publishing's *Microsoft Windows 7 In Depth*, Addison-Wesley's *User Interface Design for Mere Mortals*, Amacom's *How to Succeed in Business Using LinkedIn*, and, most recently, Que Publishing's *Blogging to Drive Business*.

Eric lives in Jackson, California. He has a master's degree in communication from California State University, Fresno, and is the owner of Butow Communications Group (BCG), a web design, online marketing, and technical writing firm.

Website: http://butow.net

LinkedIn: http://linkedin.com/in/ebutow

Lonzell Watson is the award-winning author of *Teach Yourself Visually iPad*, for which he won an international award of excellence, the honor of Distinguished Technical Communication and Best of Show 2010 from the Society for Technical Communication. He was also presented the Award of Excellence for *Teach Yourself Visually iPhoto '09* in 2009. He is the author of other popular titles, including *Canon VIXIA HD Digital Field Guide*, *Final Cut Pro 6 for Digital Video Editors Only*, and *Teach Yourself Visually Digital Video*.

Lonzell is an adjunct professor in the College of Business at Bellevue University, and he is a freelance technical writer and instructional designer whose courseware has been used to train the CIA, FBI, NASA, and all branches of the U.S. Armed Forces. He is a frequent contributor to StudioMonthly.com and is a syndicated writer with hundreds of published tutorials and tips that help demystify consumer electronics and Apple software. He holds a master's degree in instructional design and development and is the owner of Creative Intelligence, LLC, an instructional design and technical writing company.

Website: http://creativeintel.com

LinkedIn: http://www.linkedin.com/pub/lonzell-watson/6/b64/499

Dedication

To Tony Barcellos and Gene Weisskopf, two of my fellow authors and friends who keep inspiring me to write.
—Eric Butow

To Evelyn Wenzel, to whom I am forever grateful. Thank you for everything.
—Lonzell Watson

Acknowledgments

Eric Butow: My thanks as always to my family and friends. I want to thank my awesome literary agent, Carole Jelen, as well as Cindy Teeters, Greg Wiegand, and especially Michelle Newcomb. Finally, I want to thank my coauthor, Lonzell Watson, for his work on this book.

Lonzell Watson: I would like to give special thanks to Michelle Newcomb, without whom this project would not have been possible. I would like to thank my amazing agent, Carole Jelen, for all of her hard work and insight. Special thanks go to Laura Clor, to my lovely wife, Robyn, to Shannon Johnson, and Danya and Sean Platt. Finally, I want to thank my coauthor, Eric Butow, for all his hard work on this project.

We Want to Hear from You!

As the reader of this book, *you* are our most important critic and commentator. We value your opinion and want to know what we're doing right, what we could do better, what areas you'd like to see us publish in, and any other words of wisdom you're willing to pass our way.

As an editor-in-chief for Que Publishing, I welcome your comments. You can email or write me directly to let me know what you did or didn't like about this book—as well as what we can do to make our books better.

Please note that I cannot help you with technical problems related to the topic of this book. We do have a User Services group, however, where I will forward specific technical questions related to the book.

When you write, please be sure to include this book's title and author as well as your name, email address, and phone number. I will carefully review your comments and share them with the author and editors who worked on the book.

Email: feedback@quepublishing.com

Mail: Greg Wiegand
         Editor-in-Chief
         Que Publishing
         800 East 96th Street
         Indianapolis, IN 46240 USA

Reader Services

Visit our website and register this book at quepublishing.com/register for convenient access to any updates, downloads, or errata that might be available for this book.

Take a tour of the physical buttons and switches on your Galaxy Tab.

Familiarize yourself with what the four touch buttons on the front of the Galaxy Tab 7.0 do.

• See the differences between the Galaxy Tab 7.0 and the Galaxy Tab 10.1.

• View three important screens on your Galaxy Tab, including the home screen.

• Understand how to manipulate the screen.

• Learn how to interact with Android.

In this chapter, you learn about the different hardware and the common screens on both models of the Galaxy Tab.

→ Features on the Front, Back, and Sides of the Unit
→ Galaxy Tab Touch Buttons for Manipulating the Screen
→ Three Important Screens You Need to Know
→ How to Manipulate the Galaxy Tab Screen
→ How to Interact with Android

Meeting the Samsung Galaxy Tab

This book covers two models of the Galaxy Tab: the original Tab with a 7" screen and a larger version with a 10" screen.

The 7" unit, called the Galaxy Tab 7.0, runs version 2.2 of Google's Android operating system, also called Froyo.

The 10" unit, called the Galaxy Tab 10.1, runs Android version 3.1, which is also called Honeycomb.

One other crucial difference is that the Tab 7.0 connects through Wi-Fi or through a number of cell phone carriers; the Tab 10.1 connects through Wi-Fi or Verizon Wireless.

Many tasks throughout the book include information about both models. The headers for each section (or subsection) indicate in parentheses the model name and/or operating system, such as (Galaxy Tab 10") or (Android 2.2, Froyo). If you don't see an area in parentheses in the section (or subsection) name, the information applies to both models.

What About Other Galaxy Tab Models?

As we were finishing this book, Samsung had just released its "in-between" model, the Galaxy Tab 8.9. This unit has an 8.9" screen and runs Honeycomb. What's more, Samsung also announced the Galaxy Tab 7.0 Plus; this model not only has improved hardware over the original Tab 7.0 but also runs Honeycomb. Because these two new models run Honeycomb just as the Tab 10.1 does, you can still refer to the Tab 10.1 sections and instructions to learn how to use the Tab 8.9 and 7.0 Plus. (And if you've heard about the Galaxy Tab 7.7, at the time this book was published, Samsung had a web page with information but no pending release date, so we don't cover the Tab 7.7 in this book.)

Investigating the Galaxy Tab Unit

Before you work with your Galaxy Tab, it's important to take it out of the box and examine it so you can learn where all the controls and features are on the unit. If you've used (or tried) another tablet computer in the past, you might already be familiar with some of the features. If this is your first time using a tablet computer or the Galaxy Tab, though, take time to read this chapter and enjoy learning about your new Tab.

Physical Features of the Galaxy Tab 7"

The Front of the Unit

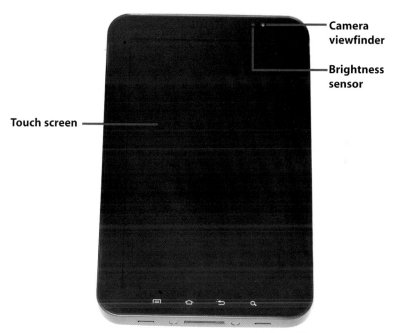

Camera
viewfinder

Brightness
sensor

Touch screen

©Eric Scott Miller

The front of the Galaxy Tab 7" includes the LCD touch screen for viewing information as well as a brightness sensor and a camera so you can take photos and/or record video of yourself.

You learn more about using the cameras to record video in Chapter 7, "Playing Music and Video," and to take photos in Chapter 9, "Capturing and Managing Photos."

The Back of the Unit

The back of the unit has only one feature: a second camera that includes a flash so you can take photos and record video using your Galaxy Tab. (Otherwise, the function of the back is to rest in your hand, of course.)

The Sides of the Unit

Aside from buttons and switches that are covered in the next section, the Galaxy Tab 7" contains a number of features on the sides of the unit.

Microphone

©Eric Scott Miller

- A microphone on the left side of the unit, which is useful for making phone calls and recording audio.

MicroSD memory card slot   *©Eric Scott Miller*

- A MicroSD memory card slot on the right side of the unit.

- A Subscriber Identity Module (SIM) card may also be on the right side of the unit next to the card slot if you purchased a data plan from the carrier when you got your Galaxy Tab. The SIM card identifies you as a unique mobile phone subscriber.

Speakers

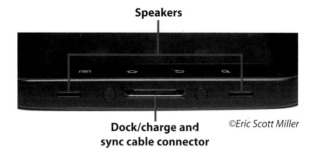

Dock/charge and   *©Eric Scott Miller*
sync cable connector

- The audio speakers on the bottom side of the unit.

- A dock/charge and sync cable connector that is also on the bottom side of the unit. You learn more about docking, charging, and syncing your Galaxy Tab in Chapter 2, "Becoming Familiar with Android."

Headphone/
microphone
©Eric Scott Miller **jack**

- A headphone and microphone jack on the top side of the unit so you can either listen to audio privately or record audio into a microphone.

Physical Features of the Galaxy Tab 10"

The Front of the Unit

Camera viewfinder

Touchscreen

The front of the Galaxy Tab 10"includes the LCD touchscreen for viewing information and a camera so you can take photos or record video of yourself.

You learn more about using the cameras to record video in Chapter 7, "Playing Music and Video," and to take photos in Chapter 9,"Capturing and Managing Photos."

The Back of the Unit

The back of the unit has only one feature: a second camera that includes a flash so you can take photos and record video using your Galaxy Tab.

The Sides of the Unit

Aside from buttons and switches that we discuss in the next section, the Galaxy Tab 10" contains a number of features on the sides of the unit.

Headphone/microphone jack

- A headphone and microphone jack on the top side of the unit so you can either listen to audio privately or record audio into a microphone.

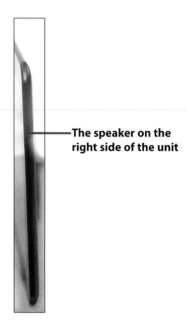

The speaker on the right side of the unit

- The audio speakers on the left and right sides of the unit.

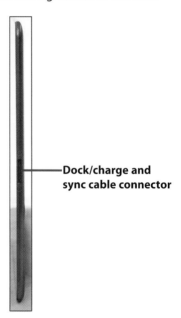

Dock/charge and sync cable connector

- A dock/charge and sync cable connector that is on the bottom side of the unit. You learn more about docking, charging, and syncing your Galaxy Tab in Chapter 2, "Becoming Familiar with Android."

The Galaxy Tab Buttons and Switches

The Galaxy Tab 7" features four touch buttons on the front of the unit below the touch screen and a power button and volume slider on the right side of the unit.

Where Are the Touch Buttons on the Galaxy Tab 10"?

There are no touch buttons on the front of the unit on the Galaxy Tab 10" (or on the Tab 8.9) because in Honeycomb, that functionality is included on the screen. You learn more about Honeycomb screen features later in this chapter.

The Four Galaxy Tab 7" Touch Buttons

There are four touch buttons on the Galaxy Tab 7" that you use frequently to manage the device and applications on it. They are (from left to right) Menu, Home, Back, and Search.

©Eric Scott Miller

Menu   Home   Back   Search

- **Home**—The Home button is the most important button because it's the button you touch to get out of a specific application, such as the Galaxy Tab web browser, and move back to the home screen so you can open another application.

  If you want to hide an application and go back to the home screen, pressing the Home button is the way to go. Pressing the Home button hides the application you currently have open.

Waiter, There's a Home Button on My Apps Screen

When you view all your applications in the apps page, you might notice there's a large Home icon at the bottom of the touchscreen. You can press this icon instead of the Home button if you prefer.

Menu area

- **Menu**—The menu button opens the Menu area at the bottom of the screen so you can access Galaxy Tab and Android operating system options and settings. You learn more about options and settings in Chapter 2, "Becoming Familiar with Android," and Chapter 3, "Customizing Android to Your Liking."

- **Back**—The Back button moves you back to the previous screen. For example, if you're on the home screen and touch the Menu button, you might decide that you don't want to change settings. Close the menu area at the bottom of the screen and go back to the home screen by pressing the Back button.

Google box

Keyboard

- **Search**—The Search button makes it easy for you to search the Web. Just click the button to open the search screen. The Google box appears at the top of the screen and the keyboard appears at the bottom of the screen so you can type in the search terms into the box. You learn more about using the onscreen keyboard in Chapter 2.

The Power Button

The power button performs a number of important functions on your Galaxy Tab.

©Eric Scott Miller

Power button on the
Galaxy Tab 7"

Power button on the Galaxy Tab 10"

- Turns on the unit when you press the button. The power button is on the right side of the Galaxy 7" unit and on the top of the Galaxy Tab 10" unit. The Galaxy Tab boots up and is ready for you to use in about 20 seconds.

- Turns off the unit when you press the button for about 10 seconds.

- If you press and hold the button for a few seconds while the unit is on, the Galaxy Tab automatically goes into sleep mode and locks the device.

- When the unit is in sleep mode, press the power button and hold it for a few seconds to wake up the Galaxy Tab.

What Happens if I Don't Turn Off the Galaxy Tab?

If the Galaxy Tab is idle for a long period of time, the unit goes into sleep mode automatically. Sleep mode drains very little battery power, so if the Galaxy Tab is frequently in sleep mode, you won't need to recharge your battery as often. Refer to Chapter 14, "Troubleshooting Your Galaxy Tab," for information about expected battery life and strategies for extending that lifespan.

Volume Control Buttons

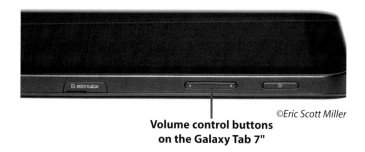

©Eric Scott Miller

**Volume control buttons
on the Galaxy Tab 7"**

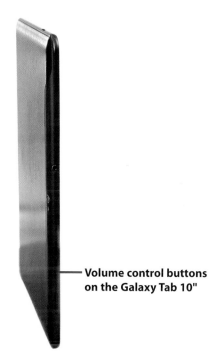

**Volume control buttons
on the Galaxy Tab 10"**

There are two volume control buttons on the device—one that turns the volume up and one that turns the volume down. What device the buttons control depends on what you have connected to the Galaxy Tab.

If you're listening to audio through the Galaxy Tab speakers, the unit remembers the volume settings for the external speakers and sets the volume accordingly. If you decide to connect headphones to the unit, the Galaxy Tab adjusts to the headphone volume the unit has in memory. When you remove the headphones, the unit readjusts the volume to the speaker volume.

You might want to check your volume settings for your headphones and external speakers so you don't get any nasty surprises. You learn more about setting the volume in Chapter 3.

Galaxy Tab Screens

There are three important screens that are mainstays of your Galaxy Tab experience no matter which Galaxy Tab model you use.

The Lock Screen (Galaxy Tab 7")

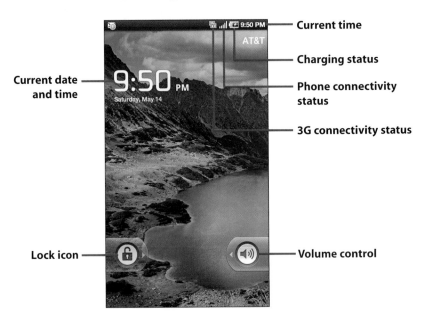

Current time

Charging status

Phone connectivity status

Current date and time

3G connectivity status

Lock icon

Volume control

The lock screen is the default state of the Galaxy Tab when it first boots.

The lock screen shows the black status bar at the top of the screen, the current date and time, and the Lock icon. The status bar keeps you apprised of what's happening with your Galaxy Tab at a glance.

More About the Status Bar

You can expand the status bar downward by pressing your finger on the bar and dragging it downward. You see the status bar window overtake the rest of the screen and show you the current date at the top of the bar. You also see any Android notifications and/or any navigation options available for a specific screen. You can close the window by pressing your finger on the scrollbar at the bottom of the window and moving it up to the top of the window.

Clicking the lock icon either prompts you for a password or, if you don't have a password, opens to the home screen or the application you were working on before you put the unit to sleep. You learn more about password protecting your Galaxy Tab in Chapter 3.

The Lock Screen (Galaxy Tab 10")

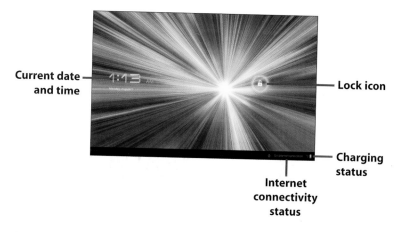

Current date and time

Lock icon

Charging status

Internet connectivity status

The lock screen is the default state of the Galaxy Tab when it first boots.

The lock screen shows the current date and time, the current status of your Bluetooth and Internet connections, the amount of charge you have in your battery, and the Lock icon if you don't have a password. The black status bar at the bottom of the screen keeps you apprised of what's happening with your Galaxy Tab at a glance. You can slide the Lock icon in any direction to open the applications screen.

If your Galaxy Tab is password protected, the password box appears in place of the Lock icon. You must tap the password box, type your password, and then tap the OK button to open the home screen or the application you were working on before you put the unit to sleep. You learn more about password-protecting your Galaxy Tab in Chapter 3.

The Applications Screen (Galaxy Tab 7")

**The Applications icon on the
home screen**

The applications screen is your command center where you can access all the applications available on the Galaxy Tab. Tap the Applications icon at the bottom of the home screen to view the applications screen.

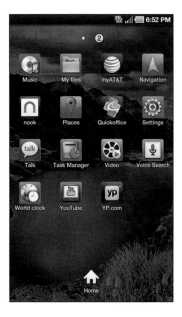

When you tap an application icon, the application launches. If you have more than one page of application icons on the applications screen, dots appear on either side of the menu buttons at the bottom of the screen. You can scroll between pages by clicking one of the buttons or dragging or flicking left and right. You learn more about dragging and flicking later in this chapter.

The Applications Screen (Galaxy Tab 10")

The Apps icon

The applications screen is your command center where you can access all the applications available on the Galaxy Tab. Tap the Apps icon at the top right of the screen to view all stored applications.

When you tap an application icon, the application launches. If you have more than one page of application icons on the applications screen, dots appear on either side of the menu buttons at the bottom of the screen. You can scroll between pages by tapping one of the buttons or dragging or flicking left and right. You learn more about dragging and flicking later in this chapter.

The Applications Screen (Galaxy Tab 7")

**A list of incoming mail on the
Email application screen**

After you press an application button on the applications screen, the application launches and takes up the entire screen. For example, if you open the Email application, a list of your incoming mail appears on the screen.

The Applications Screen (Galaxy Tab 10")

After you tap the Apps icon on the home screen, the application launches and takes up the entire screen. For example, if you open the Google Search application, the search term box appears on the screen.

Manipulating the Screen

Like many tablets these days, the Galaxy Tab doesn't come with a stylus (essentially a stick) for manipulating elements on the screen. Instead, you use your fingers and change the orientation of the Galaxy Tab itself to make it do what you want. Although the examples in this section are for the Galaxy Tab 7", you manipulate elements on the Galaxy Tab 10" screen in the same way. If there are different instructions for manipulating the screen for the Tab 10" model, we'll note them in a different subsection.

Tapping an Element

Unlike a desktop or laptop computer, you don't have a mouse installed on your Galaxy Tab, so there is no cursor that you can see. However, when you quickly tap an element with your finger, the Galaxy Tab performs an action. For example, when you tap an application icon, the Galaxy Tab launches the application.

You can also double-tap, which is two quick taps in the same location, to perform a specific function. For example, you can double-tap an image to zoom in and double-tap again to zoom out.

Pinching

Apple set the standard for multitouch screen gesture requirements with its iPad, and the Galaxy Tab follows the same standard. That is, a multitouch screen can recognize different gestures that use multiple finger touches, and one of them is the pinching gesture.

You pinch when you touch the screen with both your thumb and forefinger and bring them together in a pinching motion. This is also called pinching in, and it has the same effect as zooming in. For example, you can get a closer view of a web page in the browser by pinching. You can also pinch outward, which has the same effect as zooming out, by touching the screen with your thumb and forefinger together and moving them apart.

Dragging and Flicking

You can drag up and down the screen (or even left to right if an app allows it) by touching the top of the screen and moving your finger to drag content the length of the screen. If you want to move more content down the screen, remove your finger, touch the top of the screen, and drag your finger down the length of the screen again. You can drag a page of content up by touching the bottom of the screen and dragging your finger upward.

Dragging can become cumbersome, though, if you have to drag through a long document such as a web page or spreadsheet. The Galaxy Tab makes it easy for you to drag through large chunks of content by flicking. That is, after you touch the top (or bottom) of the screen, move your finger quickly down (or up) and then lift your finger at the last moment so the content scrolls after you lift your finger. You can wait for the content to stop scrolling when you reach the beginning or end of the content, or you can touch anywhere on the screen to stop scrolling.

Screen Rotation and Orientation

Your Galaxy Tab has two screen orientation modes—vertical and horizontal—and it knows which way it's oriented. By default, the Galaxy Tab screen orientation changes when you rotate the unit 90 degrees so the screen is horizontal, or you can rotate it another 90 degrees so the screen is vertical again. Nearly all default apps, such as the Browser, use both orientations. However, there might be times when you don't want the Galaxy Tab to automatically change its screen orientation when you move the unit. For example, you might want to view a web page only in vertical orientation.

Setting Autorotation (Galaxy Tab 7")

You can set the autorotation setting on or off as you see fit.

1. Press the Menu button.

2. Slide the status bar to the bottom of the screen.

3. Tap the Orientation Lock button to lock the current screen orientation. The button turns green to signify that orientation lock is on.

4. Tap the Orientation Lock button again to turn off orientation lock. The next time you rotate the unit 90 degrees, the screen will rotate automatically.

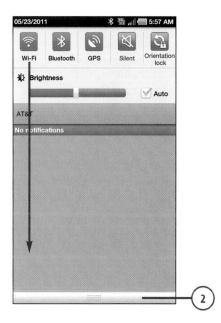

Setting Autorotation (Galaxy Tab 10")

You can set the autorotation setting on or off as you see fit.

1. In the Apps screen, tap the Settings icon.

2. Tap Screen.

3. Tap Auto-rotate Screen to lock the current screen orientation. The check box to the right of the Auto-rotate Screen text is empty to signify that orientation lock is on.

4. Tap Auto-rotate Screen again to turn off orientation lock. The next time you rotate the unit 90 degrees, the screen rotates automatically.

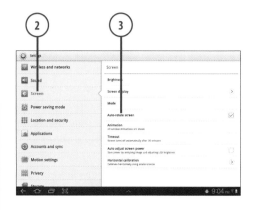

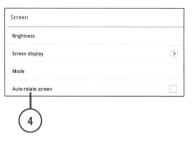

Interacting with Android

Android is a fun operating system to use; it includes a number of common elements, including sliders and switches, as well as the keyboard that you can use to enter and edit text in your Galaxy Tab.

Sliders

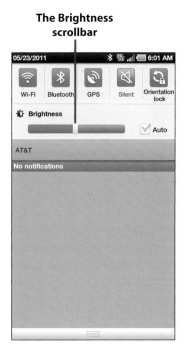

The Brightness scrollbar

A slider is a button that requires a bit more effort for you to activate. Android uses sliders to prevent you from doing something that can lead to unintended consequences. For example, if you slide the status bar to the bottom of the page, you'll see the Brightness slider so you can adjust the brightness of the screen.

Toolbars

You might run into toolbars at the top of specific screens that provide more controls over a specific function. The toolbar might disappear or the toolbar functions might be different depending on the type of app you have. For example, when you press the down arrow below the Search icon on the home screen, the Search toolbar appears so you can tell Android where to search.

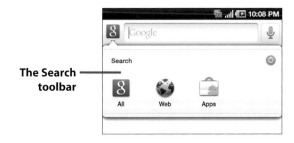

The Search toolbar

Button Lists

A button list at the top of an email message

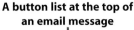

You might see button lists in different locations on the screen depending on the app you're using. For example, if you read an email message, you'll see a list of buttons at the top of the screen so you can perform certain tasks, such as reply to the message.

Tab Bars

A tab bar at the top of the Task Manager page

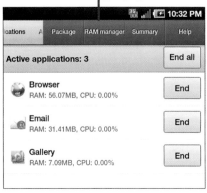

Some apps have a Tab bar at a location on the screen that contains a set of buttons that control the app. The buttons vary depending on the app; if the app doesn't have a Tab bar, you won't see one. For example, if you tap the Task Manager app you'll see a Tab bar at the top of the Task Manager page that includes a list of applications, other system information, and a help screen.

Using the Keyboard

The keyboard

The Galaxy Tab doesn't come with a physical keyboard like you find on many smartphones. Instead, you type in the text with something that looks similar to a computer keyboard. The keyboard appears at the bottom of the screen automatically when you want to enter text.

A lowercase a ———

You can type the letter by tapping the letter key. For example, if you tap the letter a on the keyboard, the lowercase letter a appears on the screen.

How Do I Capitalize a Letter?

There are two ways you can capitalize a letter:

1. Tap the Shift key, and then tap the letter you want to capitalize. You'll notice that after you tap the Shift key that all the keys on the keyboard become capitalized.

The Shift key ———

2. You can capitalize more than one letter by tapping the Shift key twice. The Shift key turns blue; this denotes that the Shift key is locked. You can unlock the Shift key by tapping the key again. You'll know the Shift key is unlocked not only because the white light on the Shift key is off, but also because all the letter keys on the keyboard are back to lowercase.

Using Special Keyboards and Characters

It's not easy typing on a screen that's only 7" wide (or even 10"), especially with an onscreen keyboard, but Android has a trick to make it a bit easier to add information.

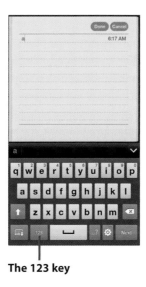

The 123 key

The standard keyboard doesn't include any numbers and not very many punctuation marks, but you can access more keys by tapping the 123 key to see all 10 digits and a number of symbols.

The 1/3 key

You can access an extended symbols keyboard by tapping the 1/3 key on the numbers and symbols keyboard. After you tap this key, the key label changes to 2/3. This signifies that you are on the second of three extended keyboards.

You can go to the third extended keyboard by tapping the 2/3 key. When you're on the third extended keyboard, you can return to the numbers and symbols keyboard by tapping the 3/3 key.

My Keyboard Doesn't Look the Same!

Your keyboard options might change somewhat depending on the app you're in. For example, if you're in the Search app, you see a .,? key to the right of the spacebar. If you're setting up your email account in the Email app, you see the @ key to the right of the spacebar because that's a key that you use often when typing an email address.

A button list of special characters

If you hold down a key on the keyboard, the letter appears, and if there are any related letters, such as a letter with an umlaut (such as ü), you see a button list above the board that lets you add the special character. If you don't want to add the special character, click the X button to close the button list.

Copying and Pasting Data (Galaxy Tab 7")

Android makes it pretty easy to copy and paste text from one app to another. In this example, you learn to copy a term from the Browser app and paste it into the Search app so you can search for the term not only on the Web but also throughout the Galaxy Tab.

1. Launch the Browser app.

2. For this example, we'll start on the Yahoo! website. Type a search term into the Yahoo! search box.

3. Hold down your finger on the search box for a couple of seconds, and then release your finger.

4. In the Edit Text menu, tap Copy All.

5. Press the Search button.

6. Hold down your finger on the Google box until it turns orange, and then release your finger.

7. In the Edit Text menu, tap Paste to insert the copied text.

Copying and Pasting Data (Galaxy Tab 10")

Android makes it pretty easy to copy and paste text from one app to another. In this example, you learn to copy a term from the Browser app and paste it into the Search app so you can search for the term not only on the Web but also throughout the Galaxy Tab.

1. Launch the Browser app.

2. On the Google home page that appears by default, type a search term into the Search field.

3. The results page displays search results as you type. Hold down your finger on the search box for a couple of seconds, and then release your finger.

4. In the Text Selection bar at the top of the screen, tap Select All. The entire word is highlighted in green.

5. Tap Copy.

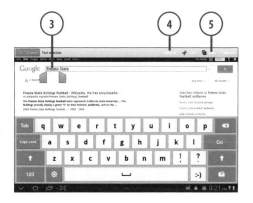

6. Tap the Home icon in the status bar.

7. Tap Apps.

8. Tap the Memo icon.

9. Hold down your finger on the Google box until a green tab appears underneath the Search box, and then release your finger.

10. In the Edit Text menu, tap Paste to insert the copied text.

6   8

10

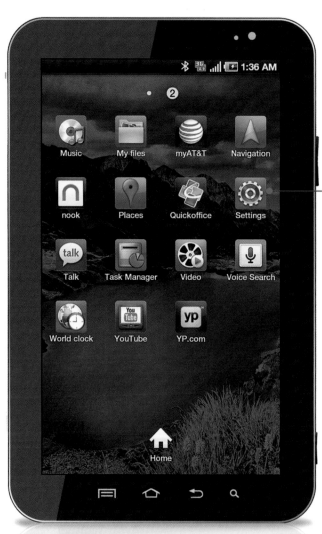

* 🔳 ᴵᴵᴵᴵᴵᴵ 📶 🔋 1:36 AM

②

Music   **My files**   **myAT&T**   **Navigation**

nook   **Places**   **Quickoffice**   **Settings**

Talk   **Task Manager**   **Video**   **Voice Search**

World clock   **YouTube**   **YP.com**

Home

Learn how to get details about the Galaxy Tab.

Learn how to set up your network.

Learn about synchronizing the Galaxy Tab with other computers.

In this chapter, you learn about your Galaxy Tab and how to connect it with other computers and networks.

→ Getting Details About the Galaxy Tab
→ Setting Up Your Network
→ Syncing the Galaxy Tab

2

Becoming Familiar with Android

You can easily find information about the Galaxy Tab so you can make changes as needed. When you finish making general changes to the Galaxy Tab, it's time to set up the network so your Galaxy Tab can connect with the Internet. Finally, you learn how to synchronize your Galaxy Tab with other devices, such as your desktop or laptop PC.

Getting Details About the Galaxy Tab

If you want to get information about the features in your Galaxy Tab from one place, you can do so in the About section of the Settings app.

Galaxy Tab 7"

1. Press the Menu button.

2. Tap Settings.

3. Scroll down the list, and then tap
About Tablet.

4. See the model number for your
Galaxy Tab.

5. See the Android firmware,
Baseband, and Kernel versions.

6. See the build number for your
Galaxy Tab.

7. Tap Status.

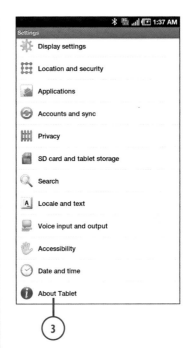

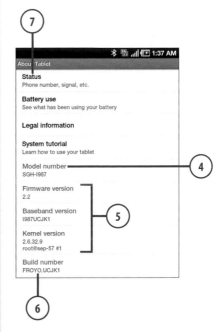

8. View the status of your Galaxy Tab, including battery status and charge level, phone number, signal strength, your Wi-Fi MAC address, and the current uptime (that is, how long your Galaxy Tab has been on continuously). You need to scroll down to see the Wi-Fi MAC address, Bluetooth address, and uptime.

9. Press the Back button.

10. Tap Battery Use to view apps and services that have used battery power.

11. Tap Legal Information to view legal information about your Galaxy Tab.

12. Tap System Tutorial to learn how to use the Galaxy Tab.

Galaxy Tab 10"

1. Tap the Apps icon.

2. Tap Settings.

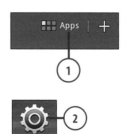

3. Scroll down the settings list and tap About Tablet.

4. See the model number for your Galaxy Tab.

5. See the Android firmware and Kernel versions.

6. See the build number for your Galaxy Tab.

7. Tap Status.

8. View the status of your Galaxy Tab, including battery status and charge level, your IP address, your Wi-Fi MAC address, your Bluetooth address (if any), your Tab's serial number, and the current uptime (that is, how long your Galaxy Tab has been on continuously).

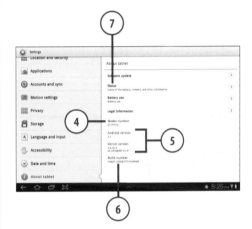

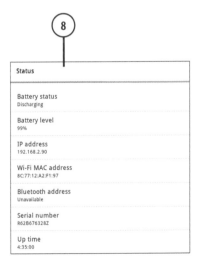

Status	
Battery status	
Discharging	
Battery level	
99%	
IP address	
192.168.2.90	
Wi-Fi MAC address	
8C:77:12:A2:F1:97	
Bluetooth address	
Unavailable	
Serial number	
R62B676328Z	
Up time	
4:35:00	

9. Tap Back in the staus bar at the bottom-left corner of the screen.

10. Tap Software Update to get any Galaxy Tab or Android updates from Samsung.

11. Tap Battery Use to view apps and services that have used battery power.

12. Tap Legal Information to view legal information about your Galaxy Tab.

Setting Up Your Network (Galaxy Tab 7")

Now that you're familiar with the details about your Galaxy Tab and accessing the Settings app, you need to use the Settings app to do one very important setup task: connect your Galaxy Tab to the Internet. Depending on the phone carrier you use, you can connect with the Internet through a Wi-Fi connection or through a 3G connection. You can also connect to other networks securely using a Virtual Private Network (VPN).

I Don't Have a Wireless Network…What Do I Do?

If you don't have a Wi-Fi network but you do have a high-speed Internet connection through a telephone (DSL) or cable (broadband) provider, you have several options. First, call your provider and ask for a new network modem that enables wireless connections. Ask how much that costs—some providers might upgrade your box for free.

Another option is to keep your current box and add a wireless base station of your own, such as ones offered by Apple and Microsoft.

Setting Up Wi-Fi

1. Press the Menu button.

2. Tap Settings.

3. Tap Wireless and Network.

4. Tap Wi-Fi Settings.

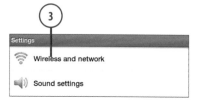

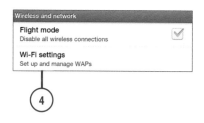

5. Tap Wi-Fi if Wi-Fi is not turned on.

6. Tap Add Wi-Fi Network.

7. Type the network SSID into the Network SSID field.

8. Tap the down arrow to set the security level.

9. Select the security level; the default is Open.

10. Tap Save.

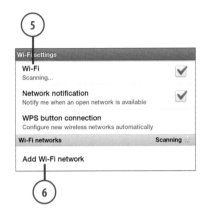

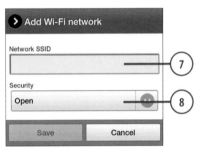

It's Not All Good

Be Secure First!

Your wireless network equipment at home should have security enabled. You'll know that security is enabled on the Wi-Fi network when you view the Wi-Fi Settings screen and see a padlock next to the Wi-Fi network in the list. When you select the Wi-Fi network for the first time, you should be asked to supply a password.

If you don't require a password, strongly consider adding one, because unsecured networks send encrypted data—such as passwords and credit card numbers—through the air. Anyone else who has a Wi-Fi connection can tap into your unsecured network and see what you're doing online. If you need more information, consult your network equipment documentation or the manufacturer's website.

>>> Go Further

DISABLE WIRELESS CONNECTIONS ON A PLANE

When you're flying, the flight attendants always remind you to turn off your wireless devices during takeoffs and landings. You can quickly disable your wireless connections until you get to a safe flying altitude and the pilot gives you permission to turn on wireless devices again. Here's how:

1. Press the Settings button.

2. Tap Settings.

3. Tap Wireless and Network.

4. Tap Airplane mode.

The check box turns green to inform you that wireless connections are disabled. Tap Airplane mode again to enable wireless connections.

Setting Up 3G

1. Press the Menu button.

2. Tap Settings.

3. Tap Wireless and Network.

4. Tap Mobile Networks.

5. Tap Network Operators.

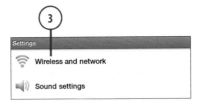

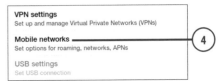

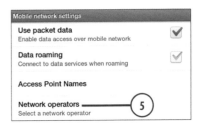

6. If you have only one network you use with your Galaxy Tab, such as AT&T, then the default setup is grayed out so you can't select it.

It's Not All Good

Be Sure You Roam When You Want

The Mobile Network Settings screen lets you engage in data roaming, which enables your Galaxy Tab to connect to wireless networks that are outside of your data plan. This is useful when you travel, but if you accidentally leave data roaming on while you travel and your Galaxy Tab connects to an outside wireless network, you'll be charged for it. Fortunately, Samsung realized that you don't want to get a nasty surprise on your next phone bill, and data roaming is turned off by default. You can turn on data roaming in the Mobile Network Settings screen by tapping Data Roaming. Just be sure to turn it off when you're finished. You can also contact your wireless data provider about its data roaming plans in case you plan to leave data roaming on intentionally.

Setting Up a VPN

A VPN lets users in a public network (such as the Internet) transfer private data by making it appear to the users that they're in a private network of their own. For example, you can set up a VPN between yourself and your boss at the office so you can send private company data securely.

1. Press the Settings button.

2. Tap Settings.

3. Tap Wireless and Network.

4. Tap VPN Settings.

5. Tap Add VPN.

6. Tap the VPN to which you want to connect.

7. Enter the VPN information, such as the VPN name and server.

How to Disconnect from Your VPN

Disconnect from the VPN by opening the Notifications panel at the top of the screen, tapping the VPN notification name, and then tapping Disconnect.

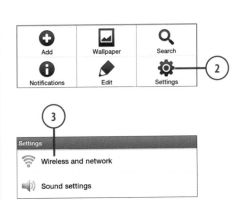

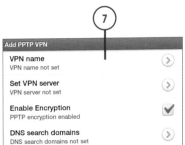

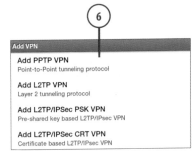

Setting Up Your Network (Galaxy Tab 10")

Now that you're familiar with the details about your Galaxy Tab and accessing the Settings app, you need to use the Settings app to do one very important setup task: Connect your Galaxy Tab to the Internet. Depending on the phone carrier you use, you can connect with the Internet through a Wi-Fi connection. You also can connect to other devices and networks using a Bluetooth connection or through a VPN.

I Don't Have a Wireless Network...What Do I Do?

If you don't have a Wi-Fi network but you do have a high-speed Internet connection through a telephone (DSL) or cable (broadband) provider, you have several options. First, call your provider and ask for a new network modem that enables wireless connections. Ask how much that costs—some providers might upgrade your box for free.

Another option is to keep your current box and add a wireless base station of your own, such as ones offered by Apple and Microsoft.

Setting Up Wi-Fi

1. On the home screen, tap the Apps icon.

2. Tap Settings.

3. Tap Wi-Fi Settings.

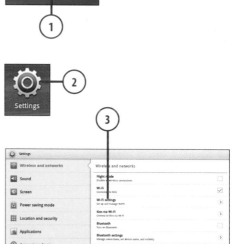

4. Tap Wi-Fi if Wi-Fi is not turned on.

5. Tap Add Wi-Fi Network.

6. Type the network SSID into the Network SSID field.

7. Tap the Security field to set the security level.

8. Select the security level; the default is Open.

9. Tap Save.

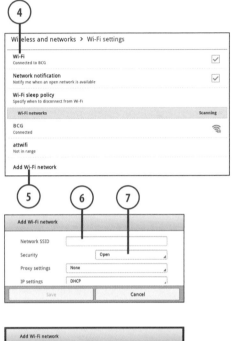

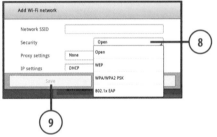

It's Not All Good

Be Secure First!

Your wireless network equipment at home should have security enabled. You'll know that security is enabled on the Wi-Fi network when you view the Wi-Fi Settings screen and see a padlock next to the Wi-Fi network in the list. When you select the Wi-Fi network for the first time, you should be asked to supply a password.

If you don't require a password, strongly consider adding one because unsecured networks send encrypted data—such as passwords and credit card numbers—through the air. Anyone else who has a Wi-Fi connection can tap in to your unsecured network and see what you're doing online. If you need more information, consult your network equipment documentation and/or manufacturer's website.

GO FURTHER: DISABLE WIRELESS CONNECTIONS ON A PLANE

When you're flying, the flight attendants always remind you to turn off your wireless devices during takeoffs and landings. You can quickly disable your wireless connections until you get to a safe flying altitude and the pilot gives you permission to turn on wireless devices again. Here's how:

1. Press the Settings button.

2. Tap Settings.

3. Tap Wireless and Network.

4. Tap Flight mode.

The check box turns green to inform you that wireless connections are disabled. Tap Airplane mode again to enable wireless connections.

Setting Up Bluetooth

1. Tap the Apps icon.

2. Tap Settings.

3. Tap Bluetooth to turn on Bluetooth.

4. Tap Bluetooth Settings.

5. Tap Visible if you want your Galaxy Tab to be discovered by other computers and/or devices that you can connect to using a Bluetooth connection.

6. Tap Find Nearby Devices.

7. Tap on a found device to connect with that device. You can rescan for devices by tapping Scan for Devices.

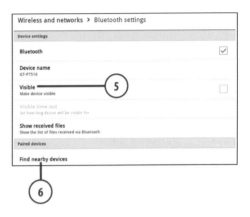

Setting Up a VPN

A VPN lets users in a public network (such as the Internet) transfer private data by making it appear to the users that they're in a private network of their own. For example, you can set up a VPN between yourself and your boss at the office so you can send private company data securely.

1. Tap the Apps icon.

2. Tap Settings.

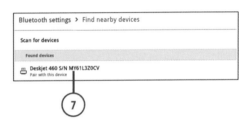

3. Tap VPN Settings.

4. Tap Add VPN.

5. Tap the VPN to which you want to connect.

6. In the next screen, enter the VPN information, such as the VPN name and server.

How to Disconnect from Your VPN

Disconnect from the VPN by opening the Notifications panel at the top of the screen, tapping the VPN notification name, and then tapping Disconnect. It's as simple as that.

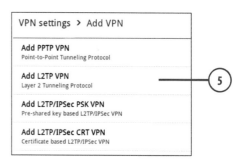

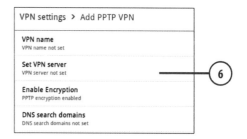

Syncing the Galaxy Tab

Synchronizing your Galaxy Tab with your desktop or laptop computer has a number of advantages.

The Galaxy Tab stores a backup of its contents on your desktop or laptop every time you sync both devices, so if you lose your data on the Galaxy Tab—or lose the Galaxy Tab itself—you can restore the data from the backed up copies on your computer. What's more, if you have music, photos, or video on your computer, you can choose and copy a selection of those files onto your Galaxy Tab.

Android prefers Windows when it comes to syncing, and that's no surprise considering that Windows is the leading operating system for desktop PCs by far. This chapter describes how to sync music with the Galaxy Tab in Windows. Later chapters cover how to sync other types of data, such as contacts.

Can I Sync Between the Galaxy Tab and the Mac OS?

Syncing music from iTunes on the Mac OS to the Galaxy Tab requires additional software to download for your Mac. Salling Software (www.salling.com) produces Salling Media Sync, a utility that syncs music and photos with Android devices. Salling offers a fully functional trial version at no cost and charges only $14.99 for the full version, which offers significantly faster syncing.

Galaxy Tab 7"

It's easy to sync music files in Windows Media Player, the default music and multimedia player in Windows, to your Galaxy Tab 7".

1. Connect the Galaxy Tab to your computer with the USB cable that came with your Galaxy Tab if you haven't done so already.

2. Press the Menu button.

3. Tap Settings.

4. Tap Accounts and Sync.

5. By default, your applications sync automatically at any time. If you don't want to sync background data, tap Background Data; if you don't want applications to sync data automatically, tap Auto-sync.

6. Add an account to sync by tapping Add Account.

7. Add an integrated social networking account, a corporate account, or a Google account.

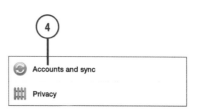

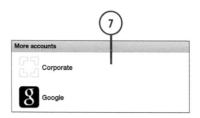

Go Further

SYNC WITH ITUNES

It's also easy to sync your Galaxy Tab with iTunes. You can mount the USB drive on the Galaxy Tab; then, on your computer, you can drag songs from iTunes and drop them to that drive. You can also sync to iTunes wirelessly by downloading the TuneSync app from the Android Market or from Highwind Software (www.highwindsoftware.com) for only $4.99. Highwind also makes a free Lite version if you want to check it out first, but this version limits playlists to 20 songs.

Galaxy Tab 10"

1. Connect the Galaxy Tab to your computer with the USB cable that came with your Galaxy Tab if you haven't done so already.

2. Tap the Apps icon.

3. Tap Settings.

4. Tap Accounts and Sync.

5. By default, your applications sync automatically at any time. If you don't want to sync background data, tap Background Data; if you don't want applications to sync data automatically, tap Auto-sync.

6. Add an account to sync by tapping Add Account.

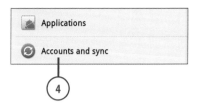

7. Add an integrated social network-ing account, a server account, a corporate account, a Google account, or a Samsung account.

Learn how to password-protect your Galaxy Tab.

Learn how to set parental restrictions.

Learn about setting alert sounds.

Learn how to change keyboard settings.

Learn about modifying screen wallpaper.

Your Galaxy Tab isn't just a static system that forces you to work with it. It's malleable so you can change many attributes of the system to work the way you prefer. The topics in this chapter include the following:

→ Password-Protecting the Galaxy Tab
→ Setting Parental Restrictions
→ Changing the Date and Time
→ Modifying Your Wallpaper
→ Setting Alert Sounds
→ Changing Keyboard Settings

Customizing Android to Your Liking

Password-Protecting the Galaxy Tab

One of the first things you should do when you set up your Galaxy Tab is password-protect it so that unauthorized persons can't use your Galaxy Tab or gain access to the data stored on it.

Galaxy Tab 7"

1. Press the Menu button.

2. Tap Settings.

3. Tap Location and Security.

4. Tap Set Screen Lock.

5. Tap Password.

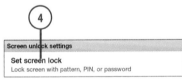

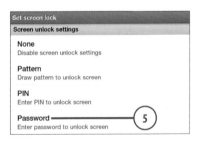

6. Type your password in the Select Password screen. The password must be at least four characters. A couple of seconds after you tap the letter, the letter turns into a dot to hide what you just entered. Tap Continue.

7. Retype the password in the Confirm Password screen (which is identical to the Select Password screen), and then tap OK.

The next time you log in to your Galaxy Tab, you are prompted to type in your password.

>>> Go Further

WHAT IF I CAN'T REMEMBER MY PASSWORD?

If you can't remember your password, your only recourse is to reset your Galaxy Tab so that you wipe all the data from it and start from scratch. Unfortunately, this means that all your other data will be wiped off the unit as well.

1. Turn your Galaxy Tab off if it isn't already. You might need to remove the battery to turn off the unit.

2. Press and hold the Power and Volume Up buttons.

3. When you see the Samsung logo, release the Power button but continue to hold the Volume Up button.

4. When the recovery screen appears, tap the Volume Down button until wipe data/factory reset is highlighted.

5. Press the Power button.

6. In the next screen, press the Volume Down button until Yes—Delete All User Data is highlighted.

7. Press the Power button.

8. After the Galaxy Tab wipes the system data, press the Power button to reboot the system.

Galaxy Tab 10"

1. Tap the Apps icon at the top-right corner of the home screen.

2. Tap Settings.

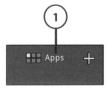

3. Tap Location and Security.

4. Tap Configure Lock Screen.

5. Tap Password.

6. Type your password in the Select Password screen, and then tap Continue. The password must be at least four characters. A couple of seconds after you tap the letter, the letter turns into a dot to hide what you just entered.

7. Retype the password in the Confirm Password screen, and then tap OK.

8. The next time you log in to your Galaxy Tab, you will be prompted to type your password in the Enter Password to Unlock screen.

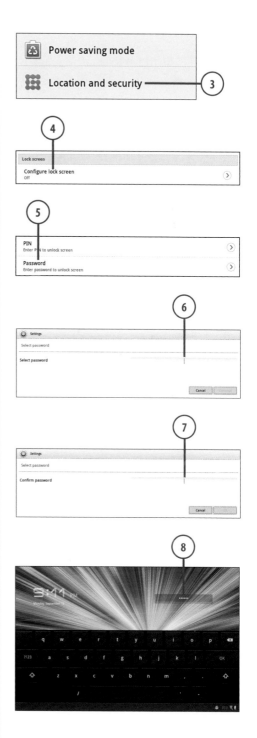

Changing Your Password

It's a good idea to change your password regularly so you have the peace of mind knowing that you're keeping one step ahead of potential thieves.

Galaxy Tab 7"

1. Press the Menu button.

2. Tap Settings.

3. Tap Location and Security.

4. Tap Change Screen Lock.

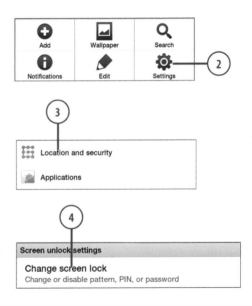

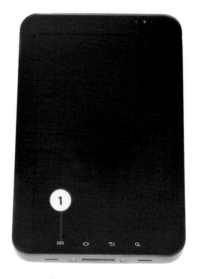

5. Type your password in the
   Confirm Password screen, and
   then tap Continue.

6. Tap Password.

7. Type your password in the Select
   Password screen. The password
   must be at least four characters. A
   couple of seconds after you tap
   the letter, the letter turns into a
   dot to hide what you just entered.
   Tap Continue.

8. Retype the password in the Confirm Password screen (which is identical to the Select Password screen), and then tap OK. The next time you log in to your Galaxy Tab you are prompted to type in your new password.

Go Further

ENTER A PATTERN OR NUMERIC PIN

The Galaxy Tab gives you one of three options for password-protecting your unit: a text password, a numeric PIN (such as the one you use for an ATM card, or a pattern that you can draw on the screen). In the Screen Unlock Settings screen, tap Pattern or PIN to create a new pattern or numeric PIN, respectively. Then follow the step-by-step instructions.

Galaxy Tab 10"

1. Tap the Apps icon at the top-right corner of the home screen.

2. Tap Settings.

3. Tap Location and Security.

4. Tap Configure Lock Screen.

5. Type your password in the Confirm Password screen, and then tap Continue.

6. Tap Password.

7. Type your password in the Choose Your Password screen, and then tap Continue. The password must be at least four characters. A couple of seconds after you tap the letter, the letter turns into a dot to hide what you just entered.

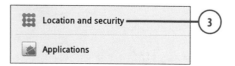

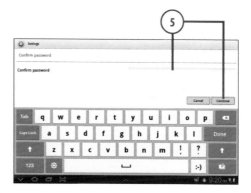

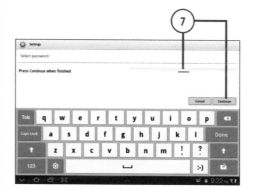

8. Retype the password in the
Confirm Password screen, and
then tap OK.

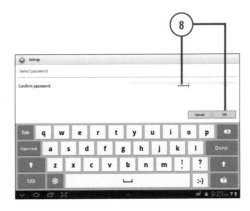

Setting Parental Restrictions

Neither Android 2.2 nor Android 3.1 have parental restrictions for specific
applications built in aside from the pattern, PIN, or text password used for full
access to the Galaxy Tab.

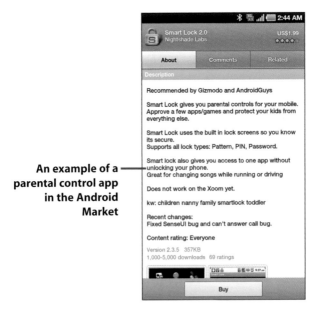

An example of a parental control app in the Android Market

However, you can find parental control apps in the Android Market
(https://market.android.com). Search for "parental control" or "parental controls," read the user reviews for each app, and then decide whether you want
to download an app to see if it works for you.

Changing the Date and Time

You can set the date and time for your Galaxy Tab, change the time zone, change the date format, and display whether you want to display the time as standard 12-hour or 24-hour (military) time.

Galaxy Tab 7"

1. Press the Menu button.

2. Tap Settings.

3. Tap Date and Time.

4. Tap Automatic to release the date, time, and time zone information from the information provided by your network.

5. Tap Set Date.

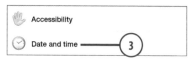

6. Tap the month, date, or year to change the date information. You can also tap the + or – buttons above and below the month, date, or year to move the information up or down one month, one date, or one year, respectively.

7. Tap Set.

8. Tap Select Time Zone.

9. Tap the time zone for your locality.

10. Tap Set Time.

11. Tap the hour and/or minute to change the time information. You can also tap the + or – buttons above and below the hour or minute to move the hour or minute up or down one hour or one minute, respectively.

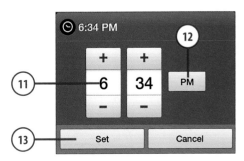

12. Tap the AM or PM button to change the time of day between AM and PM.

13. Tap Set.

14. Tap Use 24-hour Format to change the format to 24-hour time. Note that the time on the status bar reflects the change. You can return to 12-hour time by tapping Use 24-hour Format again.

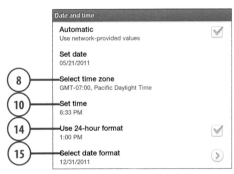

15. Tap Select Date Format.

16. Change the date format by tap-
    ping one of the three format
    options. If you don't want to
    change the date format, tap
    Cancel.

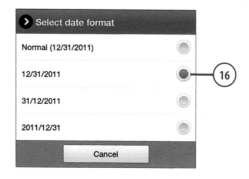

Galaxy Tab 10"

1. Tap the Apps icon at the top-right
   corner of the home screen.

2. Tap Settings.

3. Scroll down the Settings list, and
   then tap Date and Time.

4. Tap Set Date.

5. Tap the month, date, and/or year to change the date information. You can also tap the up or down arrows to move the information up or down one month, one date, or one year, respectively.

6. Tap Set.

7. Tap Set Time.

8. Tap the hour and/or minute to change the time information. You can also tap the up or down arrows to move the hour or minute up or down one hour or one minute, respectively.

9. Tap the AM or PM button to change the time of day between AM and PM.

10. Tap Set.

11. Tap Select Time Zone.

12. Tap the time zone for your locality in the Select Time Zone list.

13. Tap Use 24-hour Format to change the format to 24-hour time. Note that the time on the status bar reflects the change. You can return to 12-hour time by tapping Use 24-hour Format again.

14. Tap Select Date Format.

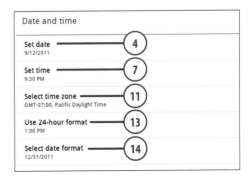

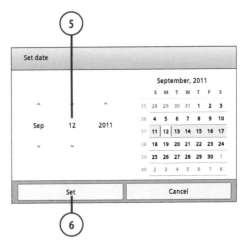

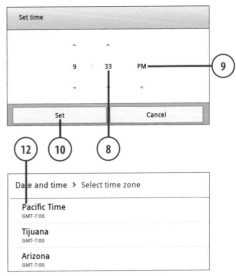

15. Change the date format by tapping one of the three formats below the selected format. If you don't want to change the date format, tap Cancel.

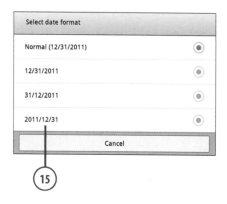

Modifying Your Wallpaper

The standard wallpaper appears behind both the lock screen and the home screen. Android makes it easy for you to change the wallpaper to whatever you want.

Galaxy Tab 7"

1. Go to the home screen if you're not there already. Press the Menu button.

2. Tap Wallpaper.

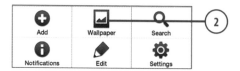

3. Select where you want to get the wallpaper by tapping Gallery, Live Wallpapers, or Wallpaper Gallery.

4. Scroll through the thumbnail images of wallpapers at the bottom of the screen. When you find one you want to see in more detail, tap the thumbnail.

5. Tap Set Wallpaper. After a few seconds the new wallpaper appears on your home screen.

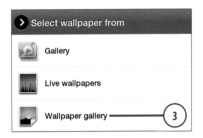

Galaxy Tab 10"

1. Go to the home screen if you're not there already. Tap the Apps icon.

2. Tap Settings.

3. Tap Screen.

4. Tap Screen Display.

5. Under Home Screen, tap Wallpaper.

6. Select where you want to get the wallpaper by tapping Gallery, Live Wallpapers, or Wallpapers.

7. Scroll through the thumbnail images of wallpapers.

8. When you find wallpaper you want, tap the thumbnail image. The new wallpaper appears on your home screen.

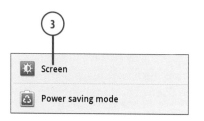

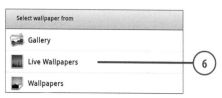

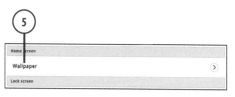

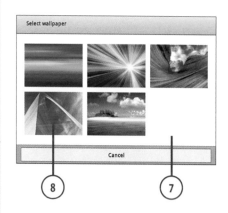

Setting Alert Sounds

If you want the Galaxy Tab to make noise when you perform different actions, such as when you tap something on the screen, you can change the alert sounds or turn them off entirely.

Galaxy Tab 7"

1. Press the Menu button.

2. Tap Settings.

3. Tap Sound Settings.

The One Guaranteed Solution for Silence

The Galaxy Tab makes certain noises by default. For example, the unit plays tones when you use the dial pad on the phone.

If you really want to ensure that the unit doesn't make any noise, the one foolproof solution is to turn off the Galaxy Tab unit.

4. Tap Vibrate.

5. By default, the Galaxy Tab vibrates only when the unit is in Silent Mode. Change the status by tapping one of the three other options. If you don't want to change the status, tap Cancel.

6. Tap Volume.

7. Change the volume for the ringtone, alarm, system, and notification volume by dragging the slider bar to the left (lower volume) or right (higher volume).

8. Tap OK.

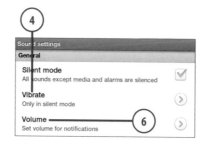

9. Tap Notification Ringtone.

10. Set the notification ringtone from the menu. This ringtone plays whenever you receive a notification. If you don't want a ringtone, scroll to the top of the list and tap Silent.

11. Tap OK.

12. Tap Audible Touch Tones to play tones when you press the keypad.

13. Tap Audible Selection to play a sound when you make a screen selection.

14. Tap Screen Lock Sounds to play sounds when you lock and unlock the screen.

15. By default, the Galaxy Tab unit vibrates when you tap soft keys and on certain user interface interactions so you know that you performed an action. If you would rather not have the unit vibrate, tap Haptic Feedback.

16. Set the haptic feedback vibration intensity by tapping Vibration Intensity.

17. Change the vibration intensity by dragging the slider bar to the left (lower intensity) or right (higher intensity).

18. Tap OK.

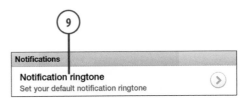

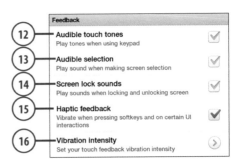

Galaxy Tab 10"

1. Tap the Apps icon.

2. Tap Settings.

3. Tap Sound.

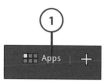

The One Guaranteed Solution for Silence

The Galaxy Tab makes certain noises by default. For example, the unit plays tones when you use the dial pad on the phone.

If you really want to ensure that the unit doesn't make any noise, the one foolproof solution is to turn off the Galaxy Tab unit.

4. Tap Vibrate.

5. By default, the Galaxy Tab vibrates only when the unit is in Silent Mode. Change the status by tapping one of the three other options. If you don't want to change the status, tap Cancel.

6. Tap Volume.

7. Change the volume for the ringtone, alarm, system, and notification volume by dragging the slider bar to the left (lower volume) or right (higher volume).

8. Tap OK.

9. Tap Notification Ringtone.

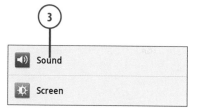

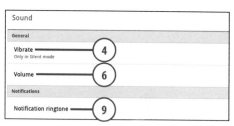

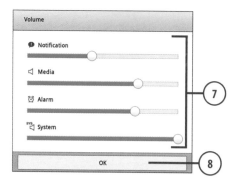

10. Set the notification ringtone from the menu. This ringtone plays whenever you receive a notification. If you don't want a ringtone, scroll to the top of the list and tap Silent.

11. Tap OK.

12. Tap Audible Selection to play a sound when you make a screen selection.

13. Tap Screen Lock Sounds to play sounds when you lock and unlock the screen.

14. By default, the Galaxy Tab unit vibrates when you tap soft keys and on certain user interface interactions so you know that you performed an action. If you would rather not have the unit vibrate, tap Haptic Feedback.

15. Set the touch feedback vibration intensity by tapping Vibration Intensity. The default intensity is Full.

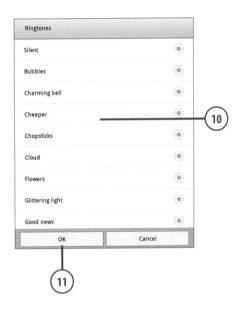

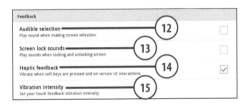

Changing Keyboard and Voice Settings

The Galaxy Tab 7" comes with two keyboards activated by default: the Samsung keyboard and the Swype keyboard. The Galaxy Tab 10" gives you more input options: the Android keyboard, the Samsung keyboard, and the TalkBack keyboard so you can use your voice to manipulate the Galaxy Tab.

The examples in this book use keyboard settings for the Samsung keyboard, which is the default keyboard the Galaxy Tab uses when you type text, as well as built-in keyboard settings that apply to all keyboards.

Galaxy Tab 7"

1. Press the Menu button.

2. Tap Settings.

3. Scroll down the menu and tap Locale and Text.

4. Tap Samsung Keypad.

5. Tap XT9 if you want the Galaxy Tab to guess what you're typing and provide you with suggestions for words so you don't have to keep typing all the time. This is similar to the auto-complete feature in word processors.

6. Tap XT9 Advanced Settings to modify the default XT9 settings. For example, you can turn automatic spelling correction on or off.

7. Tap Automatic Full Stop to automatically insert a full stop after a word by double-tapping the space bar.

8. By default, the Galaxy Tab auto-capitalizes the first word in a sentence. If the Galaxy Tab recognizes a punctuation mark and a space, the next letter is capitalized automatically unless you tap the Shift key twice to turn it off. (There are exceptions to this rule, such as when you type in the To box when you compose a new email message.) Tap Auto-capitalization to turn off auto-capitalization for words. You can turn it on again by tapping Auto-capitalization.

9. Tap Voice Input to use voice input instead of the keyboard.

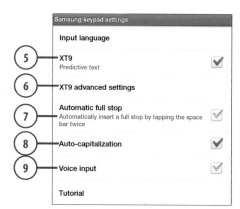

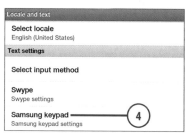

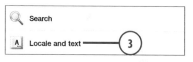

10. The Galaxy Tab tells you how to use voice input and asks if you want to enable it. Enable voice input by tapping Yes.

11. Tap Tutorial to get a quick and easy tutorial about how to use the keyboard.

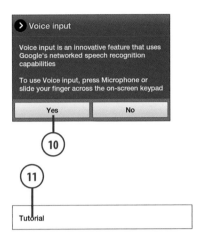

Galaxy Tab 10"

1. Tap the Apps icon.

2. Tap Settings.

3. Scroll down the Settings list, and then tap Language and Input.

4. Tap Configure Input Methods under Keyboard Settings.

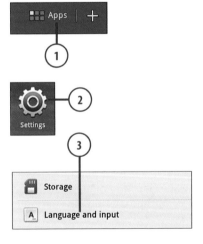

5. Scroll down the list, and then tap Settings under Samsung Keypad.

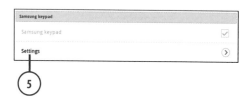

6. Tap Input Language if you want to change the default keyboard input language.

7. Tap XT9 if you want the Galaxy Tab to guess what you're typing and provide you with suggestions for words so you don't have to keep typing all the time. This is similar to the auto-complete feature in word processors.

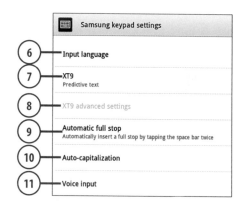

8. Tap XT9 Advanced Settings to modify the default XT9 settings. For example, you can turn automatic spelling correction on or off.

9. Tap Automatic Full Stop to automatically insert a full stop after a word by double-tapping the space bar.

10. By default, the Galaxy Tab auto-capitalizes the first word in a sentence. If the Galaxy Tab recognizes a punctuation mark and a space, the next letter is capitalized automatically unless you tap the Shift key to turn it off. (There are exceptions to this rule, such as when you type in the To box when you compose a new email message.) Tap Auto-capitalization to turn off auto-capitalization for words. You can turn it back on by tapping Auto-capitalization.

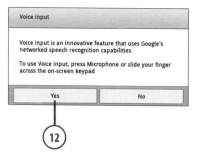

11. Tap Voice Input to use voice input instead of the keyboard.

12. After you tap Voice Input, the Galaxy Tab tells you what you need to do to use voice input. Activate voice input by tapping Yes, or cancel it by tapping No.

13. Tap Sound on Keypress to have the Galaxy Tab make a sound each time you press a key.

14. Tap Tutorial to get a quick and easy tutorial about how to use the keyboard.

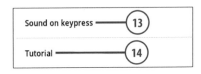

Modifying More Settings

There are too many settings in Android to cover in this book, but here are some of the more important settings that you should know about.

More Settings (Galaxy Tab 7")

1. Press the Menu button.

2. Tap Settings.

3. Tap Display Settings.

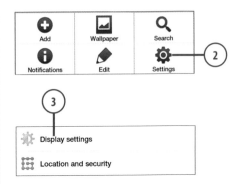

4. Set the font style, the brightness of the screen, the white and black color densities, color saturations, and whether to have Android show all window animations (which is the default), show some window animations, or not show any window animations.

5. Tap Screen Timeout.

6. Select the period of inactivity after which the screen times out and goes dark. The default is one minute. If you don't want to change the time interval, tap Cancel.

Powering Up Your Screen

After the screen goes dark, you can easily start it again by tapping the screen or pressing the Power button. If your Galaxy Tab is password (or PIN or pattern) protected, you must type your password (or PIN or pattern) to start using the Galaxy Tab again.

7. Press the Back button.

8. Tap Power Saving Mode if you would rather not save power by having the Galaxy Tab analyze the image and adjust LCD brightness automatically.

9. Tap TV Out if you want to select the settings for transmitting the Galaxy Tab screen to your TV.

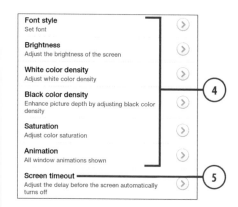

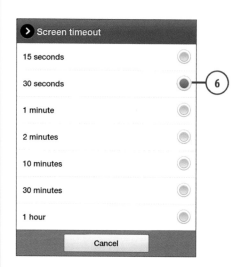

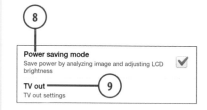

10. Press the Back button.

11. Tap Search.

12. Tap Searchable Items.

13. Choose what you want to search for on your Galaxy Tab when you search from the home page or the Browser app. By default, you can search the Web or apps installed on your Galaxy Tab, and also perform voice searches. For example, you can tap the Microphone icon in the Google box on the home screen and then speak the search terms into your Tab. You also can search for text in your contacts and text in your messages, as well as music stored on your Galaxy Tab.

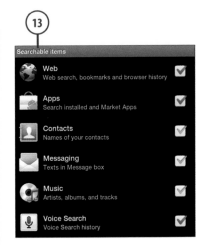

Galaxy Tab 10"

1. Tap the Apps icon on the home screen if you aren't there already.

2. Tap Settings.

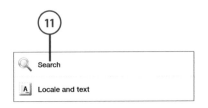

3. Tap Screen.

4. Set the brightness of the screen, the screen display to set wallpaper on your home and lock screens, the auto-rotate screen setting (on is the default), and whether to have Android show all window animations (which is the default), show some window animations, or not show any window animations.

5. Tap Timeout.

6. Select the period of inactivity after which the screen times out and goes dark. The default is one minute. If you don't want to change the time interval, tap Cancel.

7. Tap Cancel.

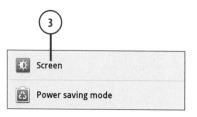

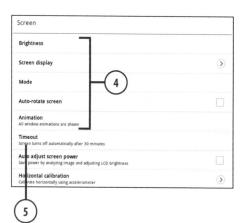

Powering Up Your Screen

After the screen goes dark, you can easily start it again by tapping the screen or pressing the power button. If your Galaxy Tab is password (or PIN or pattern) protected, you must type your password (or PIN or pattern) to start using the Galaxy Tab again.

---

8. Tap Auto Adjust Screen Power if you would rather not save power by having the Galaxy Tab analyze the image and adjust LCD brightness automatically.

9. Calibrate your screen horizontally using the built-in accelerometer by tapping Horizontal Calibration. The Galaxy Tab asks you to place the Tab on a level surface to calibrate the screen.

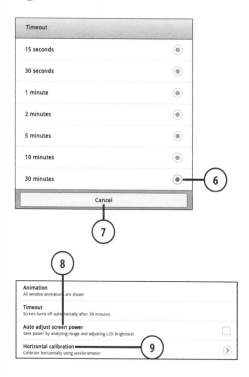

Learn how to browse the web and view websites using the built-in Browser app.

The Galaxy Tab is a great tool for viewing web pages, whether you're at home or you're on the go. No matter which Galaxy Tab model you use, the screen is much larger than a mobile phone so you can see more on the Galaxy Tab's screen. Because you can touch the screen, you can interact with web content in ways that a computer typically cannot. This chapter covers the following:

→ Browsing to a URL
→ Searching the Web
→ Viewing Web Pages
→ Bookmarking Websites
→ Returning to Previously Visited Websites
→ Deleting Bookmarks
→ Filling in Web Forms
→ Copying Text and Images from Web Pages

Browsing the Web

Browsing to a URL

It's likely that you already know how to browse to different web pages in your favorite web browser on your computer. The built-in Browser app in Android works much the same as the browser on your computer, but there are some differences.

Galaxy Tab 7"

1. Tap the Applications icon.

2. Tap Browser.

3. Tap the Address field at the top of the screen. The keyboard opens at the bottom of the screen so you can type a Uniform Resource Locator (URL), which can be a website name or a specific page in a website. You can also select from one of the search sites in the list that appears below the Address field.

4. Start typing a URL, such as samsung.com or market.android.com.

5. Tap Go on the keyboard when you finish typing.

Smarter Searching

As you type, terms that match the letter(s) you've added appear in the list below the Address field. As you type more letters, Android updates the list to give you what it thinks is a more accurate list of possible terms you're looking for. You can stop typing at any time and scroll down the list to view the terms and then tap the term to open the web page. For example, as you type the first three letters of "android" (without the quotes), you see that you get terms for android and a number of other results.

Tips for Typing a URL

The Browser app doesn't require you to type the "http://" or the "www." at the beginning of the URL. For example, if you type samsung.com or www.samsung.com, you still go to the Samsung home page. However, there may be some instances when you need to type in "http://" or even "https://" (for a secure web page) at the beginning of the URL. If you do, the Browser app lets you know so you can type in the "http://" or "https://" in the Address field.

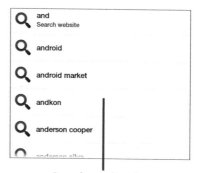

Search results when you start typing the word "android" in the Address field

Galaxy Tab 10"

1. On the home screen, tap Apps.

2. Tap Browser. (Note that you can also tap Browser in the home screen if you want.)

3. Tap the Address field at the top of the screen. The keyboard opens at the bottom of the screen so you can type a URL, which can be a website name or a specific page in a website. You can also select from one of the search sites in the list that appears below the Address field.

4. Start typing a URL, such as sam-sung.com or market.android.com.

5. Tap Go on the keyboard when you finish typing.

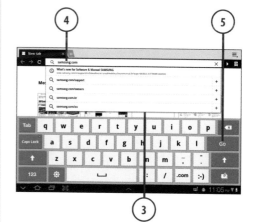

Searching the Web

The Browser app makes it easy for you to search the Web, so you don't need to know every URL of every web page out there (which is good considering there are literally billions of web pages). As you type, the Browser suggests search terms you've used in the past as well as search terms that you might be looking for.

Galaxy Tab 7"

1. Tap the Applications icon.

2. Tap Browser.

3. Tap the Address field at the top of the screen. The keyboard opens at the bottom of the screen so you can type the URL. Start typing your search term. As you type, a list appears underneath the address bar with suggestions. You can stop typing at any time and scroll down the list to find your search term; tap the search term to select it and start the search.

4. If you haven't found what you're looking for, tap Search Website in the list.

5. The results display in a Google search results page. Tap any link to go to a page; you can also tap one of the links at the bottom of the screen to view more results.

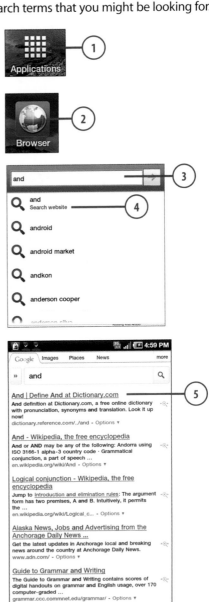

Go Further

TIPS FOR SEARCHING THE WEB

In Chapter 3, "Customizing Android to Your Liking," you learned about how to customize search settings in Android. You can also search deeper within Google itself. For example, if you put a + in front of a search term, you're telling Google that you require the word in the search results. If you put quotes around a search term ("term"), you're telling Google that you want to search for results that contain that term. Scroll to the bottom of the search page and then tap Search Tips to get more information about how you can get the most from your Google searches.

A list of search tips from Google

If you look at the top of Google's search results page, you see links so you can search for more than text terms, including Images and Places. If you click the More link, a pop-up list displays so you can search a variety of other areas within Google.

A list of more areas in which ⎯⎯⎯⎯
to search within Google

News

Buzz

iGoogle

Video

Apps

Shopping

Finance

Blogs

YouTube

Maps

Gmail

Calendar

Photos

Docs

Galaxy Tab 10"

1. On the home screen, tap Browser.

2. Tap the Address field at the top of the screen. The keyboard opens at the bottom of the screen so you can start typing your search term. As you type, a list appears underneath the address bar with suggestions. You can stop typing at any time and scroll down the list to find your search term; tap the search term to select it and start the search.

3. If you haven't found what you're looking for, tap Go.

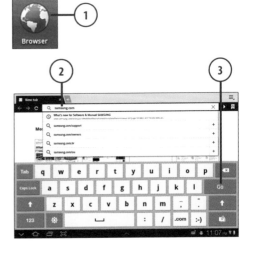

4. The results display in a Google search results page. Tap any link to go to a page; you can also tap one of the links at the bottom of the screen to view more results.

Viewing Web Pages

After you open a website, you can control what you view on the web page in several ways. These techniques let you access the entire web page and navigate between web pages in the Browser app.

Galaxy Tab 7"

1. Navigate to a web page using one of the two methods described in the previous tasks in this chapter.

2. As you view a page, you can drag up and down the page with your finger. You can also flick with your finger to scroll quickly. After you flick, the screen scrolls, decelerates, and then comes to a stop.

3. You can zoom in by double-tapping an area on the screen. Zoom out by double-tapping again.

4. While you're zoomed in, you can touch and drag left and right to view different parts of the web page.

5. Move to another web page from a link in the current web page by tapping a link. Links are usually an underlined or colored piece of text, but they can also be pictures or images that look like buttons.

Hunting for Links

Unfortunately, it isn't always easy to figure out which parts of a web page are links and which ones aren't. Back in the early days of the web, all links were blue and underlined. As web page elements have become more enhanced over time, it's now more common to find links in any color and any text style. What's more, graphics that are links aren't underlined, either.

On a computer's web browser, it's easy to find out which element is a link when you move the mouse pointer over the link because the pointer changes shape. In Android, there is no cursor, so you can't find out if a web page element is a link unless you tap it and see what happens.

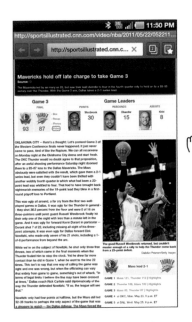

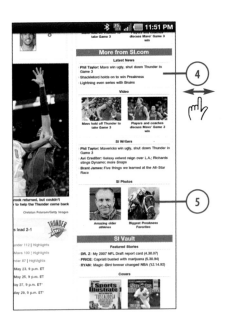

Galaxy Tab 10"

1. Navigate to a web page using one of the two methods described in the previous tasks in this chapter.

2. As you view a page, you can drag up and down the page with your finger. You can also flick with your finger to scroll quickly. After you flick, the screen scrolls, decelerates, and then comes to a stop.

3. You can zoom in by double-tapping an area on the screen. Zoom out by double-tapping again.

4. While you're zoomed in, you can touch and drag left and right to view different parts of the web page.

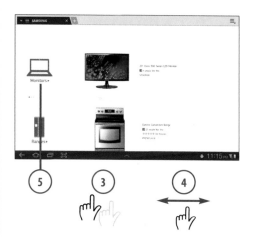

5. Move to another web page from a link in the current web page by tapping a link. Links are usually an underlined or colored piece of text, but they can also be pictures or images that look like buttons.

Bookmarking Websites

As you browse websites, you might want to save some of the websites in a list of your favorites so you can go back to them later. In browser parlance, this saving process is called bookmarking.

Galaxy Tab 7"

1. Navigate to any page in the Browser app.

2. Tap the Add Bookmark button at the top of the page.

3. In the Bookmarks list, tap the Add Bookmark button.

4. Edit the title of the bookmark. The official title of the web page is filled for you, but you can change the name by tapping the Name field and using the keyboard.

5. Select the folder you want to place the bookmark into by tapping Default.

6. Select the folder into which you want to place the bookmark. The default is the Default folder, but you can also select another folder or create a new one.

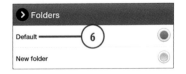

7. Tap OK.

8. The new bookmark appears in the list.

Should I Edit a Bookmark Title?

Because the titles of web pages are usually long and descriptive, it's a good idea to shorten the title to something you can recognize easily in your bookmarks list. Every bookmark also includes a thumbnail picture of what the web page looks like so you can identify the bookmark more easily. If you would rather view your bookmarks by title, press Settings and then tap List View in the menu.

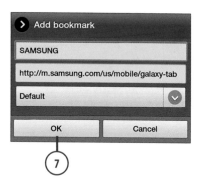

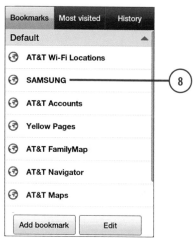

Galaxy Tab 10"

1. Navigate to any page in the Browser app.

2. Tap the Add Bookmark button at the top of the page.

3. In the Bookmarks list, tap Add Bookmark.

4. Edit the label of the bookmark. The official title of the web page is filled for you, but you can change the name by tapping the Name field and using the keyboard.

5. The web address of the page you bookmarked appears in the Address box. Change the web address of the bookmarked page if you want.

6. Select the folder into which you want to place the bookmark. The default is the Bookmarks folder, but you can also select another folder or create a new one.

7. Tap OK.

8. The new bookmark appears in the list.

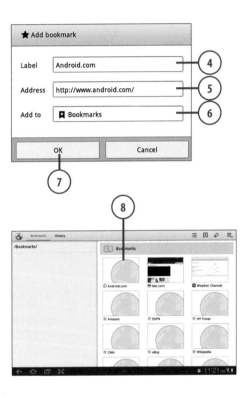

Returning to Previously Visited Websites

It's easy to return to the last page you visited in the Browser—just press the Back button. As you keep pressing the Back button, you keep going back to pages you visited. In the History page, the Browser app also keeps a list of all web pages you've visited during your browsing session.

Browsing Forward

Like any web browser, you can browse more recent pages you've viewed in your current browsing session by tapping the Forward button, which is the right-arrow button immediately to the right of the Back button.

Galaxy Tab 7"

1. Visit several web pages in the Browser app if you haven't done so already.

2. Tap Bookmarks.

3. Tap the History tab. The list of web pages you visited for the current date appears under the Today heading.

4. You can view web pages you visited on an earlier date by tapping the date range (such as Last 7 Days), and the list of web pages you visited displays underneath the date heading.

Tips for Using History

If you want to hide the history for a specific day so you can see history for another day, tap the header for the specific day. For example, if you want to hide all the web pages for today, click the Today header above the first web page in the Today list. The Today header is still visible, but you won't see the web pages. You can view the web pages again by tapping the Today header.

You can also clear the entire history database by pressing Settings and then tapping the Clear History button.

Galaxy Tab 10"

1. Visit several web pages in the Browser app if you haven't done so already.

2. Tap Bookmarks.

3. Tap the History tab. The list of your most visited web pages appears to the right of the Most Visited heading.

4. You can view web pages for the current date by tapping Today.

5. You can view web pages you visited on an earlier date by tapping the date range (such as Last 7 Days); the list of web pages you visited displays to the right of the date heading.

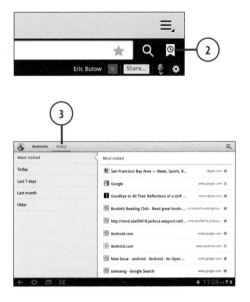

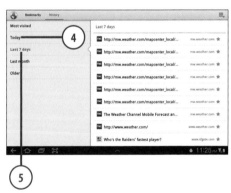

Deleting Bookmarks

If you find there are websites that you don't visit anymore or that go to obsolete or missing web pages, you need to cull your bookmark list. You can delete a bookmark from the Bookmarks list or from the History list.

Delete from the Bookmarks List (Galaxy Tab 7")

The first method uses the Bookmarks list to delete a bookmark.

1. Tap the Bookmarks button at the top of the Browser screen. The thumbnail list of bookmarks appears.

2. Tap the Edit button.

3. In the Edit Bookmark screen, tap the Delete button.

4. Tap the bookmark you want to delete in the list.

5. Tap the Delete button.

6. A dialog box asks if you want to delete the bookmark. Tap Delete to delete the bookmark instantly.

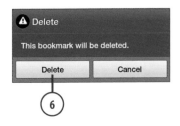

Delete from the History List (Galaxy Tab 7")

The second method uses the History list to delete a bookmark.

1. Tap the Bookmarks button at the top of the Browser screen. The thumbnail list of bookmarks appears.

2. Tap the History tab. This brings up a list of web pages you've viewed recently.

3. Tap a yellow star to the right of a website that you've viewed recently. The yellow star indicates that the site is bookmarked. After you tap the star, the Browser app immediately deletes the bookmark.

Sync Your Bookmarks

You can sync the bookmarks in your favorite Web browser on your desktop or laptop computer with the Browser app so you have maximum control over your bookmarks. You can learn more about syncing your Galaxy Tab in Chapter 2, "Becoming Familiar with Android."

Delete from the Bookmarks List (Galaxy Tab 10")

The first method uses the Bookmarks list to delete a bookmark.

1. Tap the Bookmarks button at the top of the Browser screen. The thumbnail list of bookmarks appears.

2. Hold your finger on the bookmark until the Bookmark menu appears.

3. In the Bookmark menu, tap Delete Bookmark.

4. Tap OK to delete the bookmark instantly.

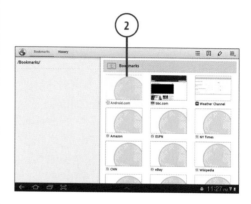

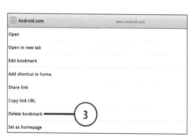

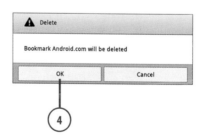

Delete from the History List (Galaxy Tab 10")

The second method uses the History list to delete a bookmark.

1. Tap the Bookmarks button at the top of the Browser screen. The thumbnail list of bookmarks appears.

2. Tap the History tab. This brings up a list of the most recent web pages you've viewed.

3. Hold down your finger on a website you've viewed recently that contains an orange star to the right of the name. The orange star indicates that the site is bookmarked.

4. Tap Delete Bookmark. The Galaxy Tab informs you that the bookmark has been deleted, and the star to the right of the website name turns to just an outline.

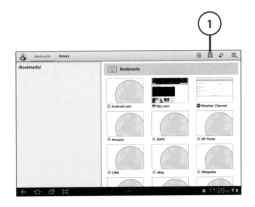

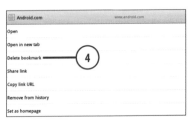

Filling in Web Forms

On many web pages, you are asked to fill in forms, such as for signing up for a company's email newsletter or to get more information about a product. Filling out web forms on your Galaxy Tab is similar to filling out forms on a computer's web browser, but there are differences.

Galaxy Tab 7"

1. Navigate to a page that you know contains a form. (The sample page is at http://code.google.com/ p/android/issues/entry? template=Feature%20request.)

2. Type in a text box by tapping in that box.

3. The keyboard appears at the bottom of the screen. Use the keyboard to type text into the box.

4. Tap the Go button when you finish typing.

5. Select an item in a pull-down menu by tapping the menu.

6. Tap an item in the menu to select it. If the menu list is long, touch and drag up and down to view more selections.

7. Tap the Done button.

8. The selected item appears in the list.

Special Menus

Some websites use special menus that are built from scratch. In these cases, the menu looks exactly like the one you get when you view the web page on a computer. If the web page is well-constructed, it should work fine on the Galaxy Tab. However, it might be a little more difficult to make a selection.

Galaxy Tab 10"

1. Navigate to a page that you know contains a form. (The sample page is at http://code.google.com/p/android/issues/entry?template=Feature%20request.)

2. Type in a text box by tapping in that box. The keyboard appears at the bottom of the screen. Use the keyboard to type text into the box.

3. Tap the Go button when you finish typing. You can also tap Next to go to the next box in the form.

4. Select an item in a pull-down menu by tapping the menu.

5. Tap an item in the menu to select it. If the menu list is long, touch and drag up and down to view more selections.

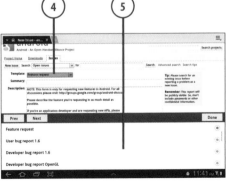

6. The selected item appears in the list.

Copying Text and Images from Web Pages

The Browser app treats web pages like other documents. That is, you can copy text and images from a web page you view in a browser to another app.

Copying a Block of Text (Galaxy Tab 7")

You can select text from web pages to copy and paste into other documents such as email messages or your own text documents.

1. Navigate to a web page in the Browser app if you haven't done so already.

2. Hold down your finger on the first word in the block of text and then release your finger. The first word is highlighted in blue with "handles" at the beginning and end of the word.

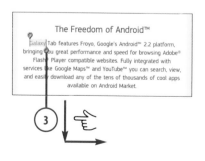

3. Hold down your finger on the bottom handle (the one on the right side of the word) and drag over the text you want to copy. When finished, release your finger.

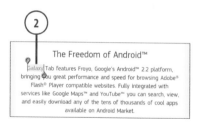

4. The selected text is highlighted in blue.

5. In the pop-up menu that appears above the selected text, tap Copy.

6. Android informs you that the text has been copied to the clipboard. You can now go to another application, such as Email (or an email form on another web page), and paste the text into a text area.

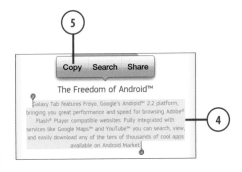

Copying an Image (Galaxy Tab 7")

In addition to being able to copy and paste text from the Browser app, you can also copy images from a web page and save them to an email message or a photo collection.

1. Go to a web page that includes an image on the page.

2. Tap and hold your finger on that image for a couple of seconds, and then release your finger.

3. A pop-up menu for the image appears. Tap Save Image. This saves your image to the Photos app so you can view and use it in any app where you select images from your photo albums.

4. The downloaded file appears as an icon in the status bar.

5. Drag the status bar to the bottom of the screen.

6. Tap the image filename to open the file in the photo album.

7. In the photo album screen, press Menu.

8. Tap Share. You can share your image through a Bluetooth device or in an instant message. You learn more about Bluetooth in Chapter 12, "Adding New Hardware," and more about instant messaging in Chapter 5, "Sending Email and Instant Messages."

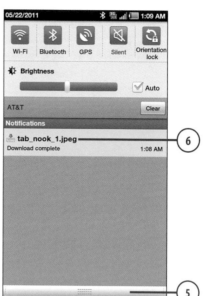

Copying a Block of Text (Galaxy Tab 10")

You can select text from web pages to copy and paste into other documents, such as email messages or your own text documents.

1. Navigate to a web page in the Browser app if you haven't done so already.

2. Hold down your finger on the first word in the block of text and then release your finger. The first word is highlighted in blue with "handles" at the beginning and end of the word.

3. Hold down your finger on the bottom handle (the one on the right side of the word) and drag over the text you want to copy. When finished, release your finger.

4. The selected text is highlighted in blue.

5. In the menu bar that appears at the top of the screen, tap Copy.

6. Android informs you that the text has been copied to the clipboard. You can now go to another application, such as Email (or an email form on another web page), and paste the text into a text area.

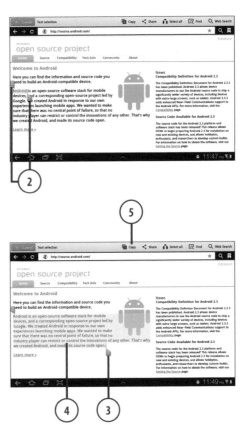

Copying an Image (Galaxy Tab 10")

In addition to being able to copy and paste text from the Browser app, you can also copy images from a web page and save them to an email message or a photo collection.

1. Go to a web page that includes an image on the page.

2. Tap and hold your finger on that image for a couple of seconds, and then release your finger.

3. A pop-up menu for the image appears. Tap Save Image. This saves your image to the Photos app so you can view and use it in any app where you select images from your photo albums.

4. The downloaded file appears as an icon in the status bar. Tap the icon.

5. Tap the image filename to view the filename and download status.

6. Tap the name to view the image in the photo album.

7. Tap the image in the photo album.

8. Tap Share in the upper-right corner of the screen. You can share your image on social networking sites, on Picasa, through a Bluetooth device, as well as in a Gmail or email message. You learn more about sharing pictures in Chapter 9.

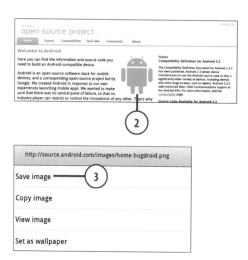

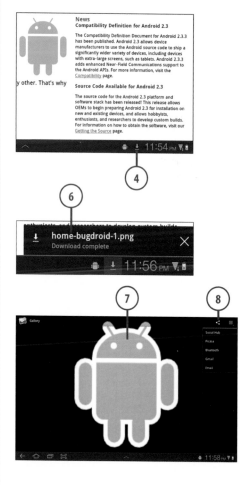

Send and receive email from your ISP or an email service.

Send and receive instant messages.

Your Galaxy Tab makes it easy for you to read and respond to email messages when you're on the go. Before you start, though, you need to configure your email account(s) using standard protocols, such as POP and IMAP, or connect with more proprietary systems such as Exchange and Yahoo!. Then you need to learn how to use the built-in Email app.

Email isn't the only way to communicate. The Galaxy Tab also contains a built in Messaging app so you can configure your instant message settings to communicate using standard text message (SMS) and multimedia message (MMS) services.

In this chapter, you learn about the following:

→ Configuring Email
→ Reading Email
→ Composing a New Message
→ Creating Your Own Signature
→ Deleting and Moving Messages
→ Searching Through Email
→ Configuring Email Settings
→ Sending and Receiving Instant Messages
→ Configuring Instant Message Settings

Sending Email and Instant Messages

Configuring Email (Galaxy Tab 7")

Following is a complete checklist of the information you need to set up your Galaxy Tab to use a traditional email account. If you have an email service such as Exchange, Google Gmail, or

Yahoo! you won't need all this. However, if you don't configure the email settings, you can't use webmail services in other apps (like Gmail) to do things like email web page links or photos, so you need some of this information no matter what.

- Email address

- Account type (POP or IMAP)

- Incoming mail server address

- Incoming mail user ID

- Incoming mail password

- Outgoing mail server address

- Outgoing mail user ID

- Outgoing mail password

>>> Go Further

DO I USE POP OR IMAP?

If you're not sure whether to use POP or IMAP as your account type, keep the following in mind:

Post Office Protocol, or POP, retrieves and removes email from a server. Therefore, the server acts as a temporary holding place for email. If you receive email using both your Galaxy Tab and your computer, it's more difficult to share your email messages using POP. You need to either set up your email to go to one device and some to another device, or you need to set up one device so it doesn't remove email from the server so another device can retrieve the email as well.

Internet Message Access Protocol, or IMAP, makes the server the place where all messages are stored. Your Galaxy Tab and computer display all email messages on the server. This is the better situation if you have multiple devices retrieving email from the same account.

1. Tap the Email icon on the home screen.

2. In the Set Up Email screen, type the email address in the high-lighted Email Address field. When you start typing, the keyboard appears at the bottom of the screen.

3. Tap the password for your email account in the Password field. As you type in the password charac-ters, they become dots so the password is hidden right away.

4. Tap Next.

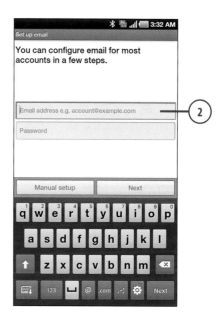

5. Tap the button that corresponds to the account type you have.

6. Type the incoming server settings into the appropriate fields.

7. Tap Next.

8. After the Galaxy Tab checks your incoming server settings, type the outgoing server settings into the appropriate fields.

9. Tap Next.

10. In the Account Options screen, the default is for the Galaxy Tab to never check your email automatically and notify you when email arrives. Make the account you added your default email account by tapping the check box.

11. Change the checking frequency by tapping the Email Check Frequency button. The default frequency is to never check your email automatically. You can have the Tab check for new email as often as 5 minutes a day. If that's too often, you can have the Tab check every 10 minutes, 15 minutes, 30 minutes, every hour, every 4 hours, or once per day.

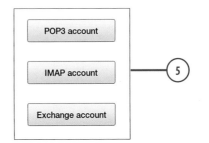

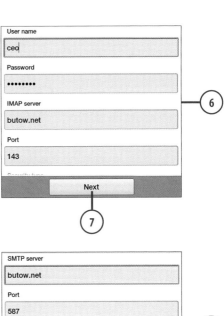

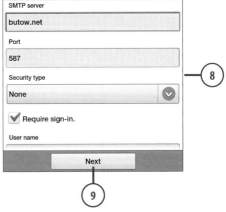

12. Tap the checking frequency in the list.

13. Tap Next.

14. In the Set Up Email page, type an optional name into the Give This Account a Name field.

15. Type your name as you want it to be displayed in outgoing messages.

16. Tap Done. A list of your email messages appears in your Inbox screen.

What Happens if the Settings Won't Verify?

If your settings don't verify, a dialog box displays, asking you to tap the Edit Details button to return to the previous screen and double-check all the information you entered. When something is wrong, it often comes down to misspelled information, such as a misspelled word or letter that needs to be capitalized, or other information such as a different outgoing server port number.

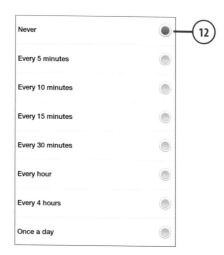

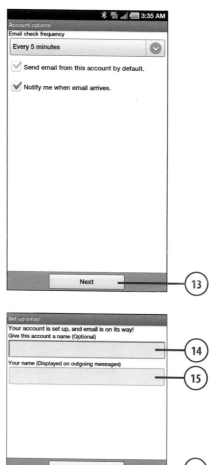

Configuring Email (Galaxy Tab 10")

Here's a complete checklist of the information you need to set up your Galaxy Tab to use a traditional email account. If you have an email service such as Exchange, Google Gmail, or Yahoo! you won't need all this. However, if you don't configure the email settings, you can't use webmail services in other apps (like Gmail) to do things like email web page links or photos, so you need some of this information no matter what.

- Email address

- Account type (POP or IMAP)

- Incoming mail server address

- Incoming mail user ID

- Incoming mail password

- Outgoing mail server address

- Outgoing mail user ID

- Outgoing mail password

>>> Go Further

DO I USE POP OR IMAP?

If you're not sure whether to use POP or IMAP as your account type, keep the following in mind:

Post Office Protocol, or POP, retrieves and removes email from a server. Therefore, the server acts as a temporary holding place for email. If you receive email using both your Galaxy Tab and your computer, it's more difficult to share your email messages using POP. You need to either set up your email to go to one device and some to another device, or you need to set up one device so it doesn't remove email from the server so another device can retrieve the email as well.

Internet Message Access Protocol, or IMAP, makes the server the place where all messages are stored. Your Galaxy Tab and computer display all email messages on the server. This is the better situation if you have multiple devices retrieving email from the same account.

1. Tap Apps, and then tap Email.

2. In the Account setup screen, type the email address in the high-lighted Email Address field. When you start typing, the keyboard appears at the bottom of the screen.

3. Tap the password for your email account in the Password field. As you type in the password charac-ters, they become dots so the password is hidden right away.

4. Tap Next.

5. Tap the button that corresponds to the account type you have.

6. Type the incoming server settings into the appropriate fields.

7. Tap Next.

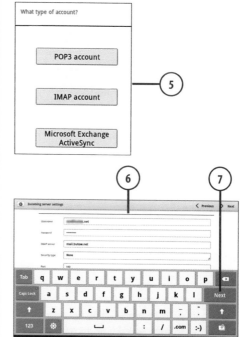

8. After the Galaxy Tab checks your incoming server settings, type the outgoing server settings into the appropriate fields.

9. Tap Next.

10. In the Account Options screen, the default is for the Galaxy Tab to never check your email automatically and notify you when email arrives. Make the account you added your default email account by tapping the check box.

11. Change the checking frequency by tapping the Inbox Checking Frequency button. The default frequency is to never check your email automatically. You can have the Tab check for new email as often as 5 minutes a day. If that's too often, you can have the Tab check every 10 minutes, 15 minutes, 30 minutes, every hour, every 4 hours, or once per day.

12. Tap the checking frequency in the list.

13. Tap Next.

14. In the Set Up Email page, type an optional name into the Give This Account a Name field.

15. Type your name as you want it to be displayed in outgoing messages.

16. Tap Done. A list of your email messages appears in your Inbox screen.

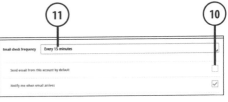

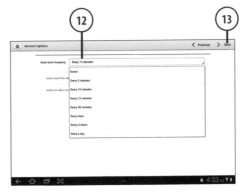

What Happens If the Settings Won't Verify?

If your settings don't verify, a dialog box displays, asking you to tap the Edit Details button to return to the previous screen and double-check all the information you entered. When something is wrong, it often comes down to misspelled information, such as a misspelled word or letter that needs to be capitalized, or other information such as a different outgoing server port number.

Reading Email (Galaxy Tab 7")

You use the Email app to navigate, read, and type your email messages. Let's begin by reading some email messages.

1. Tap the Email icon on the home screen.

2. Tap a message in the list to view it. New messages appear with the subject line in black; previously read messages appear with the subject line in gray.

3. Tap the up and down arrows at the top of the screen to move back and forth between messages.

4. Tap the button that has the sender's name on it at the top of the page.

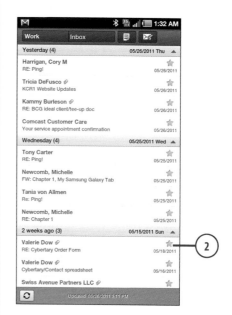

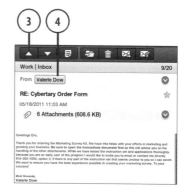

5. Tap the Add to Contact button to add the sender to your list of contacts. The Contacts app opens.

6. Tap the Add button.

7. Tap the location to which you want to save the contact.

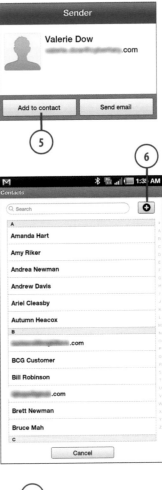

8. Type information into the New Contact screen fields if you want, and then tap Done when you're finished. (You learn more about adding a contact in Chapter 6, "Using the Calendar and Contacts to Simplify Your Life.") Press the Back button to return to the message list.

9. Tap the folder name above the list.

10. Scroll down the list to view folders within the Inbox and tap a folder to view messages within that folder.

11. The folder name appears above the folder list.

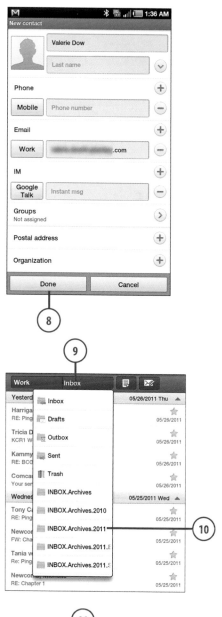

12. Tap the folder name.

13. Tap the Inbox folder.

14. Tap a message in the list.

15. Tap Delete. The Email app deletes the message automatically and displays the next message further down the list.

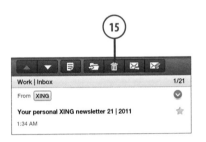

How Do You Create Folders?

You can't create folders inside your mailbox in the Email app. If you use an IMAP mail server, you can go to the web interface for that server and create a new folder there so it appears in the Email app. Unfortunately, if you use a POP email server, you cannot add folders to the server—all you have is Inbox, Sent, and Trash.

How Do I Combat Spam?

The Galaxy Tab has no spam filter built in. However, most email servers filter spam at the server level. If you use a basic POP or IMAP account from an ISP, unfortunately you might not have any server-side spam filtering. If you use an account at a service such as Gmail, you get spam filtering on the server, and spam mail goes to the Junk folder, not your Inbox.

Reading Email (Galaxy Tab 10")

You use the Email app to navigate, read, and type your email messages. Let's begin by reading some email messages.

1. Tap Apps on the home screen, and then tap Email.

2. Your list of Inbox folder messages appears with a list of folders to the left of the message. Tap a message in the list to view it. New messages appear with the subject line in bold type. A folder you're currently in is highlighted in blue in the folder list.

3. Tap the envelope icon at the top-left corner of the screen to return to your list of messages and folders.

4. Tap the button that has the sender's name on it at the top of the page.

5. Tap Add to Contact to add the sender to your list of contacts.

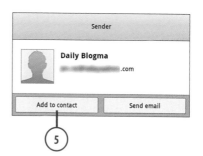

6. Tap the account you want to add the contact to. The Contacts app opens.

7. Tap New.

8. Type information into the New Contact screen fields if you want. (You learn more about adding a contact in Chapter 6, "Using the Calendar and Contacts to Simplify Your Life.") Tap Done to save the new contact and return to the message list.

9. Tap the email account name in the upper-left corner of the screen, and then tap the account name in the list.

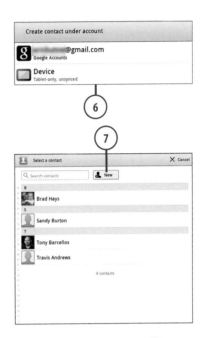

10. Scroll down the folder list to view folders within the Inbox and tap a folder to view messages within that folder.

11. The list of messages within that folder appears to the right of the folder list.

12. Scroll up the folder list until you reach the Inbox folder.

13. Tap the Inbox folder.

14. Tap a message in the list.

15. Tap the Refresh icon to refresh the message on the screen.

16. The Email app refreshes the message automatically.

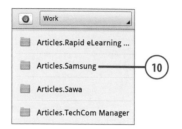

How Do You Create Folders?

You can't create folders inside your mailbox in the Email app. If you use an IMAP mail server, you can go to the web interface for that server and create a new folder there so it appears in the Email app. Unfortunately, if you use a POP email server, you cannot add folders to the server—all you have is Inbox, Sent, and Trash.

How Do I Combat Spam?

The Galaxy Tab has no spam filter built in. However, most email servers filter spam at the server level. If you use a basic POP or IMAP account from an ISP, unfortunately you might not have any server-side spam filtering. If you use an account at a service such as Gmail, you get spam filtering on the server, and spam mail goes to the Junk folder, not your Inbox.

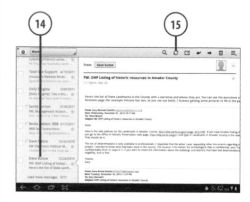

Composing a New Message

The process for composing a new message and composing a reply to a message is similar. This section covers composing a message from scratch.

Galaxy Tab 7"

1. In the Email app, tap the New Mail button.

2. Enter the recipient's address in the To field.

3. Enter an address to copy (Cc) or blind copy (Bcc) the message.

4. Tap in the Subject field, and then type a subject for the email.

5. Tap below the Subject field in the body of the email, and then type your message.

6. Tap the Send button.

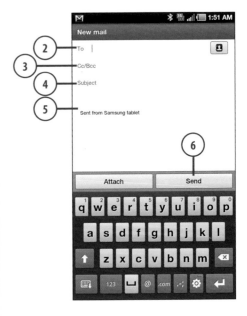

Add Attachments

If you've copied text or images to your clipboard, you can add that text or image as an attachment, just as you can with any email program on your computer. Just tap the Attach button to the left of the Send button. Then you can pick your text, image(s), contacts, or location from the Attach screen.

Galaxy Tab 10"

1. In the Email app, tap the New Mail icon.

2. Enter the recipient's address in the To field.

3. Tap +Cc/Bcc so you can enter an address to copy (Cc) or blind copy (Bcc) the message.

4. Tap in the Subject field, and then type a subject for the email.

5. Tap below the Subject field in the body of the email, and then type your message.

6. Tap Send.

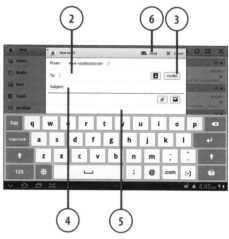

Creating Your Own Signature

You can create a signature that appears below your messages automatically. You create your signature in the Email app.

Galaxy Tab 7"

1. On the home screen, tap the Email icon.

2. Press the Settings button.

3. Tap Account Manager.

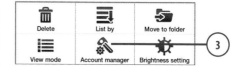

4. Tap your account name in the list.

5. In the Account Settings screen, tap Signature.

6. Type what you want the signature to say (such as your full name) in the Signature field.

7. Tap OK.

8. The signature as it will appear in your Message Composition field appears under the Signature heading.

Can I Have Multiple Signatures?

You can have only one signature per email account on your Galaxy Tab, so technically you can't have multiple signatures. However, the signature is placed in the editable area of the Message Composition field, so you can edit it like the rest of your message and create multiple signatures that way.

Account manager

Work

[redacted].net ✓ — 4

Account settings

General settings

Account name
Work ⟩

Your name
Eric Butow ⟩

Signature
Sent from Samsung tablet ⟩ — 5

Email check frequency
Every 5 minutes ⟩

Default account
Send email from this account by default ✓

Always Cc/Bcc myself
Include my email address in Cc/Bcc line ⟩

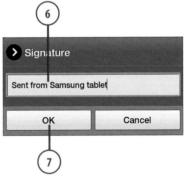

6

⟩ Signature

Sent from Samsung tablet|

OK   Cancel

7

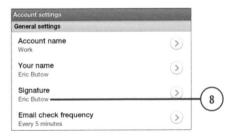

Account settings

General settings

Account name
Work ⟩

Your name
Eric Butow ⟩

Signature
Eric Butow — 8 ⟩

Email check frequency
Every 5 minutes ⟩

Galaxy Tab 10"

1. On the home screen, tap Apps.

2. Tap Email.

3. Tap Menu.

4. Tap Settings.

5. Tap your account name in the list if you have more than one. If you have only one account, the information for that account appears automatically.

6. In the Account Settings screen, tap Signature.

7. Type what you want the signature to say (such as your full name) in the Signature field.

8. Tap OK.

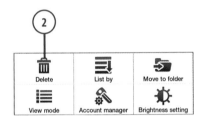

Deleting Messages

When you view a message, you can tap the Delete icon and move the message to the trash.

Galaxy Tab 7"

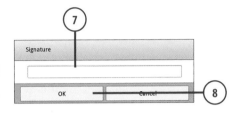

1. In the Email app, go to any mailbox and any subfolder, such as your Inbox, and then press the Settings button.

2. Tap Delete.

3. Tap a check box at the right side of the message entry in the list. The check box turns green. You can select multiple check boxes if you want to delete multiple messages.

4. Tap the Delete button to delete the selected messages.

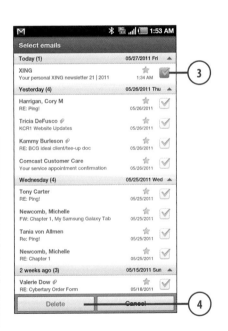

Can I Move Messages to Other Folders?

Unfortunately, you can't move messages in the Email app from one folder to another. If you use an IMAP server, you can log in to the web interface for that server and move messages around there. The next time you log in to the Email app, the app reflects the changes you made in the IMAP server. If you're using a POP server, though, the only way you can move messages is to do so in another email program like one on your desktop or laptop computer.

Galaxy Tab 10"

1. In the Email app, go to any mailbox and any subfolder, such as your Inbox.

2. Tap the message you want to delete.

3. Tap the Trash icon.

4. Tap a check box at the left side of the message entry in the list. You can select multiple check boxes if you want to delete multiple messages.

5. Tap the Trash icon to delete the selected messages.

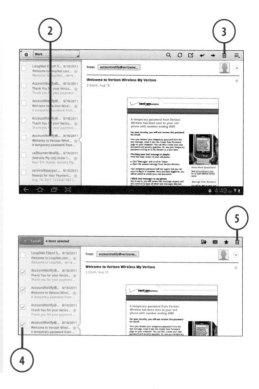

Searching Through Email

By default, the Galaxy Tab doesn't let you search through your email messages. You can change this quickly and then search text in your email messages.

Galaxy Tab 7"

1. Tap the Email icon on the home screen.

2. Press the Search button.

3. Tap All, and then choose whether you want to search for the term in the entire message (All), just the sender name, or just the title of the message. All is the default.

4. Type the search term into the Search Email field.

5. As you type, updated results display below the field. In my example, I typed amad into the field and the Amador County subject appears in the list. Tap a message to open it.

What's the Continue Searching on Server Link?

If you use an IMAP server, you can search other locations on your server (such as other email accounts) for the search term you entered by tapping the Continue Searching on Server link. After you tap this link, more results (if any) appear underneath your original search results. If you use another type of email service, such as POP, you won't see this link.

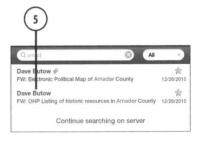

Galaxy Tab 10"

By default, the Galaxy Tab 10" doesn't let you search through your email messages. You can change this quickly and then search text in your email messages.

1. Tap the Search icon.

2. Type the search criteria into the Search Mail field. As you type, updated results display below the field.

3. Tap the Done key.

4. The results appear on the screen. In my example, I typed amador into the field, and the Amador County subject appears in the list. Tap a message to open it.

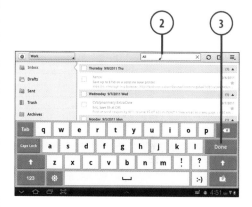

Configuring Email Settings (Galaxy Tab 7")

The Galaxy Tab enables you to update your email account settings as needed.

1. Follow the steps from earlier tasks in this chapter to open the Email app if you aren't there already. Then press the Settings button.

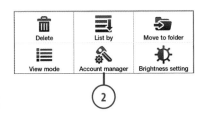

2. Tap Account Manager.

3. Tap your account in the Account Manager list.

4. Change your account name by tapping Account Name.

5. Add or change your name by tapping Your Name.

6. Add or change your signature by tapping Signature as you did earlier in this chapter.

7. Change the email checking frequency by tapping Email Check Frequency as you did earlier in this chapter.

8. Tap Default Account if you don't want to send email from this account by default.

9. Tap Always Cc/Bcc Myself if you always want to include the account's email address in a message's Cc/Bcc line.

10. Choose to Cc yourself (your email address is visible to the sender in the Cc field) or Bcc yourself (your email address is not visible to the sender).

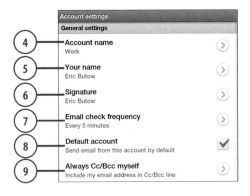

11. Tap Email Notifications to specify whether the Galaxy Tab should notify you when email arrives.

12. Select a ringtone, or no ringtone at all, by tapping Select Ringtone.

13. Tap Vibrate to specify when the Galaxy Tab should vibrate in response to an email arriving. It can vibrate every time an email arrives or only when the Galaxy Tab is in silent mode. Or you can set it back to Never Vibrate.

14. Change your incoming settings (as you did with a new account earlier in this chapter) by tapping Incoming Settings.

15. Change your outgoing settings (as you did with a new account earlier in this chapter) by tapping Outgoing Settings.

16. Tap Forward with Files if you don't want to include attached files in a message you're forwarding to someone else.

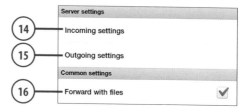

Configuring Email Settings (Galaxy Tab 10")

The Galaxy Tab enables you to update your email account settings as needed.

1. Follow the steps from earlier tasks in this chapter to open the Email app if you aren't there already. Then tap the Settings icon.

2. Tap Settings.

3. Tap your account in the Account manager list if there is more than one. If not, your account appears on the screen automatically.

4. Change your account name by tapping Account Name.

5. Add or change your name by tapping Your Name.

6. Add or change your signature by tapping Signature as you did earlier in this chapter.

7. Change the Inbox checking frequency by tapping Inbox Check Frequency as you did earlier in this chapter.

8. Tap Default Account if you don't want to send email from this account by default. Scroll down for more options.

9. If you always want to add your email address in the Cc or Bcc box, tap Always Cc/Bcc Myself.

10. Tap Email Notifications to specify whether the Galaxy Tab should notify you when email arrives.

11. Select a ringtone, or no ringtone at all, by tapping Select Ringtone.

12. Tap Vibrate to specify when the Galaxy Tab should vibrate in response to an email arriving. It can vibrate every time an email arrives or only when the Galaxy Tab is in silent mode. Or you can set it back to Never Vibrate.

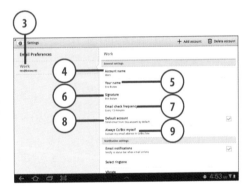

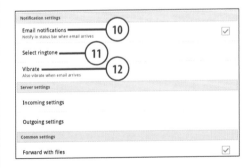

13. Change your incoming settings (as you did with a new account earlier in this chapter) by tapping Incoming Settings.

14. Change your outgoing settings (as you did with a new account earlier in this chapter) by tapping Outgoing Settings.

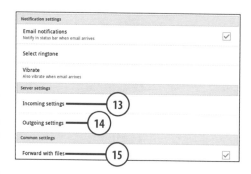

15. The Forward with Files check box is checked by default. This means that if you forward a message that includes one or more file attachments, the Email app will send the files with the forwarded message. Turn off this feature by tapping the check box.

16. Tap Email Preferences.

17. Determine the size of the text in your messages by tapping Message Text Size. The default is Normal, but the size can vary from Tiny to Huge.

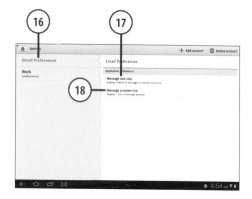

18. Tap Message Preview Line to determine how many lines of text in the message will appear in the message list. The default is 1 line; the number of lines varies from None to 3 lines.

Sending and Receiving Instant Messages

Galaxy Tab 7"

The built-in Messaging app lets you send and receive instant messages.

1. Tap the Applications icon.

2. Tap Messaging.

3. Tap the New Message button.

4. Type the phone number or name of a contact to whom you want to send the message in the To field. As you type, the Galaxy Tab tries to match a name or email address with one that exists in your Contacts database, so you can choose that name from a list below the To field. If the recipient's email address isn't in your Contacts database, or if you prefer to type the email address, you can do that in the To field.

5. You can also add a recipient from your Contacts list by tapping the Contacts button.

6. Type the message you want to compose in the Enter Message Here field.

7. Tap Send. Your message (and any replies) appear in the text area between the To and Enter Message Here fields.

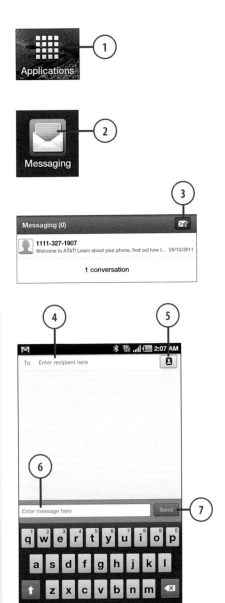

Galaxy Tab 10"

The Galaxy Tab 10" has the Google
Talk instant messaging app built in
so you can send messages to and
receive messages from other Google
Talk users.

1. Tap the Talk icon on the home
   screen.

2. Your Status appears on the Talk
   screen so you can send a status
   message. If you don't have a
   Google account, follow the steps
   to create one.

3. Tap Status Message.

4. Type a new status message in the
   Status Message box.

5. Tap Save.

6. Tap Available to change your
   availability status to others in
   Google Talk. The options are
   Available, Busy, and Invisible. You
   can also sign out of Google Talk.

7. Tap Allow Video and Voice Chats
   if you want text chats only.

8. Tap Change to a Recently Used
   Status to view a history of your
   recent status updates. You can
   also clear your status history.

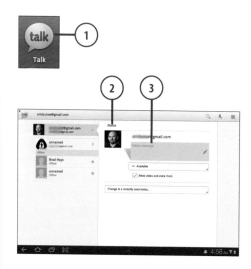

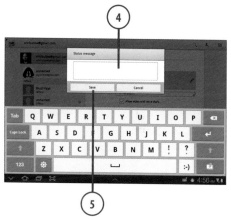

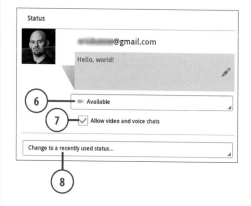

Configuring Instant Message Settings (Galaxy Tab 7")

You can change your instant message settings in the Settings app so you can manage your messages to your liking, set Cell Broadcast settings, and determine how you want to be notified of new messages that come into your message Inbox.

1. Tap the Applications icon to view your apps if you haven't done so already.

2. Tap Messaging, and then press the Settings button.

3. Tap Settings.

4. Tap Delete Old Messages if you want to turn off the default of deleting old message as limits are reached. You can set those storage limits in the next step.

5. Change the number of text messages stored in each conversation by tapping Text Message Limit.

6. Type the message limit in the box or tap the + and – buttons to move the number up and down one message, respectively.

7. Tap Set.

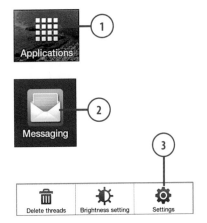

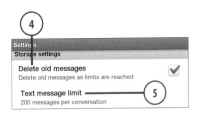

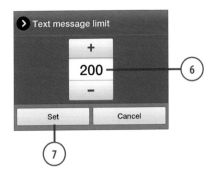

8. Manage messages stored on your SIM card by tapping Manage SIM Card Messages. If there are any messages on the SIM card, they display on the Text Messages on SIM Card screen. If there aren't any, the screen displays the message "No messages on the SIM card." Press the Back button to return to the Settings screen.

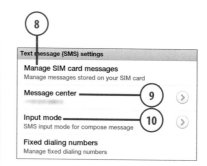

9. If you find that you can't send text messages, it might be because your carrier has a different message center number than the one that came with your Galaxy Tab. Change your default message center phone number by tapping Message Center.

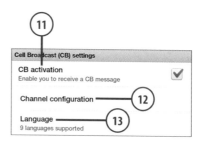

10. Tap Input Mode to set the SMS input mode for composing messages. The default is Automatic, but you can also choose from GSM alphabet and Unicode.

11. Tap CB Activation if you want to receive CB messages on your Galaxy Tab.

12. Tap Channel Configuration to configure the CB channels you want to receive. The default is all channels.

13. Tap Language to configure the languages of the CB broadcasts you want to receive. The default is all languages your version of the Galaxy Tab supports (for example, nine languages including English).

14. Tap Notifications if you don't want notifications to display in the status bar at the top of the screen.

15. Tap Select Ringtone to change the ringtone that sounds when you receive messages.

16. You can select from the default ringtone, a number of other ringtones, or silent mode.

17. After you select the ringtone, tap OK.

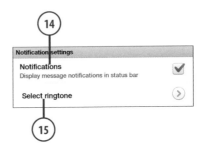

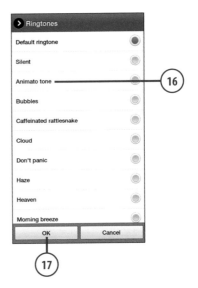

Configuring Instant Message Settings (Galaxy Tab 10")

You can change your instant message settings in Google Talk's settings screen so you can manage your messages to your liking, set Cell Broadcast settings, and determine how you want to be notified of new messages that come into your message Inbox.

1. Tap the Talk icon in the home screen.

2. Tap Menu.

3. Tap Settings.

4. By default, the Galaxy Tab signs into Talk automatically when you turn on the unit. If you don't want to do this, tap Sign in Automatically.

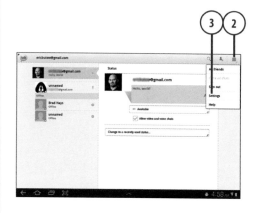

5. If you want to show your Google Talk friends that you're on a mobile device when you're talking to them, tap Mobile Indicator.

6. By default, Google Talk sets the status to Away when your screen turns off. If you want your status to remain the same regardless of your screen status, tap Set Status to Away When the Screen Is Turned Off to clear the checkbox.

7. Change how you want the Galaxy Tab to notify you when you receive a new message by tapping IM Notifications. The default is a system bar notification, but you can also have the system open a dialog box or turn notifications off.

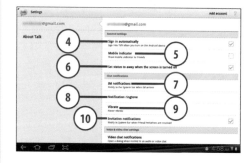

8. Tap Notification Ringtone to change the ringtone that sounds when you receive messages.

9. Tap Vibrate to have the unit vibrate when a new message comes in, vibrate only when the system is silent, or never (which is the default).

10. If you don't want the system bar to tell you when Google Talk has received friend invitations, tap Invitation Notifications. Scroll down to see more options.

11. Change how you want to have the system notify you of a video chat request by tapping Video Chat Notifications. You can either have the system open a dialog box (the default) or notify you on the system bar.

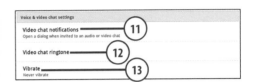

12. Change the video chat request ringtone by tapping Video Chat Ringtone and choosing a ringtone from the list.

13. If you would rather have the unit vibrate when you receive a video chat request, tap Vibrate. You can have the unit vibrate every time, only when the system is silent, or never (which is the default). Scroll down to see more options

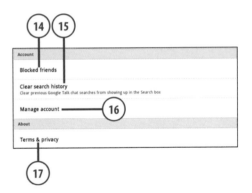

14. View all friends you have blocked by tapping Blocked Friends.

15. You can clear all previous Google Talk chat searches in Google Talk's search box by tapping Clear Search History.

16. Tap Manage Account to open the Accounts and Sync page within the Settings screens so you can manage sync information with your Google services.

17. Tap Terms & Privacy to open a Browser window and view terms and privacy information for Google Talk.

Monitor the day's weather, news, and your personal schedule, and track stocks from one convenient location.

Track your appointments and events.

Store and search all your contacts.

In this chapter, you learn how to organize your daily schedule, news, and information. You also learn how to add and search contacts and calendar events.

→ Putting Together Your Daily Briefing
→ Choosing a Weather Forecast for Your Briefing
→ Tracking Stocks
→ Selecting Your News Settings
→ Checking and Adding to Your Personal Schedule
→ Setting Up Contacts Accounts
→ Managing Contacts
→ Using Contacts
→ Creating Calendar Events
→ Using Calendar Views

6

Using the Calendar and Contacts to Simplify Your Life

Your Samsung Galaxy Tab is highly capable of helping you organize your busy life. The preinstalled Contacts and Calendar widgets help you improve your daily efficiency by enabling you to manage personal contacts and schedule important appointments. Depending on which cellular carrier you have, the Daily Briefing widget or the News and Weather widget provide a snapshot for the day's important information. Let's take a close look at what the Contacts, Calendar widgets, and Daily Briefing/News and Weather widgets can do for you.

Putting Together Your Daily Briefing (Galaxy Tab 7")

The Daily Briefing/News and Weather widget enables you to monitor the weather forecast, news, financial information, and your own personal schedule. You can customize the widget to display your local forecast.

Choosing a Weather Forecast

Follow these steps to display the forecast for a different city.

1. From any home screen, tap the Applications icon.

2. Depending on your Galaxy Tab model or carrier, tap the Daily Briefing or News and Weather widget icon. The first screen of the widget opens to display a default forecast.

3. Tap the + button located in the bottom-left corner of the screen to add a new forecast.

4. Tap Add to open the Add screen.

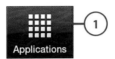

5. Tap in the Search Field and begin to type the name of the city for which you want to add a forecast. As you start to type the name of the city, a list of matching cities appears in the list below.

6. Tap the check box next to the desired city in the list to select it.

7. Tap Save to add the city to your city list.

8. Tap the newly added city within the city list to display the forecast.

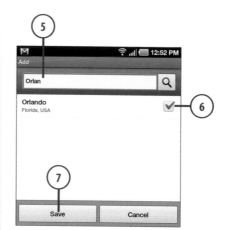

Adding Additional Forecasts

You can add additional forecasts by tapping the add button located in the bottom-left corner of the screen; then tap Add and type in a new city. You can navigate among the multiple forecasts by tapping the forward or back arrows located at the top of a weather forecast screen.

Updating Forecasts and Other Settings

By default, the weather forecast has to be manually refreshed by tapping the Refresh icon at the bottom-right corner of the screen. You can further customize your forecasts by tapping the Menu key located on your Galaxy Tab and then tapping Settings. You can set the forecast to auto refresh by tapping the Weather option in the Settings menu and then tapping Auto Refresh to choose an interval.

Tracking Stocks

You can configure the Daily Briefing or News and Weather widget so that you can monitor a desired stock for a company. So how do you search through all the stocks to find the one that you want to track?

1. From a forecast screen, press your finger on the screen and flick it to the left to access the finance screen.

2. Tap the screen to add a stock.

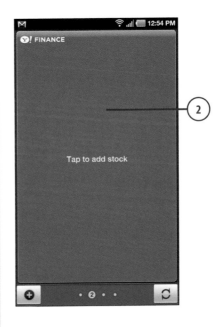

3. Type the name of the stock that you want to track.

4. Tap Search to view a list of results for the stock.

5. Tap the check box next to the stock that you want to track.

6. Tap Save to add the stock and add it to your briefing.

7. Tap the name of the stock that you just added to view the stock summary.

Adding Additional Stocks

You can add an additional stock by tapping the Add button located in the bottom-left corner of the screen, choosing Add again, and then typing in a new stock. You can navigate between multiple stocks by tapping the forward or back arrows located at the top of a stock's information screen.

Refreshing Stocks and Other Settings

By default, your stock information has to be manually refreshed by tapping the Refresh icon at the bottom-right corner of the screen. You can further customize your stock information by tapping the Menu key located on your Galaxy Tab, and then Tapping Settings. You can set the stock to auto refresh by tapping the Finance option in the Settings menu and then choosing Widget Auto Refresh to select an interval.

Selecting Your News Settings

You can browse the latest world, national, and local news stories by customizing your news home page.

1. From a finance screen, press your finger on the screen and flick it to the left to access the news screen. You can scroll up and down to view the list of today's news topics.

2. Tap a story to read.

Adding a Bookmark for a Story and Other Settings

You can bookmark an interesting story by tapping the Menu key. Your Galaxy Tab makes it easy to perform a word search in a news story as well as adjust screen brightness, print stories, share pages, and more.

3. Options for filtering and customizing your news are located at the very top of the screen. Tap the Settings option.

4. Tap Customize Home Page.

5. Toggle the categories to customize the news you see when you access your news home screen. Tap a new category to add it to your home screen.

6. Tap the Back key to return to the previous screen.

7. Tap Set Local Preferences.

8. Tap in the ZIP field to access the keyboard.

9. Tap the SYM key on the keyboard to switch the keyboard to Symbol mode.

10. Enter your ZIP code.

11. Tap Go and the city appears below the entry box.

12. Tap Local News to browse local news stories.

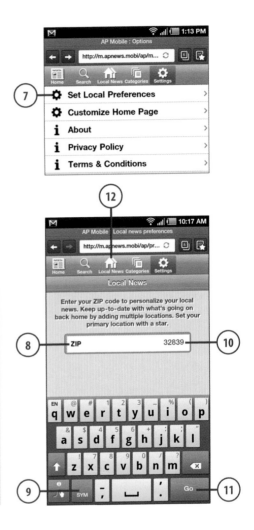

It's Not All Good

Refreshing News Stories

By default, your news results must be refreshed manually. If you have not manually refreshed your news results for a couple days, you need to do so before tapping a story to read. If you fail to do so and then tap an old news story, you are taken to an empty news page. You can set news topics to auto refresh by tapping the Menu key on your Galaxy Tab from a news results page and then tapping Settings. You can choose the news option from the Settings list and then tap Widget Auto Refresh to select an interval.

Checking and Adding to Your Personal Schedule

The fourth and final page of the Daily Briefing or News and Weather widget is dedicated to your personal schedule. The day's activities entered into your Galaxy Tab Calendar appear on this final page, where you can also add new events.

1. From the News headline home screen, press your finger on the screen and flick it to the left to access your schedule for today. The information that you have already added into the Calendar widget for this day is displayed on this screen. You can also add new events to the schedule.

2. Tap the screen to add an event to your schedule.

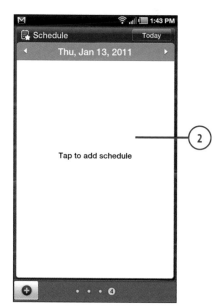

3. Tap in the field to access the keyboard.

4. Type a title for the new event.

5. Tap the Time button in the From field to specify a beginning time for the event.

6. Tap the plus and minus buttons in the hour and minute fields to designate a new time.

7. Tap the PM button to toggle between PM and AM.

8. Tap Set when you're finished.

9. Tap the Time button in the To field to specify an end time for the event. This field is automatically adjusted to an hour later than the time set in the From field. Adjust the end time for the event in the same manner as setting the begin time.

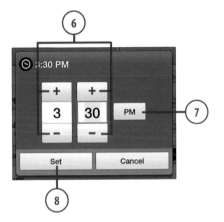

10. Scroll down and tap in the location field to enter an address.

Mapping an Address

Do you need to locate the address you entered? You can tap the map icon located at the end of the address field to pinpoint the address you have entered for the event.

Adding an Alarm

Do you need a little extra help remembering important events? You can instruct your Tab to issue an alarm as a helpful reminder before a scheduled event. Simply tap the Alarm field and choose a time.

11. Tap in the Note field and enter notes regarding the event.

12. Tap Done. The event has now been added to Today's schedule.

Staying Up to Date (Galaxy Tab 10")

The Daily Briefing/News and Weather widget aren't available on the Galaxy Tab 10" because as of this writing there weren't very many applications available for tablets running Honeycomb. That doesn't mean you can't find alternatives on the Android Market site, however. Several well-reviewed free apps are available.

- If you're looking for news, search for News360 for Tablets.

- AccuWeather, which is one of the components in the Galaxy Tab 7.0 Daily Briefing widget, has a separate AccuWeather for the Honeycomb app.

- The Stock Alert Tablet Edition app enables you to view all sorts of information about stocks.

This section gives you a brief look at these three apps so you can get the information you're looking for on your Galaxy Tab 10". Start by downloading the apps. (You can find out how to download apps in Chapter 11, "Enhancing Your Galaxy Tab with Apps.") You can also explore the Market to see what other apps might meet your needs.

Choosing a Weather Forecast

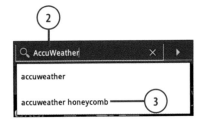

Follow these steps to display the forecast for a specific city in AccuWeather:

1. Tap Market on the home screen.

2. Tap Search Market and type AccuWeather.

3. Tap accuweather honeycomb in the list.

4. Tap AccuWeather for Honeycomb on the Apps screen.

5. Tap Download.

6. On the Download & Allow Access screen, tap OK. The Galaxy Tab downloads and installs the Stock Alert Tablet Edition app automatically.

7. After the Galaxy Tab downloads and installs the app, tap Open.

8. Tap I Agree in the Terms and Conditions screen.

9. Type your location in the form of City, State (like Jackson CA) into the Add Location box, and then tap the Search button.

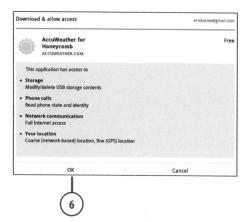

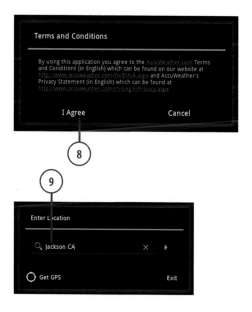

10. Tap the city or town on the search results page.

11. Tap the newly added city or town to display the current condition.

12. View the 15-day forecast for the city or town by tapping 15-Day Forecast. You can scroll down the days to see the forecasted conditions for the next 15 days.

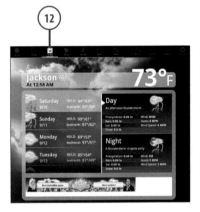

Adding Additional Forecasts

You can add additional forecasts by tapping Locations in the top-right corner of the screen; then tap Add Location and type in a new city. You can navigate among the multiple forecasts by tapping Locations and then selecting the location from the Locations list.

Updating Forecasts and Other Settings

By default, the weather forecast must be manually refreshed by tapping the Refresh icon at the upper-right area of the screen. You can further customize your forecasts by tapping Settings at the far upper-right corner of the screen, such as changing the units and time format.

Tracking Stocks

You can configure the Stock Alert Tablet app so that you can monitor a desired stock for a company.

1. Tap Market on the home screen.

2. Tap Search Market and type Stock.

3. Tap stock alert tablet in the list.

4. Tap Stock Alert Tablet Edition on the Apps screen.

5. Tap Download.

6. On the Download & Allow Access screen, tap OK. The Galaxy Tab downloads and installs the Stock Alert Tablet Edition app automatically.

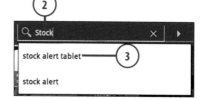

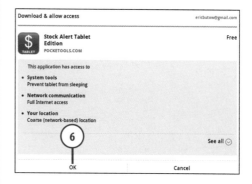

7. After the Galaxy Tab downloads and installs the app, tap Open.

Launching Stock Alert Tablet Edition from the Home Screen

After you install the Stock Alert Tablet Edition app, the system installs a link icon on the home screen. Tap on this icon to launch the app from the home screen the next time you want to run it.

8. If this is your first time starting Stock Alert Tablet, tap Accept to accept the End User agreement.

9. Tap the Add Stock icon to add a stock.

10. Type the name of the company with the stock that you want to track. You can also type the stock ticker name.

11. Tap Search to view a list of results for the stock. Tap the name of the stock that you want to track from the list of search matches.

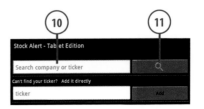

12. Scroll down the stock list in the left column if necessary. Tap the name of the stock that you just added to view the stock summary.

Adding Additional Stocks

You can add an additional stock by tapping the Add Stock icon, typing in a new stock ticker in the ticker box directly underneath the Search box, and then tapping Add. You can navigate between multiple stocks by scrolling up and down your list of stocks in the left column and then tapping the stock you want to view.

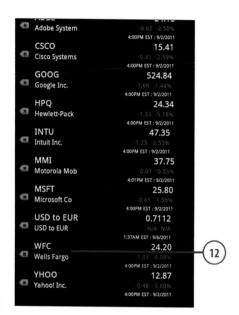

Refreshing Stocks

By default, your stock information must be manually refreshed by tapping the Refresh Rates icon above the list of stocks in the left column on the screen.

Selecting Your News Settings

You can browse the latest world, national, and local news stories by customizing your news settings in News360. However, before you can do so you need to create a News360 account.

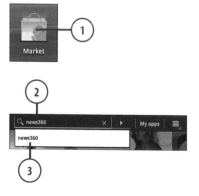

1. Tap Market on the home screen.

2. Tap Search Market and type News360.

3. Tap news360 in the list.

4. Tap News360 for Tablets on the Apps screen.

5. Tap Download.

6. On the Download & Allow Access screen, tap OK. The Galaxy Tab downloads and installs the News360 for Tablets app automatically.

7. After the Galaxy Tab downloads and installs the app, tap Open.

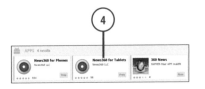

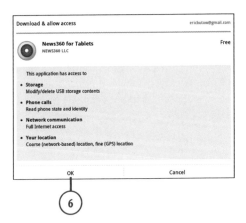

8. Tap Create New Account.

9. Choose how you want to authenticate with News360. You can either use your Facebook or Twitter account information. This example uses a connection through a Facebook account.

10. In the Facebook screen, type your email account and password, and then tap Log In.

11. Give the new device a name in the Name New Device screen, and then tap Save Device.

12. Tap Continue to close the Welcome window.

13. The list of top stories appears. You can scroll up and down the list and tap a story title to read it.

Bookmarking a Story by Saving It to the Tab

You can bookmark an interesting story while you're reading it by tapping the plus icon in the upper-right corner of the screen. When you return to the main News360 page (tap the News360 icon in the upper-left corner of the screen) tap Saved in the upper-right area of the screen. You'll see a list of stories that you've saved that you can read when you're online or not con-nected to the Web. Be mindful, though, that the more stories you add the more room consumed on your Tab, and that could affect system performance.

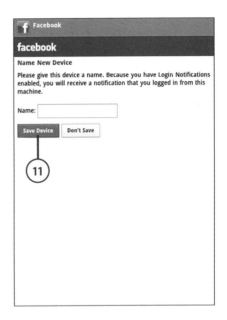

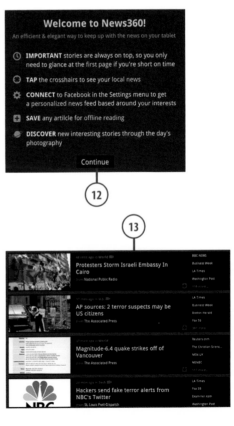

14. Options for filtering and customizing your news are located at the upper-right corner of the screen. Tap the Search icon to search for articles or topics.

15. Tap the Settings icon to open the settings page.

16. You can change your current account options, connect to other social networking sites with which you have accounts, change your application settings, submit feedback, and get product support. Return to the News360 home screen by tapping the News360 icon.

17. You can add categories to your My Interests list by tapping the wrench icon to the right of the My Interests category header.

18. Tap Add Section to add a section to the My Interests list.

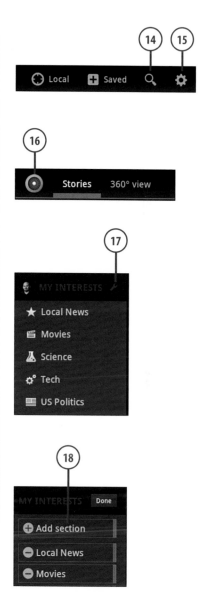

19. Scroll through the list of topics and tap one or more topics in the list that you want to add as a new section.

20. Search for a topic by tapping Search Topics and typing the topic you want to search for.

21. Tap the Search button.

22. Tap the thumbnail of the matches you want to add as a new section.

23. Tap Done.

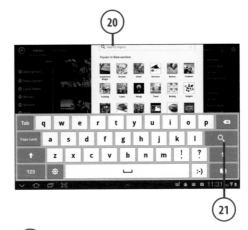

24. The app adds all the topics you added to the My Interests section list and displays any stories for the section category on the screen.

25. In the My Interests list, scroll down to the bottom of the list, and then tap Update My Interests.

26. Analyze your Facebook profile and news feeds for topics so News360 can provide news stories based on your preferred topics. Tap Start.

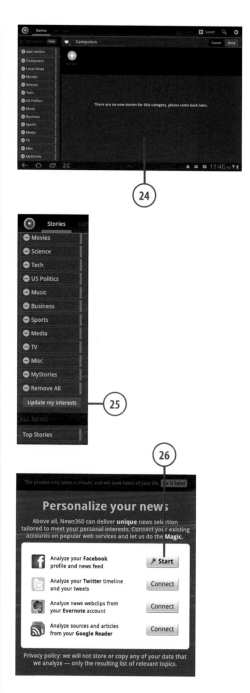

27. After News360 analyzes your pro-
    file and news feeds, the app tells
    you how many topics it found in
    your Facebook profile. Tap
    Continue.

28. Scroll up and down in the Edit
    Your Interests screen to view the
    various categories and the topics
    within them. You can remove a
    category by tapping the X button
    in the upper-right corner of the
    category area.

29. Tap Finish.

30. Tap a category in the My Interests
    list that contains topics you
    added in the Edit Your Interests
    screen.

31. Tap a topic thumbnail image to
    view more information about the
    topic and to receive a list of news
    stories related to the topic.

32. The left side of the screen shows information about the topic as well as links to related topics in blue.

33. Scroll up and down the stories list to view the list of headlines. Tap the headline to read the story.

34. Add this topic to the My Stories category by tapping Add to My Stories.

It's Not All Good

Refreshing News Stories

By default, News360 refreshes news stories when the app finds new stories to post in your headlines list. If you want to refresh your headlines list manually, you must move to another category and then return to your original category. If you want to return to the Top Stories category and refresh that category's headlines list, tap the News360 icon in the upper-left corner of the screen. The Top Stories screen appears and displays the latest headlines.

Managing Contacts (Galaxy Tab 7")

The Contacts widget enables you to manage all the important information you receive from colleagues, friends, and prospective business associates. Think of your Galaxy Tab as a virtual filing cabinet or Rolodex where you can store contact information such as names, addresses, emails, and notes. If you collect contacts with other social networking services, you can also configure Contacts to sync information between accounts.

Setting Up Contacts Accounts

The Galaxy Tab can synchronize its contacts information with multiple accounts, such as Google, Corporate Exchange, other email providers, and social networking sites such as Facebook, Twitter, and Myspace. Information on your Galaxy Tab is updated when you make changes to information in your accounts. Setting up a contacts account is easy.

1. Tap the Menu key from any home screen.

2. Tap Settings.

3. Tap Accounts and Sync.

4. Tap Add Account.

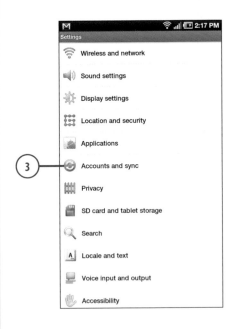

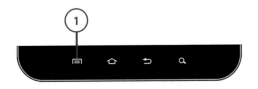

5. Tap an account that you want to set up.

6. Follow the prompts to set up each account that you would like to add. The accounts you add appear in the Manage Accounts area of the Accounts and Sync Screen.

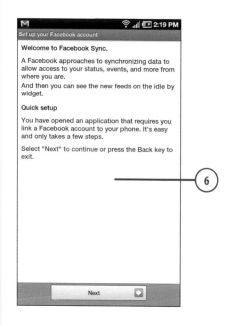

Adding Contacts

You can store contact information for family, friends, and colleagues for quick access and to send messages. Let's look at the Contacts widget.

1. From any home screen, tap Applications.

2. Tap the Contacts widget icon. A list of all contacts appears.

3. Tap the Add button located at the bottom-left corner of the screen to access a new contact form.

4. The accounts you have set up for synchronization appear in the Save Contact To prompt. Tap the account for which you want to synchronize this contact.

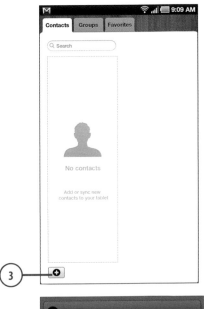

5. Tap in the First Name field to reveal the keyboard and enter the first name of the contact. You can tap the arrow icon, located at the end of the last name field, to add a Name Prefix, Middle Name, Name Suffix, Phonetic Given Name, Phonetic Middle Name, and Phonetic Family Name to the contact. There is no need to use the Shift key on the keyboard to capitalize the name, because the Galaxy Tab does this automatically.

6. Tap the Done button on the keyboard to advance to the next field.

7. Continue to type data into the fields and tap Done on the keyboard to skip any fields you don't want to fill.

Don't Worry About Formatting

You don't need to type parentheses or dashes for the phone numbers you enter. The Galaxy Tab formats the number for you.

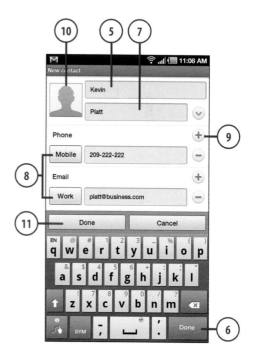

8. Tap the labels within fields to reveal a pop-up menu with other labels to choose from. Tap the Back key if you want to dismiss the pop-up list.

9. Tap the plus icon in a Phone field to add an additional field, or tap the minus button to remove a field.

10. Tap the Photo ID field to select a photo from an album or to take a photo to assign to the contact.

11. Tap the Done button to complete the new contact.

Assigning Contacts to Groups

You can assign a contact to one of three groups (Family, Friends, or Work) by Tapping in the Groups field located toward the bottom of the New Contact sheet and then tapping a group.

Updating a Contact

You can update a contact by first tapping an existing contact in the Contacts list and then tapping Edit located at the bottom right of the screen. The contact sheet opens so that you can edit or add information.

Displaying Contacts

You can control how your contacts are listed by setting sorting and display preferences. After you launch the Contacts widget, you can tap the Menu key on the Galaxy Tab and choose Display Options. The Display Options screen provides you the following viewing options: View Only Contacts with Devices, Sort by First Name, Sort by Last Name, Display Contacts by First Name First, Display Contacts by Last Name First.

Searching for Contacts

Your list of contacts is sure to grow the longer you have your Galaxy Tab. So how do you search your large list of contacts for a specific contact?

1. From any home screen, tap Applications.

2. Tap the Contacts widget icon. A list of all contacts displays.

3. Tap in the Search field. The keyboard appears.

4. Start typing the name of the contact you are looking for. As soon as you begin to type, the widget provides a list of possible results matching the text you have typed. Continue typing until you have narrowed the search.

5. Tap the name to reveal the contact information.

6. Tap the X located in the Search field to dismiss the search.

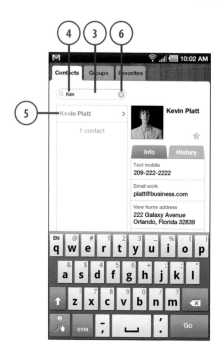

Joining Contacts

When you synchronize the contacts on your Galaxy Tab with multiple accounts, such as Facebook, Twitter, Myspace, and Google, you can have varying numbers and address information for a single contact. You can see all the contacts' numbers and addresses in a single contact entry by joining contacts. Joining contacts can help you keep your contact information up to date.

1. Tap the Contacts widget icon.

2. Hold your finger to a contact that you want to join with another contact. A contextual menu appears. You can also tap the Menu key on your Galaxy Tab to access the Join Contact option under the More menu.

3. Tap Join Contact in the contextual menu.

4. Tap the same contact in the list to reveal entries synchronized with other accounts. The second entry is now joined with your Galaxy Tab contact. The information for both entries in each account has merged. You can unjoin the contacts by tapping the minus sign next to the entry you want to unlink. You can also choose which entry is the primary entry for your Galaxy Tab.

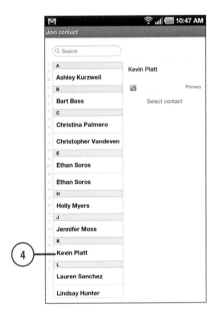

Using Contacts

After you have entered a contact in your Galaxy Tab, you can utilize a few functions and displays directly from the Contacts page.

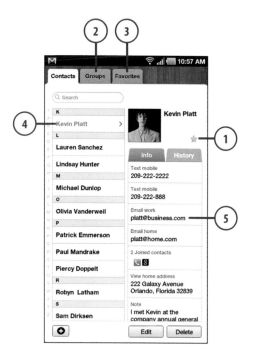

1. Tap the star icon to the right of the contact to set that contact as a favorite.

2. Tap the Groups tab to view the list of contacts you have assigned to a group.

3. Tap the Favorites tab to view the list of contacts you have designated as favorites.

4. Press and hold your finger on a contact's name to Send a Namecard via Bluetooth, Gmail, or messaging. Think of a namecard as an electronic business card.

Managing Contacts

After a contact has been entered into your Galaxy Tab, many of the things you would care to do with a contact can be found by pressing your finger to a contact and holding, such as Join Contact, Add to Favorites, Add to Group, Set Default, Send Namecard.

5. Tap a Contact's email address into the Info field to compose a new email to that contact.

Managing Contacts (Galaxy Tab 10")

The Contacts widget enables you to manage all the important information you receive from colleagues, friends, and prospective business associates. Think of your Galaxy Tab as a virtual filing cabinet or Rolodex where you can store contact information such as names, addresses, emails, and notes. If you collect contacts with other social networking services, you can also configure Contacts to sync information between accounts.

Setting Up Contacts Accounts

The Galaxy Tab can synchronize its contacts information with multiple accounts, such as Google, Corporate Exchange, other email providers, and social networking sites such as Facebook, Twitter, and Myspace. Information on your Galaxy Tab is updated when you make changes to information in your accounts. Setting up a contacts account is quite easy.

1. Tap the Apps icon from the home screen.

2. Tap Settings.

3. Tap Accounts and Sync.

4. Tap Add Account.

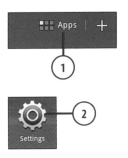

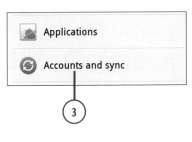

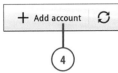

5. Tap an account that you would like to set up.

6. Follow the prompts to set up each account that you would like to add. The accounts you add appear in the Manage Accounts area of the Accounts and Sync Screen.

Adding Contacts

You can store contact information for family, friends, and colleagues for quick access and to send messages. Let's take a look at the Contacts widget.

1. From any home screen, tap Apps.

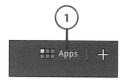

2. Tap the Contacts widget icon. A list of all contacts appears.

3. Tap the New button located at the upper-right corner of the screen to access a new contact form. If you have a Google Contacts account, the widget asks you whether you want to create a new contact in your Google Contacts database or on the tablet.

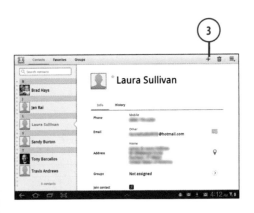

4. Tap in the First Name field and enter the first name of the contact. You can tap the arrow icon, located at the end of the last name field, to add a Name Prefix, Middle Name, Last Name, and Name Suffix to the contact. There is no need to use the Shift key on the keyboard to capitalize the name because the Galaxy Tab does this automatically.

5. Tap the Next button on the keyboard to advance to the next field.

6. Continue to type data into the fields and tap Next on the keyboard to skip any fields you don't want to fill.

Don't Worry About Formatting

You don't need to type parentheses or dashes for the phone numbers you enter. The Galaxy Tab formats the number for you.

7. Tap the labels within fields to reveal a pop-up menu with other labels to choose from. Tap the Back key if you want to dismiss the pop-up list.

8. Tap the plus icon in a Phone field to add an additional field, or tap the minus button to remove a field.

9. Tap the silhouette to the left of the contact name to select a photo from an album or to take a photo to assign to the contact.

Assigning Contacts to Groups

You can assign a contact to one of three groups (Family, Friends, or Work) by tapping in the Groups field located toward the bottom of the New Contact sheet and then tapping a group.

10. Tap the Done button to complete the new contact.

Updating a Contact

You can update a contact by first tapping an existing contact in the Contacts list and then tapping the Edit icon located at the upper right of the screen next to the New icon. The contact sheet opens so that you can edit or add information.

Displaying Contacts

You can control how your contacts are listed by setting sorting and display preferences. After you launch the Contacts widget, you can tap the Settings icon located at the upper-right corner of the screen, tap Settings, and then choose Display Options. The Display Options screen provides the following viewing options: List by First Name, List by Last Name, Display Contacts by First Name First, and Display Contacts by Last Name First.

Searching for Contacts

Your list of contacts is sure to grow the longer you have your Galaxy Tab. So how do you search your large list of contacts for a specific contact?

1. From the home screen, tap Apps.

2. Tap the Contacts widget icon. A list of all contacts displays.

3. Tap in the Search field and use the keyboard to type the name of the contact you are looking for. As soon as you begin to type, the widget provides a list of possible results. Continue typing until you have narrowed the search.

4. Tap the name to reveal the contact information.

5. Tap the X located in the Search field to dismiss the search.

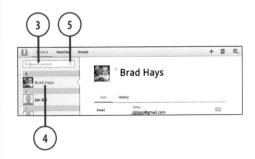

Joining Contacts

When you synchronize the contacts on your Galaxy Tab with multiple accounts, such as Facebook, Twitter, Myspace, and Google, you can have varying numbers and address information for a single contact. You can see all the contacts' numbers and addresses in a single contact entry by joining contacts. Joining contacts can help you keep your contact information up to date.

1. In the Apps screen, tap the Contacts widget icon.

2. Hold your finger to a contact that you want to join with another contact. A contextual menu appears.

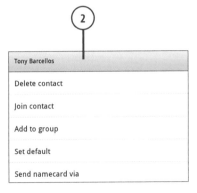

3. Tap Join Contact in the contextual menu.

4. Tap Join. The second entry is now joined with your Galaxy Tab contact. The information for both entries in each account has merged. You can unjoin the contacts by tapping the minus sign next to the entry you want to unlink. You can also choose which entry is the primary entry for your Galaxy Tab.

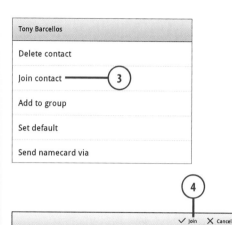

Using Contacts

After you have entered a contact in your Galaxy Tab, you can utilize a few functions and displays directly from the Contacts page.

1. Tap the star icon to the left of the contact name to set that contact as a favorite.

2. Tap the Groups tab to view the list of contacts you have assigned to a group.

3. Tap the Favorites tab to view the list of contacts you have designated as favorites.

4. Press and hold your finger on a contact's name in the contact list to Send a Namecard via Bluetooth, Gmail, or messaging. Think of a namecard as an electronic business card.

5. Tap the email icon to the right of the contact's email address to compose a new email to that contact.

Managing Contacts

After a contact has been entered into your Galaxy Tab, many of the things you would care to do with a contact can be found by pressing your finger to a contact and holding, such as Join Contact, Add to Favorites, Add to Group, Set Default, Send Namecard.

Managing Your Busy Schedule (Galaxy Tab 7")

The Calendar widget enables you to manage all your appointments and events from one convenient location. Calendar enables you to view a busy schedule in multiple views such as Day, Week, Month, and as a List. You can also instruct Calendar to send you a little reminder before an event, in the form of an alert, to help ensure that you never miss a meeting and are always on time.

Creating Calendar Events

Your Galaxy Tab was designed for you to be mobile while still enabling you to manage the important stuff, such as doctor appointments, business meetings, and anniversaries. The Calendar widget enables you to add important event dates to calendars to help ensure that you do not overlook them.

1. Tap Applications from any home screen.

2. Tap the Calendar widget icon. By default, the calendar opens to the Month view. The current date is circled.

3. Tap the date for which you want to add an event. The date becomes highlighted.

4. Tap the + button at the top right.

5. Tap in the title field and enter a title for the event.

6. Tap on the Time button in the From field to enter the end time of the event. You can also use the controls under the Date tab to designate an event for a future date and not just the date you specified in step 3. When you tap the date tab, a calendar opens, enabling you to select a future date.

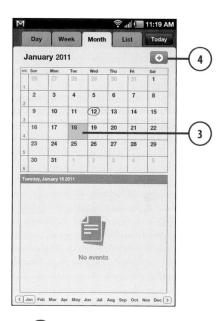

7. Tap the controls to enter the start time for the event.

8. Tap Set.

9. Tap the Time button in the To field to bring up the controls, and adjust the end time for the event in the same manner as setting the begin time.

10. Tap Repeat if you need to set a repeating cycle for the event.

11. Tap Calendar if you want to store the event information in a calendar from another account, such as your Google Calendar.

12. Enter a location, or just skip this field.

13. Tap Alarm to choose an alarm time for the event.

14. Tap to enter a note.

15. Tap Done to complete the event.

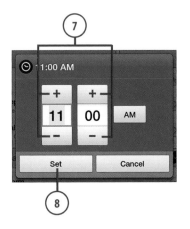

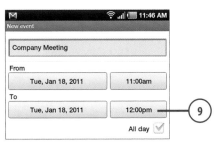

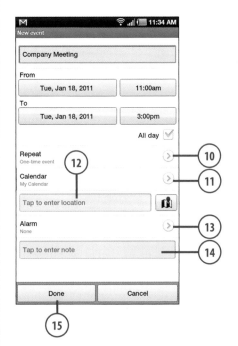

Using Calendar Views

There are four views in which you can view the contents of your calendar: Day, Week, Month, and List. In this section, we look at each view.

Day View

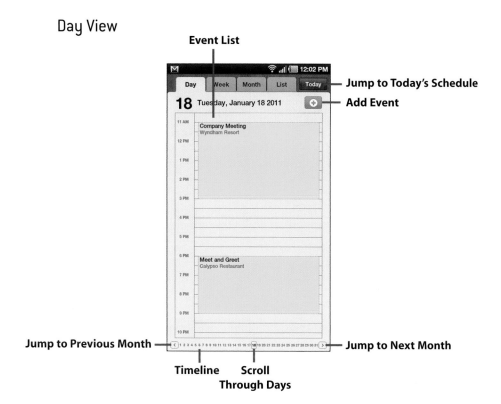

The Day view comprises a list of current events blocked for each half hour, with a section at the bottom that allows you to scroll through days and jump to the next or previous month.

You can press your finger to the list and flick up or down to scroll through the list. All events scheduled with duration of All Day are located at the top of the list.

The timeline located at the bottom of the screen enables you to scroll or tap forward or backward through days on the calendar. You can also press your finger to the list and swipe left or right to move backward or forward through the schedule in daily increments. Tap the arrows located at each end of the timeline to jump to the previous or next month. The Today button, located in the upper right, enables you to return to the current day's schedule, no matter where you are in the calendar.

You can tap an event in the list to view notes, edit the entry, delete the event, or send it via Bluetooth or Messaging.

Week View

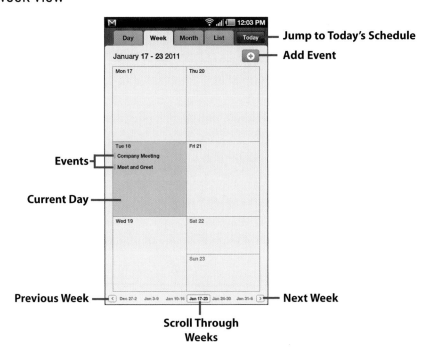

The week view is arranged into seven day parts, with Monday, Tuesday, and Wednesday located on the left and Thursday, Friday, and the weekend on the right. The timeline located at the bottom enables you to scroll or tap forward or backward one week at a time, and the arrows located at each end let you jump to the previous or next month.

Each event for that week is found in its respective scheduled day block. You can tap an event for any date to view notes, edit the entry, delete the event, or send it via Bluetooth or Messaging.

Month View

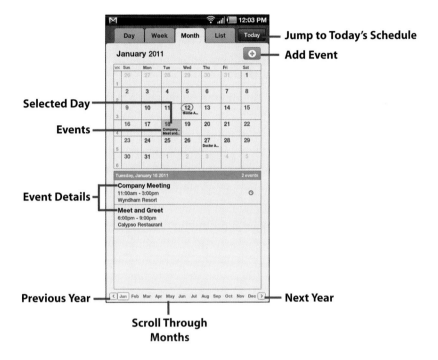

The Month view provides a broad view of events for a given month. Month view is composed of two sections: the monthly calendar and the day's event schedule.

Each section lists the events scheduled for that particular month. The current day block you are viewing is highlighted within the calendar section. Any event designated as an All Day Event is highlighted within the day block of the Calendar view.

The timeline located at the bottom of the screen becomes a monthly timeline in which you can scroll or tap a new month to view. The arrows located at each end of the timeline enable you to jump to the corresponding month of the previous or next year.

List View

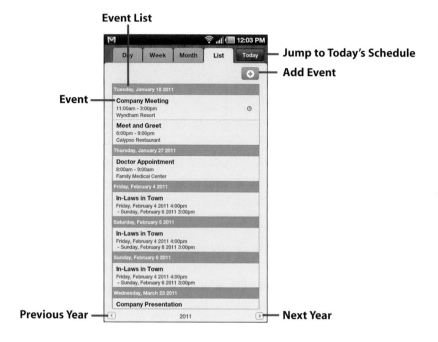

Event List

Jump to Today's Schedule

Add Event

Event

Previous Year — 2011 — Next Year

The List view provides a comprehensive view of all scheduled events for an entire year in one list. You can flick the screen upward or downward to view the entire list or use the arrows located at the bottom to jump to the previous year's event schedule or the next year's.

You can tap an event to view notes, edit the entry, delete the event, or send it via Bluetooth or Messaging.

Managing Your Busy Schedule (Galaxy Tab 10")

The Calendar widget enables you to manage all your appointments and events from one convenient location. Calendar enables you to view a busy schedule in multiple views such as Day, Week, Month, and as a List. You can also instruct Calendar to send you a little reminder before an event, in the form of an alert, to help ensure that you never miss a meeting and are always on time.

Creating Calendar Events

Your Galaxy Tab was designed for you to be mobile while still enabling you to manage the important stuff, such as doctor appointments, business meetings, and anniversaries. The Calendar widget enables you to add important event dates to calendars to help ensure that you do not overlook them.

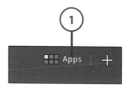

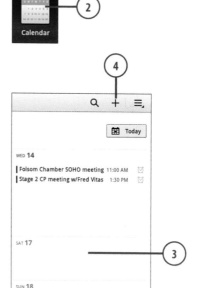

1. Tap Apps from any home screen.

2. Tap the Calendar widget icon. By default, the calendar opens to the Month view. The current date is circled.

3. Tap the date for which you want to add an event. The date becomes highlighted.

4. Tap the + button at the top-right corner of the screen.

5. Tap in the title field and enter a title for the event.

6. Tap on the Time button in the From field to enter the end time of the event. You can also use the controls under the Date button to designate an event for a future date and not just the date you specified in Step 3. When you tap the Date button, a calendar opens, enabling you to select a future date.

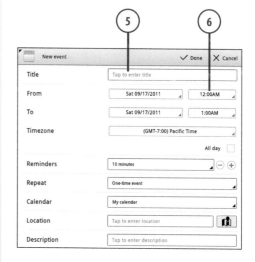

7. Tap the controls to enter the start time for the event.

8. Tap Set.

9. Tap the Time button in the To field to bring up the controls, and adjust the end time for the event in the same manner as setting the begin time.

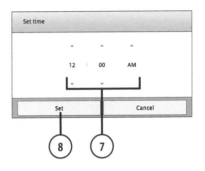

10. Tap Reminders to choose an alarm time for the event.

11. Tap Repeat if you need to set a repeating cycle for the event.

12. Tap Calendar if you want to store the event information in a calendar from another account, such as your Google Calendar.

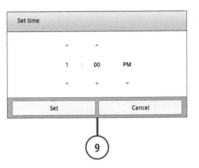

13. Enter a location, or just skip this field.

14. Tap to enter a description of the event.

15. Tap Done to complete the event.

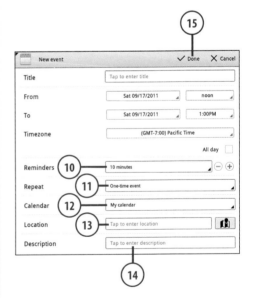

Using Calendar Views

There are four views in which you can view the contents of your calendar: Day, Week, Month, and List. In this section, we take a look at each view.

Day View

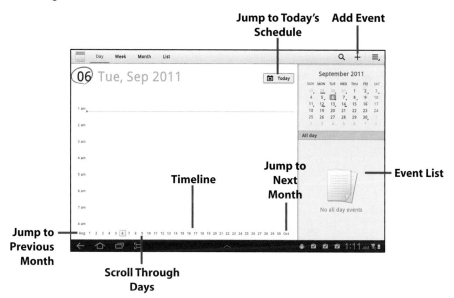

The Day view comprises a list of current events blocked for each half hour, with a section at the bottom that enables you to scroll through days and jump to the next or previous month.

You can press your finger to the list and flick up or down to scroll through the list. All events scheduled with duration of All Day are located at the very top of the list.

The timeline located at the bottom of the screen enables you to scroll or tap forward or backward through days on the calendar. You can also press your finger to the list and swipe left or right to move backward or forward through the schedule in daily increments. Tap the arrows located at each end of the timeline to jump to the previous or next month. The Today button, located in the upper right, enables you to return to the current day's schedule no matter where you are in the calendar.

You can tap an event in the list to view notes, edit the entry, delete the event, or send it via Bluetooth or Messaging.

Week View

Current Day

Add Event

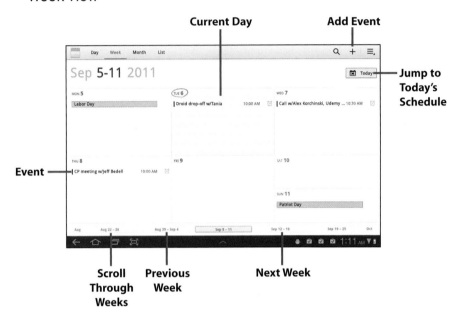

Jump to Today's Schedule

Event

Scroll Through Weeks

Previous Week

Next Week

The week view is arranged into seven day parts, with Monday, Tuesday, and Wednesday located on the left and Thursday, Friday, and the weekend on the right. The timeline located at the bottom enables you to scroll or tap forward or backward one week at a time, and the arrows located at each end let you jump to the previous or next month.

Each event for that week is found in its respective scheduled day block. You can tap an event for any date to view notes, edit the entry, delete the event, or send it via Bluetooth or Messaging.

Month View

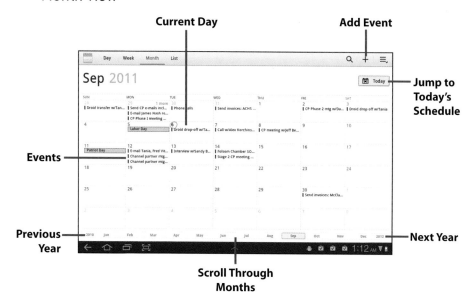

Current Day

Add Event

Jump to Today's Schedule

Events

Previous Year

Next Year

Scroll Through Months

The Month view provides a broad view of events for a given month. Month view is composed of two sections: the monthly calendar and the day's event schedule.

Each section lists the events scheduled for that particular month. The current day block you are viewing is highlighted within the calendar section. Any event designated as an All Day Event is highlighted in the day block of the Calendar view.

The timeline located at the bottom of the screen becomes a monthly timeline in which you can scroll or tap a new month to view. The arrows located at each end of the timeline enable you to jump to the corresponding month of the previous or next year.

List View

Jump to Today's Schedule

Add Event

Event

Previous Year   **Next Year**   **Event List**

The List view provides a comprehensive view of all scheduled events for an entire year in one list. You can flick the screen upward or downward to view the entire list or use the arrows located at the bottom to jump to the previous year's event schedule or the next year's.

You can tap an event to view notes, edit the entry, delete the event, or send it via Bluetooth or Messaging.

Purchase and download
music from your Tab.

Play and
manage
your videos.

Download
and manage
podcasts.

Record video.   Play and manage
your music.

In this chapter, you learn how to get the most out of the media and entertainment capabilities of the Galaxy Tab.

→ Creating a Media Hub Account
→ Downloading Movies and TV Shows Using Media Hub
→ Playing Videos
→ Recording Video
→ Copy Files with Windows Media Player
→ Connecting as a Mass Storage Device
→ Multimedia Sync for Macs and PCs
→ Adding a Podcast App
→ Purchasing Music
→ Playing Songs
→ Creating Your Own Playlists
→ Downloading Podcasts
→ Viewing YouTube Videos

Playing Music and Video

Your Galaxy Tab is a digital media player packed with entertainment possibilities as well as a camcorder capable of recording 720×480 video. You can play music, movies, TV shows, podcasts, audiobooks, and videos; read eBooks; view photos; and access YouTube. Depending on your cellular carrier, each Tab has extended services for purchasing and downloading media.

Creating a Media Hub Account (Galaxy Tab 7")

The Samsung Media Hub widget preinstalled on your Galaxy Tab is your portal to hundreds of movies and TV content available for you to rent or purchase. You need to create a Media Hub account before you can begin to purchase your favorite movies and TV shows.

1. Depending on which cellular carrier or Galaxy Tab model you have, you'll find the Media Hub icon on a home screen or under Applications. Tap the Media Hub shortcut. You can read the end user license agreement and then tap Accept. The Media Hub interface opens.

2. Press the Menu button.

3. Tap My Account to create a Media Hub account.

4. Tap Create Account.

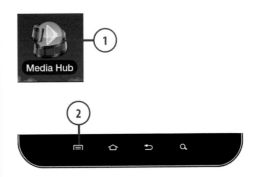

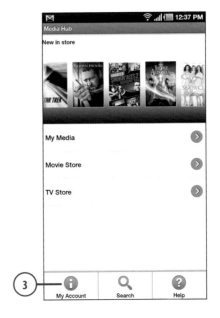

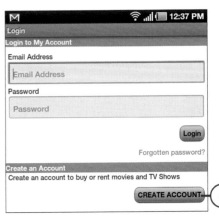

5. Type your email address for this account into the Email field.

6. Tap Next on the keyboard to progress to the next field, and do so to complete the remaining fields.

7. Tap the I Agree to the Terms and Conditions check box to select it.

Sharing Downloads

When you create a Media Hub account, every purchase is linked to your account, not just your Galaxy Tab. That means that when you purchase content, you can download that same content to another device, such as your Galaxy S phone, without having to pay again. You can also share downloads with up to five devices by connecting each device to your Media Hub account.

8. You can tap the second check box if you would like to receive email updates from Samsung.

9. Tap Create Account.

Go Further

EDITING ACCOUNT INFORMATION

You can edit your account settings, such as credit card information and contact information, from the My Account screen, which includes My Details, My Purchases, My Payment Methods, Manage My Devices, Log Out, and Reset Media Hub.

Creating a Media Hub Account (Galaxy Tab 10")

The Samsung Media Hub widget preinstalled on your Galaxy Tab is your portal to hundreds of movies and TV content available for you to rent or purchase. You must create a Media Hub account before you can begin to purchase your favorite movies and TV shows.

1. Depending on which cellular carrier or Galaxy Tab model you have, you'll find the Media Hub icon on a home screen or on the Apps screen. Tap the Media Hub shortcut. Read the end user license agreement, and then tap Accept. The Media Hub interface opens.

2. Tap the Menu button.

3. Tap My Account to create a Media Hub account.

4. Tap Create an Account.

5. Type your email address for this account into the Email Address field.

6. Tap Next on the keyboard to progress to the next field, and do so to complete the remaining fields.

7. Tap the I Agree to the Terms and Conditions check box to select it.

Sharing Downloads

When you create a Media Hub account, every purchase is linked to your account, not just your Galaxy Tab. That means when you purchase content, you can download that same content to another device, such as your Galaxy S phone, without having to pay again. You can also share downloads with up to five devices by connecting each device to your Media Hub account.

8. Tap the second check box if you would like to receive email updates from Samsung.

9. Tap Create Account.

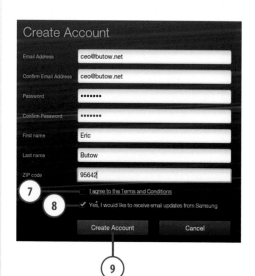

Go Further

EDITING ACCOUNT INFORMATION

You can edit your account settings, such as credit card information and contact information, from the My Account screen, which includes My Details, My Purchases, My Payment Methods, Manage My Devices, Log Out, and Reset Media Hub.

Downloading Movies and TV Shows Using Media Hub (Galaxy Tab 7")

Media Hub has a variety of content to browse, and you can preview much of it before you purchase. You also have access to summaries of movies and TV shows so that you can make an informed purchase. After you have a Media Hub account, it is very easy to browse, purchase, and rent the latest movies and TV shows.

1. Depending on which cellular carrier or Galaxy Tab model you have, you'll find the Media Hub icon on a home screen or under Applications. Tap Media Hub to access the features.

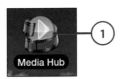

2. Flick your finger from right to left in the upper portion of the interface to scroll through what is new in the store.

3. Tap Movie Store to browse movies.

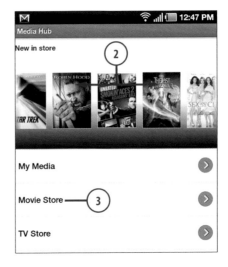

4. Movies are presented categorically, with the available categories
appearing at the top of the
screen and their results appearing
in the lower half of the screen.
Scroll through the movie categories at the top of the screen to
view another category of movies.
When the banner for the category
is centered onscreen, a new list of
results appears at the bottom of
the screen.

5. Tap the movie that you want
within the list. A summary of the
movie appears along with the
options to watch a preview, own,
or rent the movie.

6. Tap Rent or Own. If you are not
logged in to your account, the
Login to My Account screen
opens.

More on Renting and Buying

As of this publication, you can
rent on-demand videos starting
at $2.99 USD and you have up to
30 days to start watching your
video. An important thing to keep
in mind is that after you begin
watching your video, you have
anywhere between 24 to 48
hours to finish watching it. Check
each title for specifics. The price
of movies you want to purchase
and add to your permanent collection varies depending on the
release date. Movie purchases
range from $9.99 to $17.99 USD,
with newer releases on the higher
end of the scale.

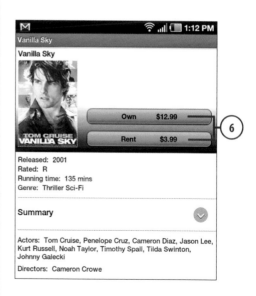

7.   Enter your Email Address and Password into the fields to log in to your account.

8.   Tap Login. This step and step 9 are not needed if you have already signed in to your account.

9.   Tap Rent or Own again.

10.   Tap Add a New Card.

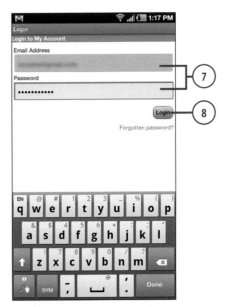

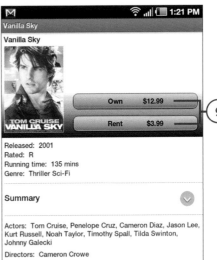

11. Enter your credit card information.

12. Tap Save Card Details. Media Hub processes your card.

13. Tap Download. You can now go to the main screen of the Media Hub app and tap the My Media option to play your movie.

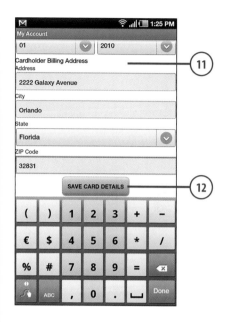

The First Time You Play

The first time you play your media, you need to connect your Tab to your computer using the data cable to unlock the file. When you access your movie for the first time, the license is activated online (not by Wi-Fi) to allow playback of the content. After you make the connection, press the Home button on your Galaxy Tab to return to the home screen. Launch Media Hub to access your media and play the movie.

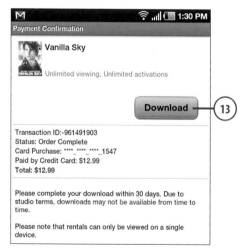

Go Further

ANOTHER WAY OF FINDING CONTENT

If you already know the name of the movie or TV show that you want to pre-view, own, or rent, you can perform a quick search of that title within Media Hub. Press the Menu button and then tap Search. As you type the name of the title into the Search field, the results appear at the bottom. Tap a search result to go straight to the preview, rent, and own options.

More Movie Libraries

If you have a Verizon Galaxy Tab, you also have the option of using the Blockbuster widget located in the Applications menu to browse and search titles. You have access to the entire mobile catalog of Blockbuster On Demand Titles and other Blockbuster content.

Downloading Movies and TV Shows Using Media Hub (Galaxy Tab 10")

Media Hub has a variety of content to browse, and you can preview much of it before you purchase. You also have access to summaries of movies and TV shows so that you can make an informed purchase. After you have a Media Hub account, it is very easy to browse, purchase, and rent the latest movies and TV shows.

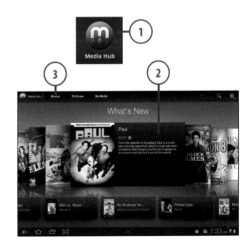

1. Depending on which cellular carrier or Galaxy Tab model you have, you'll find the Media Hub icon on a home screen or under Apps. Tap Media Hub to access the features.

2. Flick your finger from right to left in the upper portion of the interface to scroll through what is new in the store.

3. Tap Movies to browse movies.

4. Movies are presented categorically, with the available categories appearing to the left of the screen and their results appearing in the right side of the screen. Scroll through the movie categories on the left side of the screen to view another category of movies. When the banner for the category is centered onscreen, a new list of results appears at the bottom of the screen.

5. Tap the movie that you want within the list. A summary of the movie appears along with the options to watch a preview, own, or rent the movie.

6. Tap Rent or Own. If you are not logged in to your account, the Login to My Account screen opens.

More on Renting and Buying

As of this publication, you can rent on-demand videos starting at $2.99 USD and you have up to 30 days to start watching your video. An important thing to keep in mind is that after you begin watching your video, you have anywhere between 24 to 48 hours to finish watching it. Check each title for specifics. The price of movies you want to purchase and add to your permanent collection varies depending on the release date. Movie purchases range from $9.99 to $17.99 USD, with newer releases on the higher end of the scale.

7. Enter your email address and password into the fields to log in to your account.

8. Tap Sign In. This step and step 9 are not needed if you have already signed in to your account.

9. Tap Rent or Own again.

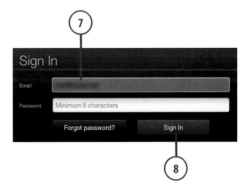

10. Tap Add Card.

11. Enter your credit card information.

12. Tap Save. Media Hub processes your card.

13. Tap the checkbox to the left of your preferred payment method in the list, and then tap Buy.

14. Tap Download. The Media Hub app downloads the file in the My Media screen. After the media file downloads, you can play your movie.

The First Time You Play

The first time you play your media, you must connect your Tab to your computer using the data cable to unlock the file. When you access your movie for the first time, the license is activated online (not by Wi-Fi) to allow playback of the content. After you make the connection, press the Home button on your Galaxy Tab to return to the home screen. Launch Media Hub to access your media and play the movie.

ANOTHER WAY OF FINDING CONTENT

If you already know the name of the movie or TV show that you want to preview, own, or rent, you can perform a quick search of that title within Media Hub. Press the Menu button, and then tap Search. As you type the name of the title into the Search field, the results appear at the bottom. Tap a search result to go straight to the preview, rent, and own options.

More Movie Libraries

If you have a Verizon Galaxy Tab, you also have the option of using the Blockbuster widget located in the Applications menu to browse and search titles. You have access to the entire mobile catalog of Blockbuster On Demand Titles and other Blockbuster content.

Playing Videos (Galaxy Tab 7")

The 7-inch high-resolution screen of your Galaxy Tab provides a great outlet for viewing your favorite videos. The Video shortcut on your Galaxy Tab was designed to make it easy for you to browse and play your downloaded and recorded videos.

1. From a home screen, tap Applications.

2. Tap Video to access your video libraries.

3. Videos are arranged in categories, including downloaded videos, recorded videos, and videos you may have grouped into folders or imported from an external device. Tap a category to view a list of videos.

4. Tap a video within the list to begin playback.

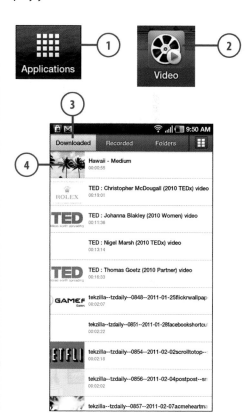

OTHER VIDEO OPTIONS

Go Further

You can choose how videos are listed, shared, and deleted, and choose playback options by pressing the Menu button. The List By options enable you to arrange a video library by Name, Date, Size, and Type. The Share Via option enables you to upload videos to YouTube, send via Messaging, AllShare, Bluetooth, and even Gmail. The Auto Play Next feature is set to Off by default, but you can configure your Galaxy Tab to automatically begin playing the next video in the list after the current video ends. You can also touch and hold your finger on a video in the list to reveal contextual menu options, such as Share via, Delete, and Details.

5. After the video has started, tap in the middle of the screen to bring up the playback controls.

6. Tap the screen brightness control to adjust the brightness level. The Auto Brightness check box appears. To manually adjust the brightness of the screen, you must first deselect Automatic Brightness, which causes a slider to appear, enabling you to adjust brightness manually.

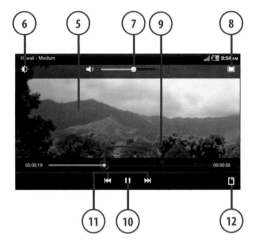

7. Slide your finger on the Volume/Channels slider to adjust the volume of the video.

8. Tap the Screen View icon to adjust scale of the video within the viewer.

9. Drag your finger across the Movie Timeline to shuttle through the video or to jump to a new location. You can also tap the timeline in a new location to jump to that location.

10. The Play button, located in the Playback controls, turns into a Pause button as the video plays. Tap the Pause button to pause the video.

11. Tap the Forward or Rewind buttons to move forward or backward through the video.

12. Tap the Bookmarks icon to mark points within the video that you can revisit at a later time.

Go Further

ANY OTHER VIDEO CONTROLS?

You bet. Press the Menu button during playback of a video to access more controls. Mosaic search breaks the video into segments and enables you to jump to a new location by tapping a video frame representation. You can also view video details and bookmarks, as well as activate subtitles for movies in which subtitles are available.

Playing Videos (Galaxy Tab 10")

The 10" high-resolution screen of your Galaxy Tab provides a great outlet for viewing your favorite videos. The Video shortcut on your Galaxy Tab was designed to make it easy for you to browse and play your downloaded and recorded videos.

1. From a home screen, tap Apps.

2. Flick to the left to view the second Apps screen page, and then tap Video to access your video libraries.

3. Videos are arranged in three categories: thumbnail images of your videos, a list of videos you've taken, and videos in your default folder. Tap a category to view a list of videos.

4. Tap a video in the list to begin playback.

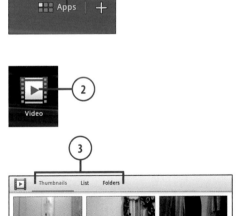

Go Further

OTHER VIDEO OPTIONS

You can choose how videos are listed, shared, and deleted, and choose playback options by pressing the Menu button. The List By options enable you to arrange a video library by Name, Date, Size, and Type. The Share Via option enables you to upload videos to YouTube, send via Messaging, AllShare, Bluetooth, and even Gmail. The Auto Play Next feature is set to Off by default, but you can configure your Galaxy Tab to automatically begin playing the next video in the list after the current video ends. You also can touch and hold your finger on a video in the list to reveal contextual menu options, such as Share via, Delete, and Details.

5. After the video has started, tap in the middle of the screen to bring up the playback controls.

6. Slide your finger on the Volume/Channels slider to adjust the volume of the video.

7. Tap the Screen View icon to adjust the scale of the video in the viewer.

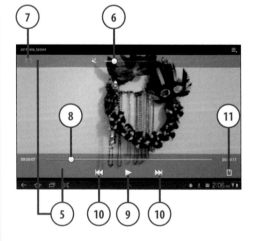

8. Drag your finger across the Movie Timeline to shuttle through the video or jump to a new location. You can also tap the timeline in a new location to jump to that location.

9. The Play button, located in the Playback controls, turns into a Pause button as the video plays. Tap the Pause button to pause the video.

10. Tap the Forward or Rewind buttons to move forward or backward through the video.

11. Tap the Bookmarks icon to mark points in the video that you can revisit later.

Go Further

ANY OTHER VIDEO CONTROLS?

You bet. Tap the menu icon in the upper-right corner of the screen during playback of a video to access more controls. Mosaic search breaks the video into segments and enables you to jump to a new location by tapping a video frame representation. You can also view video details and bookmarks, as well as activate subtitles for movies in which subtitles are available.

Recording Video (Galaxy Tab 7")

Your Galaxy Tab is capable of recording 720×480 video with its main 3-megapixel camera located on the rear of the device. The Galaxy Tab is also equipped with some very helpful features commonly found on dedicated camcorders, including white balance, a video light, manual exposure, and effects.

1. Depending on which cellular carrier or Galaxy Tab model you have, the Camera icon may be located on a home screen or under Applications. Tap the Camera icon to access the camera feature.

2. Move the mode button into the movie position to record video. Your Galaxy Tab switches to video mode.

3. Tap the recording mode icon located in the upper-left corner of the viewer to select a recording mode. The Galaxy Tab is set to Normal by default, which means you can record a video of any length. Tap Limit for MMS to record a video up to one minute long, which is suitable for sending in a multimedia message.

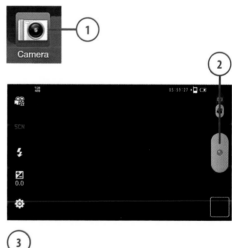

4. Tap the Flash icon to configure the built-in video light setting. By default, the flash, located next to the Camera lens on the back of the device, is set to add a little extra light to a dark scene. You can tap Off to deactivate the flash if the scene you are recording is well lit.

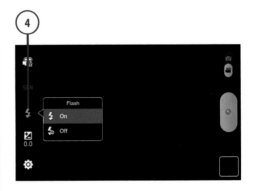

5. An image that is too light or too dark degrades the appearance of your footage. To take full advantage of the camcorder feature of the Galaxy Tab, you need to adjust the exposure level for various bright or dark lighting conditions. Tap the Exposure Value icon.

6. Drag the exposure level up to achieve a proper exposure level in a low-light shooting environment, or drag the level down for a very bright shooting environment.

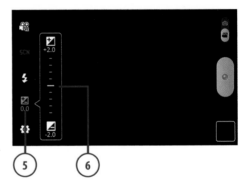

7. Tap the Settings icon in the lower-left corner of the viewer to customize more video settings.

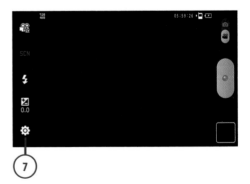

Exploring Video Settings

The video settings consist of two tabs: Video and Setup. The Video tab settings provide control over the aesthetic qualities of your video, such as white balance, effects, and video quality. White balance helps to ensure color accuracy in your videos. You can tap the White Balance setting to choose the proper light source. Use the Setup tab to deactivate audio recording and set your Galaxy Tab to review the clip immediately after you end recording. You can also reset your Tab's video settings to their default state, if needed.

8. Compose the scene in the Viewer.

9. Tap the Record button to begin recording.

10. The Record button turns into a Stop button after you begin recording. Tap the Stop button to end recording.

11. Tap the Image Viewer to review the footage you just recorded. You can also access your recorded videos by tapping the Videos or Gallery icon under Applications from any home screen.

Adding In-Camera Effects

Keep in mind that when you use any of the video effects, they become a permanent part of your video. To give yourself more choices in the future as to how you will use your video, consider purchasing a video-editing program that enables you to apply effects but still maintain a copy of your original video.

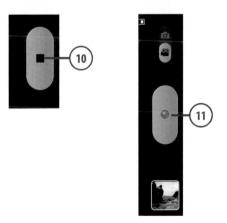

Recording Video (Galaxy Tab 10")

Your Galaxy Tab is capable of recording 720×480 video with its main 3-megapixel camera located on the rear of the device. The Galaxy Tab is also equipped with some very helpful features commonly found on dedicated camcorders, including white balance, a video light, manual exposure, and effects.

1. Depending on which cellular carrier or Galaxy Tab model you have, the Camera icon might be located on the home screen or under Apps. Tap the Camera icon to access the camera feature.

2. Move the mode button into the camcorder position to record video. Your Galaxy Tab switches to video mode.

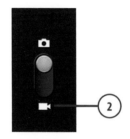

3. Tap the Flash icon to configure the built-in video light setting. By default, the flash, located next to the Camera lens on the back of the device, is set to add a little extra light to a dark scene. You can tap Off to deactivate the flash if the scene you are recording is well lit.

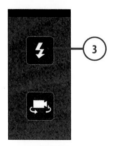

4. An image that is too light or too dark degrades the appearance of your footage. To take full advantage of the camcorder feature of the Galaxy Tab, you must adjust the exposure level for various bright or dark lighting conditions. Tap the Exposure Value icon.

5. Drag the exposure level up to achieve a proper exposure level in a low-light shooting environment, or drag the level down for a very bright shooting environment.

6. Tap the Settings icon in the lower-left corner of the viewer to customize more video settings.

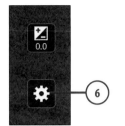

Exploring Video Settings

The video settings consist of two tabs: Video and Setup. The Video tab settings provide control over the aesthetic qualities of your video, such as white balance, effects, and video quality. White balance helps to ensure color accuracy in your videos. You can tap the White Balance setting to choose the proper light source. Use the Setup tab to deactivate audio recording and set your Galaxy Tab to review the clip immediately after you end recording. You can also reset your Tab's video settings to their default state, if needed.

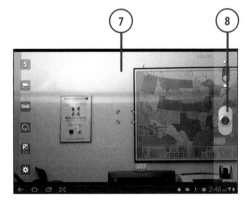

7. Compose the scene in the Viewer.

8. Tap the Record button to begin recording.

9. The Record button turns into a Stop button after you begin recording. Tap the Stop button to end recording.

10. Tap the Play button in the center of the screen to review the footage you just recorded. You can also access your recorded videos by tapping the Videos or Gallery icon under Applications from any home screen.

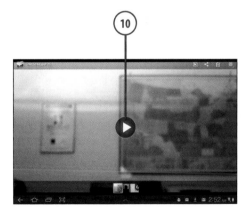

Adding In-Camera Effects

Keep in mind that when you use any of the video effects, they become a permanent part of your video. To give yourself more choices in the future as to how you will use your video, consider purchasing a video-editing program that enables you to apply effects but still maintain a copy of your original video.

Copying Files with Windows Media Player (Galaxy Tab 7")

When you connect your Galaxy Tab to your PC with the data cable, you can choose between various USB modes to synchronize your Galaxy Tab. The Media Player USB mode enables you to use just a few steps to copy files between your computer and your Galaxy Tab with Windows Media Player. Follow these steps to copy music and movies to your Galaxy Tab.

1. Connect the data cable from the Galaxy Tab to the USB port on your computer.

2. Your Tab's screen asks you to select a USB Mode. Tap Media Player to copy files using Windows Media Player. After you tap the Media Player option, your PC asks, "What do you want Windows to do?"

3. The Transfer Files Using Windows Media Player option is automatically selected. Click OK to launch Media Player.

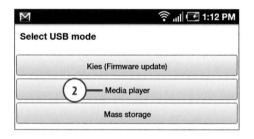

AUTOMATING THE PROCESS

Go Further

You can select the Always Perform the Selected Action check box so that each time you choose the Media Player USB option on your Tab, your PC automatically launches Windows Media Player.

Verizon Customers

If you are a Verizon customer and have V CAST Music with Rhapsody installed on your computer, you also have the choice of managing your Tab using Rhapsody.

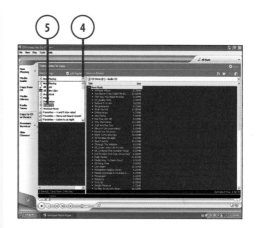

4. Windows Media Player opens with the Copy to CD or Device tab open on the far left of the interface. Click the disclosure arrow in the Items to Copy Field. A list of media available for you to copy displays.

5. Choose the Playlist that you want to copy from the drop-down list. Keep in mind that if you want to copy videos to your Tab, you could also select All Video Clips from the list.

6. The list of music you select appears in the Items to Copy field. All tracks are selected by default. You can deselect any songs that you do not want to copy.

7. Click the disclosure arrow in the Items on Device field. The list of locations in which you can copy the files is shown.

8. Click MTP Device-Card to copy to your MicroSD card in your Tab. If you don't have a memory card installed in your Tab, choose MTP Device-Phone.

CREATING A FOLDER

If you currently do not have a music folder on your Tab, you can create one from within Windows Media Player. Tap the Create Folder icon. Enter the name of the folder. Click OK.

DELETING DEVICE FILES

You can manage files on your Tab by deleting unwanted files within Windows Media Player. Select the file that you want to delete, and then click the red X.

9. Select a folder.

10. Click Copy to begin copying the files from your PC to your Galaxy Tab. The music is now available for playback by tapping the Music widget on your Tab.

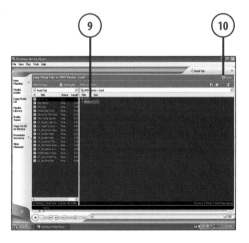

Go Further

STREAMLINE THE PROCESS

If you prefer to transfer files using the Media Player option, you can configure your Tab to use the Media Player USB mode whenever you connect to
your PC. From any home screen, press the Menu button on your Galaxy Tab
and then tap Settings. Tap Wireless and Network, choose USB Settings, and
then Select Media Player.

Copying Files with Windows Media Player (Galaxy Tab 10")

When you connect your Galaxy Tab to your PC with the data cable, you can
choose how you want to connect and/or synchronize media files with your
Galaxy Tab. One option is to sync your computer and your Galaxy Tab with
Windows Media Player. Follow these steps to copy music and movies to your
Galaxy Tab.

1. Connect the data cable from the
   Galaxy Tab to the USB port on
   your computer.

2. In the AutoPlay window on your
   PC, click Sync Digital Media Files
   to This Device using Windows
   Media Player.

Verizon Customers

If you are a Verizon customer and
have V CAST Music with
Rhapsody installed on your computer, you also have the choice of
managing your Tab using
Rhapsody.

3. Windows Media Player opens and lists media items available for you to copy to the Tab.

4. Click and drag the item(s) you want to copy to the Sync list.

5. The list of music you select appears in the Sync list. All tracks in the albums are selected by default. You can deselect any songs that you do not want to copy by right-clicking the song and clicking Remove from List.

6. Tap Start Sync to begin copying the files from your PC to your Galaxy Tab.

7. After sync is complete, the music is available for playback by tapping the Music widget on your Tab.

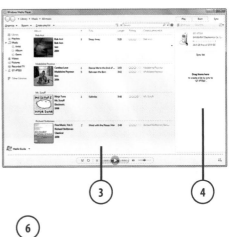

3 · 4

6

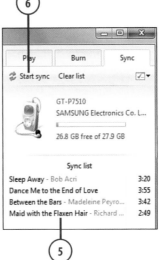

5

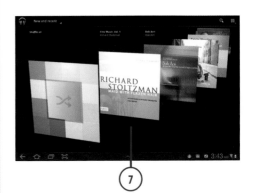

7

Connecting as a Mass Storage Device (Galaxy Tab 7")

You can drag and drop files from a PC or Mac to your Galaxy Tab by connecting as a removable disk. Follow these steps to transfer music from your PC or Mac to your Galaxy Tab, using the Mass Storage USB mode.

1. Connect the data cable to the Galaxy Tab and the USB connector to the USB port on your computer.

2. Your Tab's screen asks you to select a USB mode. Tap Mass Storage to drag and drop music files directly from your computer into a folder on your Galaxy Tab.

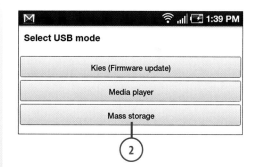

V CAST FOR VERIZON CUSTOMERS

If you are a Verizon customer and want to use VCAST Media Manager to help your Tab communicate with your PC, you can receive help with the process by changing your default USB connection settings. Do this before you connect to your PC. From any home screen, press the Menu button on your Tab and then choose Settings. Tap Wireless and Network in the Settings options. Tap USB Settings and select the Media Player or Media Storage options. Now, when you connect your Tab to your PC, a Verizon help page appears.

3. Tap Mount. Your Tab appears as a removable disk under Hard Disk Drives on your PC or mounts directly to your desktop on a Mac.

4. If you are connecting to a PC, Windows asks What Do You Want Windows to Do? (The title of this window might be different depending on the version of Windows you have.) Tap Cancel. You might have to tap Cancel twice because both your Tab and memory card may mount as two individual disks.

5. Display your Tab folders by clicking the removable disk on your computer.

6. If you do not already have a media folder, create a new folder on your Tab.

7. Locate the files that you want to transfer onto your computer and then drag them to the music folder on your Tab. The files are copied to your device.

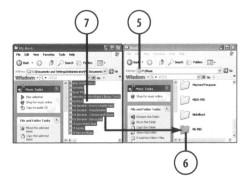

8. After you have unmounted your Tab on your computer, tap Turn Off on your Tab.

9. Disconnect the data cable from your computer and the device. When you tap the Music shortcut on your Tab, the music you have transferred is available for playback.

It's Not All Good

Ejecting Your Device

If you are connected to a Mac, make sure that you eject the device (removable drive) from your desktop before tapping Turn Off on your Tab and unplugging the device. If you don't, you get a Disk Was Not Ejected Properly warning.

Connecting as a Mass Storage Device (Galaxy Tab 10")

You can drag and drop files from a PC or Mac to your Galaxy Tab by connecting as a removable disk. Follow these steps to transfer music from your PC or Mac to your Galaxy Tab using the Mass Storage USB mode.

1. Connect the data cable to the Galaxy Tab and the USB connector to the USB port on your computer.

2. In the AutoPlay window on your computer, click Open Device to View Files using Windows Explorer to drag and drop music files directly from your computer into a folder on your Galaxy Tab. (The title of this window might be different depending on the version of Windows you have.)

3. Your Tab appears as a removable disk under Computer on your PC or mounts directly to your desktop on a Mac.

4. Display the home Tablet directory by double-clicking the removable disk in the folder tree.

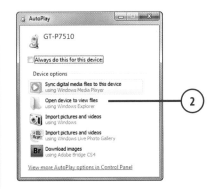

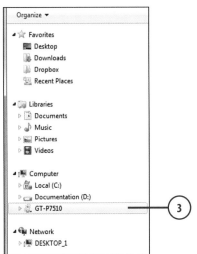

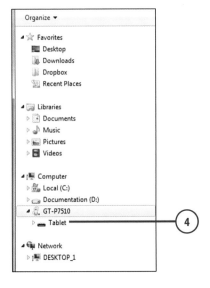

5. Display the Tablet folders by double-clicking Tablet.

6. If you do not already have a media folder, create a new folder on your Tab.

7. Locate the files that you want to transfer onto your computer, and then drag them to the Music folder on your Tab. The files are copied to your device.

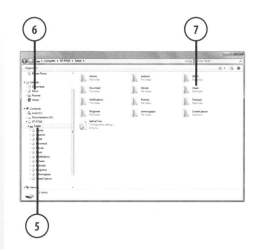

8. After you have finished copying files to your Tab from your computer, eject your device if you're on a Mac (see below) or remove the USB cable if you're on a PC.

It's Not All Good

Ejecting Your Device

If you are connected to a Mac, make sure you eject the device (removable drive) from your desktop before tapping Turn Off on your Tab and unplugging the device. If you don't, you get a Disk Was Not Ejected Properly warning.

9. When you tap the Music shortcut on your Tab, the music you have transferred is available for playback.

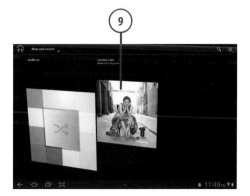

Multimedia Sync for Macs and PCs (Galaxy Tab 7")

Tucked away in your Galaxy Tab's file directory is a free desktop program called Multimedia Sync by doubleTwist. When you connect to a computer by way of the Mass Storage USB mode on your Tab, you can install Multimedia Sync by clicking the Multimedia Sync application icon, found in your Tab's file directory. Follow the prompts for installation on your computer. If you have issues installing the program from your Tab's file directory, you can download it at doubletwist.com. Multimedia Sync enables you to sync your iTunes music, videos, and photos with your Galaxy Tab.

MAC and PC Interfaces

The Multimedia Sync interface is different in Mac and PC versions. You can perform these first few steps on either version, regardless of a few interface differences.

1. After you have installed Multimedia Sync onto your computer, connect your Tab to your Mac or PC as Mass Storage.

2. Launch Media Sync on your computer. Your Tab opens under the Devices list in the sidebar on the left side of the interface.

3. Under Library, click Music to view the music files on your computer.

4. Browse to the music that you want to move to your Tab.

5. Select the music that you want, and then drag and drop it onto your device in the Devices list. The files have been copied to your Galaxy Tab.

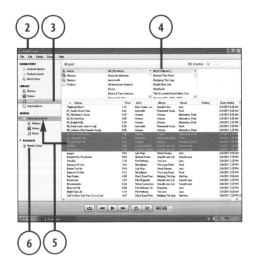

Copying Other Media

You can follow this same procedure to copy Photos, Videos, and Podcasts downloaded with iTunes to your Tab.

6. Click Playlist Setup.

It's Not All Good

Usage Restrictions

Some of the music in your Library is Digital Rights Management (DRM) protected, which means use of those files has been restricted. The files are noted with a lock icon within Multimedia Sync. These music files are from a time when music was not DRM free on iTunes. You won't be able to transfer these songs without upgrading them for a fee. Visit the iTunes Store for more information.

7. Click Import on your PC. If you are using a Mac, click Import iTunes Playlists. Your iTunes Playlists appear in the sidebar.

doubleTwist Playlists

Import your existing iTunes or Windows Media Player playlists or create new ones. After the initial import, you can re-import your playlists again from the Library menu.

Import from:
☑ iTunes ☐ WMP

[Import]   [Create New Playlist]

⑦

Importing from Windows Media Player

Windows Media Player is also selected if you are using a PC. If you don't choose to import from Windows Media Player now, you can always do so later from the Library menu.

Sync iTunes Changes

If you are using a Mac, you can select Automatically Import iTunes Playlist Changes to keep your Multimedia Sync playlists in sync with changes you make in iTunes.

8. If you are using a PC, select the Music tab at the top. If you are using a Mac, skip to step 10.

9. Select the Import New Music from Device check box to import music from your Tab to your computer.

10. Select the Sync Music to My Device check box.

11. Select the Only the Selected option if you are using a PC. Select the Selected Playlists option for a Mac.

12. Select the playlist(s) that you want to sync.

13. Click Sync. The new music on your Tab is now synced to your computer, and the playlists you selected are synced to your Tab.

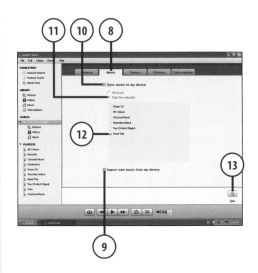

Drag and Drop

You can also drag and drop the playlists from the sidebar area to your Tab in the Devices list.

Multimedia Syncing on the Galaxy Tab 10"

The Galaxy Tab 10" doesn't include Multimedia Sync because Honeycomb (that is, Android 3.1) doesn't support USB connections. doubleTwist does offer the doubleTwist AirSync app for $4.99 in the Android Market that works with the Tab 10", but you need to connect with your computer that contains iTunes using Wi-Fi. If you don't have Wi-Fi, you'll need to set up your own Wi-Fi router (and Wi-Fi hardware on your computer if necessary) so your computer and your Tab 10" can communicate.

Adding a Podcast App (Galaxy Tab 7")

DoggCatcher is a highly rated podcast manager available in the Android Market (currently $2.99 USD) that can help you grow your podcast library.

1. After you have installed the DoggCatcher app on your Tab, tap the DoggCatcher shortcut. A list of feeds appears in which you can flick the page up or down to view the complete list.

2. Press the Menu button on the Galaxy Tab.

3. Tap Add Feed in the menu to search for a new feed. A list of recommended sources appears.

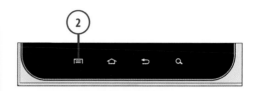

Downloaded Feeds

As you download feeds, they appear under the Audio, Video, and News tabs located at the top of the interface.

4. Tap a source to view the feed offerings. A list of feeds appears along with brief descriptions for each feed.

5. The icons located to the far right of each selection indicate whether the feed is audio, text, or video. Tap Preview Feed to review a selection before adding it to your list.

6. Tap Add Feed to acquire that selection for your collection.

7. Press the Back button on the Galaxy Tab.

8. If you don't see a featured feed that you like, you can perform a search. Tap Search Feeds.

9. Tap in the Search field to access the keyboard and enter your search keywords.

10. Tap Search. A list of search results displays.

11. Use the Back button on the Galaxy Tab to go back to your main list of Feeds.

12. Press the Menu button on the Tab.

13. Tap Update Feeds to manually update each feed in the list.

14. Tap Download Queue to view the progress of each of your downloads as they occur.

15. Tap Media Buttons to change the size of interface buttons.

16. Tap Add Feed to choose from a list of featured feeds or perform a search for a new feed.

17. Tap Preferences to configure DoggCatcher settings, including feed updates, media player settings, notifications, and advanced settings.

18. Tap More for further DoggCatcher support.

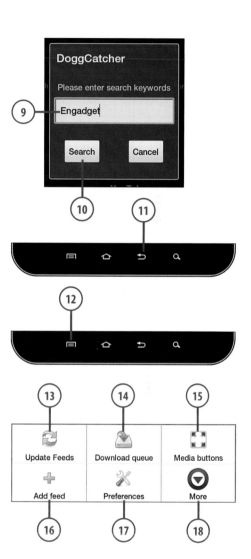

Go Further

AUTOMATICALLY UPDATING FEEDS

By default, feeds are set to automatically update on a configurable interval. You can tap the Menu button on your Tab and choose Preferences to change the interval.

Go Further

DELETING FEEDS

If you want to delete a feed, tap and hold your finger to a downloaded feed. A pop-up menu displays that includes an option to Delete Media. You can configure the Auto Delete settings by tapping a feed source and then tapping the Menu button on your Tab. Tap Feed Options to edit DoggCatcher's Auto Delete Policy. Feeds are automatically deleted after you listen to them.

Podcast Search

The program Multimedia Sync also offers a portal where you can search for audio and video podcasts. Just click Podcast Search in the sidebar under doubleTwist.

Adding a Podcast App (Galaxy Tab 10")

Although DoggCatcher doesn't support Honeycomb as of this writing, there are a few podcast apps on the Android Market to help you grow your podcast library. One popular podcast manager is BeyondPod for Honeycomb, and the lite version is free. If you want all the bells and whistles BeyondPod has to offer, you can purchase an unlock key for $6.99.

1. After you have installed the BeyondPod app, tap Press "Back" to Continue.

2. In the All Feeds screen, tap a podcast to view it.

3. Tap Download if you want to download the RSS feed, or tap Stream to stream the feed directly to BeyondPod and read it when it's finished. After you download the stream, tap Play.

4. In the Player screen, tap the Play button to play the podcast.

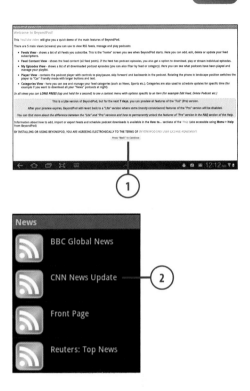

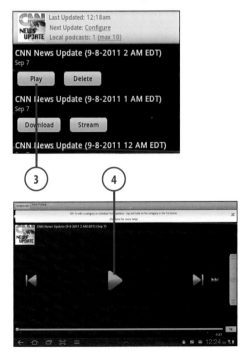

5. Tap My Episodes to view all your downloaded feeds.

Downloaded Feeds

As you download feeds, they appear in the My Episodes screen so you can view them at your leisure.

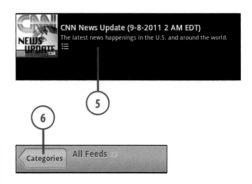

6. Tap Feeds in the upper-left corner of the screen, and then tap Categories to view all podcast categories.

7. Tap the category in which you want to search. For example, when you tap Business and Finance you see a list of podcasts in that category on the Feeds screen.

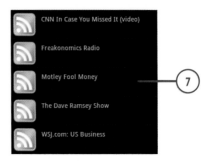

8. Tap Menu in the status bar (it has three horizontal lines).

9. Tap Add Feed.

10. You can browse popular feeds in the Browse Popular Feeds area.

11. You can import feeds in the Import Feeds area.

12. Search for feeds by typing in the Search for feeds box and then tapping Go.

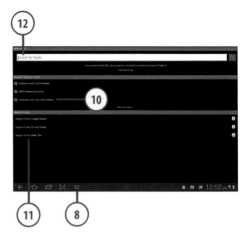

13. Tap Back twice on the status bar to go back to the category list.

14. Tap Feeds.

15. Tap a category in the list.

16. Tap Menu in the status bar.

17. Tap Update to manually update each feed in the list.

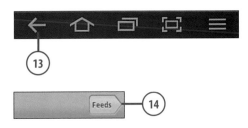

AUTOMATICALLY UPDATING FEEDS

By default, feeds are set to automatically update on a configurable interval. You can change the interval by tapping Menu in the status bar, tapping More, tapping Settings, and then tapping Feed Update Settings to change the interval.

18. Tap Menu in the status bar.

19. Tap More.

20. Tap Settings to configure BeyondPod settings, including feed updates, player settings, notifications, and advanced settings.

Go Further

DELETING FEEDS

If you want to delete a feed, tap and hold your finger to a downloaded feed. A pop-up menu displays that includes an option to Delete Feed.

Purchasing Music (Galaxy Tab 7")

There are two primary ways for you to purchase and download music directly from your Galaxy Tab. You can download music using a proprietary app provided by your cellular carrier, such as V CAST Music from Verizon. You can download a music app from Android Market that enables you to shop for and purchase music, such as Amazon MP3. (The Amazon MP3 app is free in the Android Market.) Follow these steps to browse and purchase music from your Tab using Amazon MP3. You need an Amazon.com account to make purchases in Amazon MP3.

1. After you have installed Amazon MP3, tap the Amazon MP3 icon to launch the app.

2. Tap in the Search field to access the keyboard and enter a keyword search for an album, song, or artist.

3. At the bottom of the screen, tap either the Free Song of the Day or Daily Deal Album to take advantage of those deals.

4. Content is grouped into three main categories: Bestsellers, New Releases, and Browse by Genre. Tap Bestsellers.

5. Tap an album that you would like to purchase. A page opens, giving you the opportunity to preview songs, buy individual songs, or purchase the entire album. Tap the price to purchase the entire album. The price button turns into a Buy button.

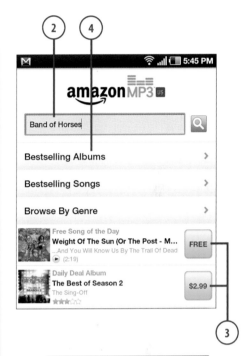

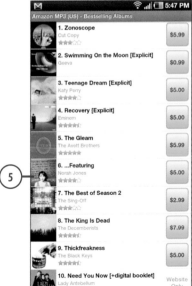

6. Tap the top price of the album to be given the option to buy. The price button turns into a Buy button.

7. Tap Buy to purchase the album. You are prompted to sign in to your Amazon.com account if you are not already logged in.

8. Enter your Amazon.com information.

9. Read the terms of use, and then select the check box agreeing to the terms.

10. Tap Sign In to begin downloading the album. Charges are made to the credit card designated in your Amazon.com account.

Amazon MP3 on Your Desktop

Keep in mind that you can also go to the Amazon MP3 website to browse, purchase, and download your favorite music to your computer. The Multimedia Sync program discussed earlier in this chapter also has a desktop portal to Amazon MP3. Click the Music Store option located in the sidebar under doubleTwist.

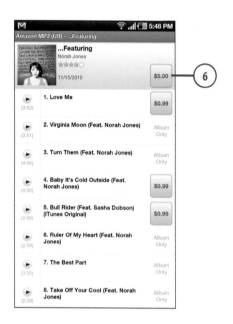

Purchasing Music (Galaxy Tab 10")

There are two primary ways for you to purchase and download music directly from your Galaxy Tab. You can download music using a proprietary app provided by your cellular carrier, such as V CAST Music from Verizon. You can download a music app from Android Market that enables you to shop for and purchase music, such as Amazon MP3. (The Amazon MP3 app is free in the Android Market.) Follow these steps to browse and purchase music from your Tab using Amazon MP3. You need an Amazon.com account to make purchases in Amazon MP3.

1. After you have installed Amazon MP3, tap the Amazon MP3 icon in the Apps screen to launch the app.

2. Tap Store.

3. Tap in the Search Amazon MP3 field to access the keyboard and enter a keyword search for an album, song, or artist.

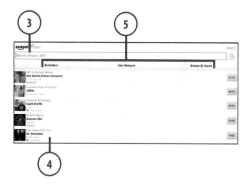

4. At the bottom of the screen, tap either the Free Song of the Day or Daily Deal Album to take advantage of those deals.

5. Content is grouped into three main categories: Bestsellers, New Releases, and Browse by Genre. Tap Bestsellers.

6. Tap an album that you would like to purchase. A page opens, giving you the opportunity to preview songs, buy individual songs, or purchase the entire album.

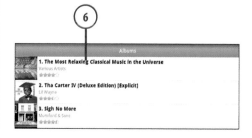

7. Tap the top price of the album to be given the option to buy. The price button turns into a Buy button.

8. Tap Buy to purchase the album. You are prompted to sign in to your Amazon.com account if you are not already logged in.

9. Type your email address and password.

10. Read the terms of use, and then select the check box agreeing to the terms.

11. Tap Sign In to begin downloading the album. Charges are made to the credit card designated in your Amazon.com account.

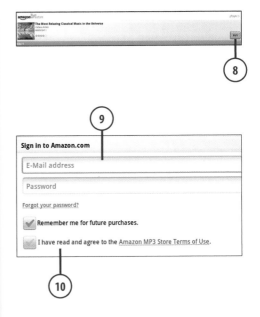

Amazon MP3 on Your Desktop

After you download your album you can save it to your Galaxy Tab 10", or you can save it to your Amazon Cloud Drive. If you save to the latter, you can access the songs not only on the Amazon MP3 app on your Tab 10" but also your computer(s) and any other Android device(s).

Playing Songs (Galaxy Tab 7")

The Music Player shortcut on your Galaxy Tab was designed to make it easy for you to browse and play your music collection. A great set of headphones can enhance the enjoyment of your favorite music. The ability to browse your Galaxy Tab's music library and understanding your playback options are a big step toward getting the most out of your Galaxy Tab's many entertainment possibilities.

1. Depending on which Galaxy Tab model or cellular carrier you use, the shortcut to the music player might be located on the main home screen or in the Applications menu. Tap the Music shortcut on your Tab.

2. The music player categorizes your music library into five categories: Songs, Playlists, Albums, Artists, and Genres. Tap the Playlists tab to choose a song for playback.

3. Tap Recently Added to view the new music that you recently transferred.

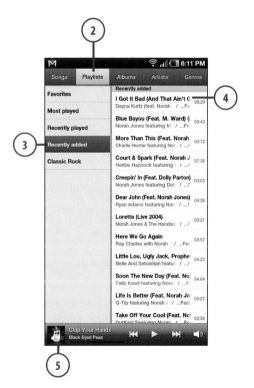

More Categories

In the Playlist tab, you can access songs that you have marked as Favorites, along with tracks that your Tab has determined you play the most, located under Most Played. You can also access the most recent tracks you have played.

4. Tap a Song in the list for playback. The small player controls appear.

5. A thumbnail of the cover appears for the song you tapped. Tap the album cover thumbnail to make the graphic open full screen. The larger playback controls disappear after a few moments, but you can tap the screen to bring them back.

6. Tap the Info icon to view media information regarding the track being played. Tap the icon again to hide the info.

7. Tap the Favorites button that is shaped like a star to add a track to your list of favorite songs.

8. Tap the Volume button to mute a track. You can also slide your finger across the scale to adjust the volume.

9. Tap Shuffle to play songs in random order.

10. Use the Playback controls to play, pause, reverse, or forward playback, and to move to the next or previous tracks.

11. Tap Repeat to repeat the current song, repeat all songs, and disable repeat mode.

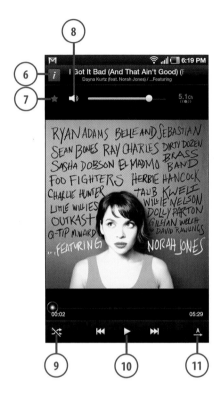

MORE PLAYBACK VIEWS

If you press the Back button on your Galaxy Tab from this full-screen playback, you'll see playback controls located at the bottom of the screen (in vertical orientation) that are very similar to the controls in full-screen mode. If you hold the Tab in the horizontal orientation, the controls are located at the top right of the screen. Tap the graphic associated with the track to return to the full-screen mode.

Go Further

MUSIC PLAYER SETTINGS

You can improve the sound quality of the music you listen to by adjusting the Music Player Equalizer settings. Tap the Menu button on your Tab, and then tap Settings to use presets made to enhance specific genres of music, such as Rock, Pop, Jazz, and Classic. You can also add effects, such as Bass Enhancement and Music Clarity, under the Effects options. Tap the Music menu option to choose the types of categories that are displayed in Music Player.

BE A SLACKER

Preinstalled on your Galaxy Tab is a very cool app named Slacker Radio that enables you to personalize your own radio stations. Just enter an artist to listen to, and Slacker Radio programs a station for that artist chock full of similar music from other artists. You must create a Slacker Radio account before you can use the Slacker application. Just tap the Slacker widget, and the Create Account option is located at the bottom of the screen when your Tab is held in a vertical orientation. Keep in mind that other free personalized radio options are available in the Android Market, too, such as Pandora Radio.

Playing Songs (Galaxy Tab 10")

The Music Player shortcut on your Galaxy Tab was designed to make it easy for you to browse and play your music collection. A great set of headphones can enhance the enjoyment of your favorite music. The ability to browse your Galaxy Tab's music library and understanding your playback options are a big step toward getting the most out of your Galaxy Tab's many entertainment possibilities.

1. Depending on which Galaxy Tab model or cellular carrier you use, the shortcut to the music player might be located on the main home screen or in the Applications menu. Tap the Music shortcut on your Tab.

2. Flip through the album covers and tap the cover for playback.

3. Tap Shuffle to play songs in random order.

4. Tap the song to begin playing the song in the Now playing screen.

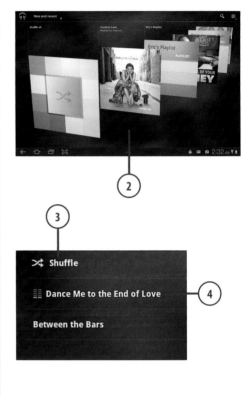

5. Use the Playback controls to play, pause, reverse, or forward playback, and to move to the next or previous tracks in the queue.

6. Tap Shuffle to play songs in random order.

7. Tap Repeat to repeat the current song, repeat all songs, and disable repeat mode.

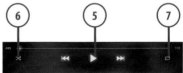

MORE PLAYBACK VIEWS

If you go to another screen from this full-screen playback, you'll see playback controls located at the bottom of the screen that are similar to the controls in full-screen mode. You can play and pause the track, go to the previous track in your queue, or go to the next track in your queue.

Creating Your Own Playlists (Galaxy Tab 7")

Playlists are a great way to create a compilation of your favorite songs for playback on your Galaxy Tab. Use playlists as an opportunity to organize the best songs from your favorite artists, acoustic selections, party music, classic rock, orchestral masterpieces, relaxation tracks, and more.

1. Depending on which Galaxy Tab model or cellular carrier you use, you'll find the shortcut to the music player on the main home screen or in the Applications menu. Tap the Music shortcut on your Tab.

2. Tap the Playlists category.

3. Press the Menu button located on your Tab.

4. Tap New Playlist.

5. Type the name of the new playlist into the field.

6. Tap Done. The new playlist is created.

7. Now your job is to choose the music that will go into the newly created playlist. Tap a category tab at the top of the screen to select songs.

8. A check box appears next to each song, album, artist, and genre. Tap a check box to select it for the playlist.

9. Tap Add at the bottom of the screen to add the selection to the playlist.

REMOVING AND ADDING SONGS IN A PLAYLIST

Go Further

You can remove songs from a playlist by selecting the playlist and then pressing the Menu button on the Galaxy Tab. Tap Remove in the menu and then select the track(s) you want to remove by tapping the check box next to the item. Tap Remove at the bottom of the screen. You can add a song by pressing the Menu button on your Tab and then tapping Add music. You can then select music and choose Add at the bottom of the screen.

Creating Your Own Playlists (Galaxy Tab 10")

Playlists are a great way to create a compilation of your favorite songs for playback on your Galaxy Tab. Use playlists as an opportunity to organize the best songs from your favorite artists, acoustic selections, party music, classic rock, orchestral masterpieces, relaxation tracks, and more.

1. Depending on which Galaxy Tab model or cellular carrier you use, you'll find the shortcut to the music player on the main home screen or in the Applications menu. Tap the Music shortcut on your Tab.

2. The music player categorizes your music library into six categories: New and Recent, Albums, Artists, Songs, Playlists, and Genres. Tap the Playlists tab to choose a song for playback, and then tap the plus icon to create a new playlist.

3. Type a name for the new playlist, and then tap OK.

4. The playlist appears in the Playlists screen.

5. Tap Playlists, and then tap Songs in the menu.

6. Tap the right triangle at the right side of the song in the list.

7. Tap Add to Playlist.

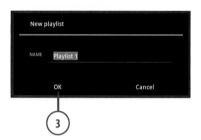

8. Select the playlist to which you want to add the song. The Music app adds the song to the playlist. If you create a new playlist, you must type the new playlist name and tap OK to create it.

9. Tap Songs, and then tap Playlists.

10. Tap the playlist on the screen.

11. Tap the song in the list to play it.

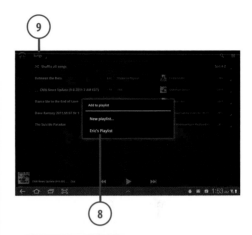

REMOVING AND ADDING SONGS IN A PLAYLIST

You can remove songs from a playlist by selecting the playlist and then pressing the right triangle at the right side of the song in the list. Tap Remove in the menu, and then select the track(s) you want to remove by tapping the check box next to the item. Tap Remove at the bottom of the screen. You can add a song by pressing the Menu button on your Tab and then tapping Add music. You can then select music and choose Add at the bottom of the screen.

Viewing YouTube Videos (Galaxy Tab 7")

The high-resolution screen of the Galaxy Tab, along with its portability and built-in video camera, makes it great for viewing and sharing videos online, anywhere and anytime. The preinstalled YouTube widget gives you the capability to browse and view videos posted by users from around the world, as well as upload videos taken with your Galaxy Tab, as soon as you take them.

1. Tap the YouTube widget on your home screen. A list of featured videos appears in three categories: Most Viewed, Most Discussed, and Top Rated. You can choose the View All option located at the end of each category to access a comprehensive list.

More Categories

You can view more YouTube categories by pressing the Menu button located on your Galaxy Tab and then choosing Categories.

2. Tap the video icon located at the top of the interface to access your Tab's video camera and record a video. After you finish recording your video, your Galaxy Tab gives you the option of uploading to YouTube. You need to create a YouTube account before you can post your videos.

3. Tap the Search icon to perform a keyword search for a YouTube video.

4. Tap the Information icon located to the far right of each video in the list to read the video description.

5. Tap the disclosure arrow to reveal the entire video description.

6. Tap Rate to rate the video using a five-star rating system. You need to be logged into your YouTube account before you can rate videos.

7. Tap Comments to read the comments that other viewers have written for the video.

8. Tap Favorite to add this video to your Favorites list, which you can return to at a later time.

9. Tap Share to share the video via Bluetooth, Gmail, or Messaging.

Other Sharing Options

Other sharing options might appear in this list if you have downloaded apps that allow for additional sharing features.

10. Tap Flag to flag a video as inappropriate. You need to be logged in to your YouTube account to flag a video.

11. Tap the thumbnail to begin to play the video.

12. Tap the user's tab to visit the YouTube member's channel and view a list of all of the videos that member has uploaded.

13. Tap Subscribe to be sent notifications when this YouTube member uploads any new videos.

14. Press the Menu button on your Tab to upload your previously recorded videos to your channel and to customize your YouTube Settings. You can also access your YouTube account from this menu.

Viewing YouTube Videos (Galaxy Tab 10")

The high-resolution screen of the Galaxy Tab, along with its portability and built-in video camera, makes it great for viewing and sharing videos online, anywhere and anytime. The preinstalled YouTube widget gives you the capability to browse and view videos posted by users from around the world, as well as upload videos taken with your Galaxy Tab as soon as you take them.

1. Tap the YouTube widget on the home screen. A list of featured videos appears in three categories: Recommendations (also called Top Favorited), Most Viewed, Most Discussed, and Most Popular (also called Top Rated).

More Categories

You can view more YouTube categories by tapping Browse and then tapping one of the categories. All is the default category.

2. Tap Your Channel to view videos you've uploaded to YouTube. Upload videos you've taken with your Tab's camcorder by tapping Upload. You must create a YouTube account before you can post your videos.

3. Tap Search YouTube to perform a keyword search for a YouTube video.

4. Information about the video appears below the video.

5. Tap the full-screen icon to view the video on the entire screen.

6. Rate the video by tapping the thumbs-up or thumbs-down icon. You must be logged in to your YouTube account before you can rate videos.

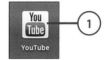

7. Tap the user's name to visit the YouTube member's channel and view a list of all the videos that member has uploaded. You can also subscribe to that member's channel if you want.

8. Tap Comments to read the comments that other viewers have written for the video.

9. Tap Share to share the video via Bluetooth, Gmail, or Messaging.

Other Sharing Options

Other sharing options might appear in this list if you have downloaded apps that allow for additional sharing features, such as BeyondPod.

---

10. In the Related videos area, tap the thumbnail to play the video.

11. Tap Menu.

12. Tap Favorite to add this video to your Favorites list, which you can return to at a later time.

13. Tap Save to if you have created one or more playlists in the YouTube website and you want the video to be added to your specified playlist.

14. Tap Copy URL to copy the URL of the video you're watching to the clipboard so you can paste it into another document such as an email message.

15. Tap Flag to flag a video as inappropriate. You must be logged in to your YouTube account to flag a video.

16. Tap Settings to customize your YouTube app settings.

Purchase and read books with
the Amazon Kindle widget.

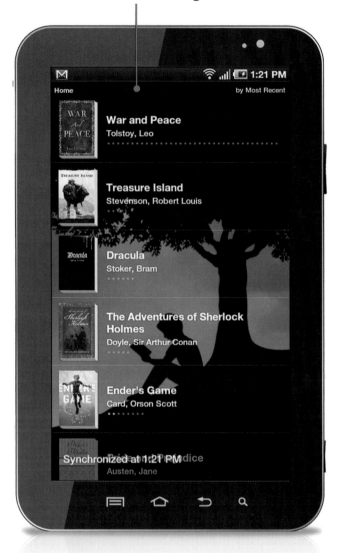

Find out how to purchase books using the Amazon Kindle app and how to read them on your Galaxy Tab.

8

→ Logging In to Your Account
→ Purchasing Books
→ Using Reading Aids
→ Adding Bookmarks, Highlights, and Notes
→ Organizing Your Books

Reading and Managing Books

Whether your Galaxy Tab runs Android 2.2 or 3.1, it offers a great outlet for you to enjoy books. The Amazon Kindle app that is preinstalled on your Galaxy Tab is stylish eReader that enables you to browse, purchase, download, and read eBooks from your device. The Galaxy Tab 10" also comes preloaded with the Google Books app, along with three free books. You can download the Google Books app for free on the Android Market for the Galaxy Tab 7".

Both the Amazon Kindle and Google Books apps enable you to enhance your reading experience by offering reading aids such as the ability to increase font size and change background color. If you prefer a different eReader, you can shop the Android Market for other readers, such as Kobo and Nook, and then download and add books from other sources. Consider trying out a few of the available readers to see which one you like the best.

Logging In to Your Account

Before you can begin using Amazon Kindle, you must first have an Amazon.com account to purchase or download Kindle-compatible book files (.mobi files). The Amazon Terms and Conditions box opens. Follow these directions for both the Android 2.2 and 3.1 Tabs.

1. Depending on which carrier you use for your device, you'll find the Amazon Kindle application icon on your home screen or under the Applications icon. Tap the Kindle app icon to launch the application.

2. Read the Terms and Conditions and then tap Accept. You only have to do this the first time you launch the Amazon Kindle widget.

3. Type the email address for your Amazon account into the email address field. If you do not have an Amazon.com account, you can use your finger to scroll down to the bottom of the screen and tap the Create One Now field to set one up.

4. Tap in the next field and type your Amazon.com password into the second field.

5. Tap Register to create your Kindle account and log in.

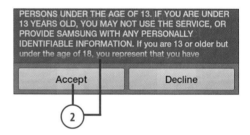

Purchasing Books

Although you can find many free books in the Amazon library, purchasing a book in the bookstore is made easy. After you set up your 1-Click account, you can purchase books with just a simple tap of your finger. Although the Kindle store only displays in landscape orientation on the Honeycomb Galaxy Tab 10.1, you can follow the same steps for both the 7" and 10" models.

1. After launching the Amazon Kindle application, press the Menu button on your 7" Galaxy Tab. Skip to step 2 if you are using the Galaxy Tab 10".

2. Tap Kindle Store to begin browsing for books to purchase.

3. Tap Books to begin browsing titles. If you already know the name of the book you want to purchase, you can tap in the search field located at the top of the screen to begin typing.

4. Tap the category you want to browse. A list of titles appears. You can flick your finger up or down on the screen to move up and down the list. If you want to browse more results in this category, you can scroll down to the bottom of the screen and tap Show More Results.

5. Tap a book to choose it and to read customer reviews, and receive more product details. You can also review a trial sample of the book by tapping Try a Sample.

6. You can set up your Amazon Kindle account so that you can make purchases with a single tap of your finger. Tap Buy Now with 1-Click.

7. You need an existing Amazon.com account to set up 1-Click. Tap in the email address field and then type in the email address associated with your existing Amazon.com account.

8. Tap the next field and type your Amazon.com password. If you are new to Amazon.com you can tap the option button to register as a new customer.

9. Tap Go on the keyboard. A Confirm screen displays.

10. You can instruct Amazon Kindle to remember the password so you don't have to enter it each time. Tap an option on the Confirm screen.

Talking About Security

If you are not the only user of your Galaxy Tab, you might want to consider choosing Not Now or Never on the Confirm screen so there is some level of security to prevent unauthorized purchases. You can also deactivate 1-Click within your 1-Click account settings.

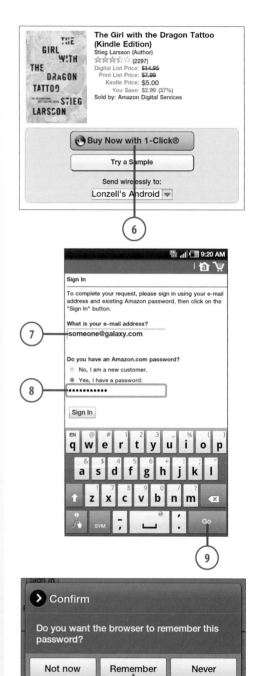

11. The shipping and payment information for your Amazon.com account is automatically entered into your Kindle account. Enter the mobile number for your Galaxy Tab. You can find this number under the Settings icon under the About Tablet option. Your mobile number is used only to match your 1-Click settings to your Galaxy Tab.

12. Tap Turn 1-Click On.

13. Return to the book you want to purchase.

14. Tap Buy Now with 1-Click. The book downloads to your Galaxy Tab and you can access it from the Amazon Kindle apps home screen.

Changing Account Settings

If you need to edit information in your Amazon account, such as adding a new credit card or editing a shipping address, you can do so from the Manage Your Kindle page on Amazon.com.

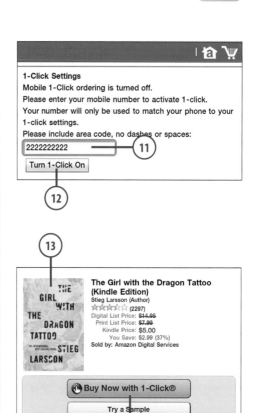

Using Reading Aids (Galaxy Tab 7")

Your Galaxy tab contains many options for enhancing your eBook experience, including changing background color, font size, jumping to locations within the book, and organizing your book titles.

1. Tap the book you want to read from your Amazon Kindle app home screen. If a Reading Tips dialog opens, you can tap Dismiss.

Go Further

ABOUT LOCATIONS

The Kindle app does not use page numbers. Instead it uses what is referred to as locations, and for a very good reason. The Locations slider is located at the bottom of the screen when you touch the screen. Locations are independent of screen size or the size of the font you have chosen, which means you can read *The Great Gatsby* using Amazon Kindle on your Android phone or Galaxy tab and use locations to jump to the same place within the book on either device. You can slide the location slider to jump to a new location within the book.

2. Tap the right side of the book page to progress to the next page. You can tap the page on the left side to revisit the previous page. You can also flick your finger on the screen left or right to turn pages.

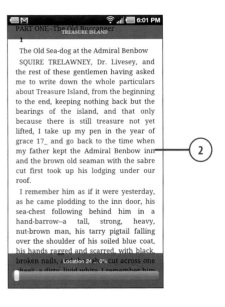

3. Press the Menu key on the Galaxy Tab.

4. Tap View Options to customize font size and background color.

5. Tap a font size to change the book font.

6. Tap a new background color.

7. To be able to adjust screen brightness from this menu, you first need to turn off the automatic brightness feature. Tap the bottom field to access the display settings.

8. Tap Brightness.

9. Tap the Automatic Brightness check box to deselect it.

10. Tap OK. You can adjust the brightness manually from here.

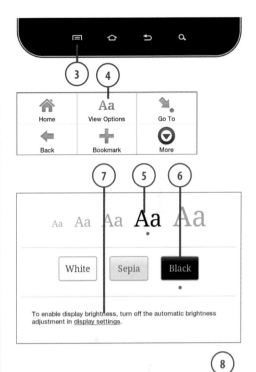

11. Tap the Back key to return to the View Options. The brightness slider appears at the bottom.

12. Adjust the brightness level by sliding your finger on the control.

13. Press the Menu key to return to the View Options.

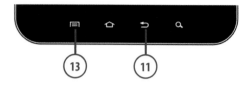

Jumping to Specified Locations

You can tap the Go To feature under the Menu key options to jump to a specified location within the book, such as Cover, Table of Contents, Beginning, Location, My Notes & Marks.

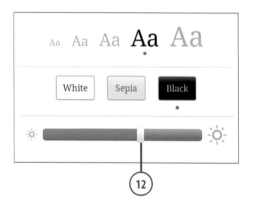

14. Tap More.

15. If you want to find where a certain word or phrase was used in the book, you can use the search function to locate it. Tap Search.

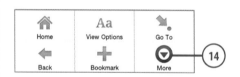

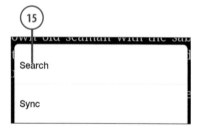

16. Type a word or phrase into the search field.

17. Tap Go on the keyboard.

18. A list of locations where that phrase was used appears, along with a brief excerpt. Tap the location in the list to jump to that location.

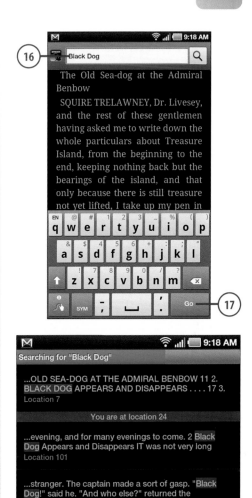

SYNCHRONIZING BETWEEN ANDROID DEVICES

You can access Kindle books located on your other Android devices from your Galaxy Tab. From the home screen of your Kindle app, you can tap the Menu key and choose Sync to synchronize your last page read, including bookmarks, highlights, and notes, between devices.

Using Reading Aids (Galaxy Tab 10")

Your Galaxy tab contains many options for enhancing your eBook experience, including changing background color, font size, jumping to locations within the book, and organizing your book titles.

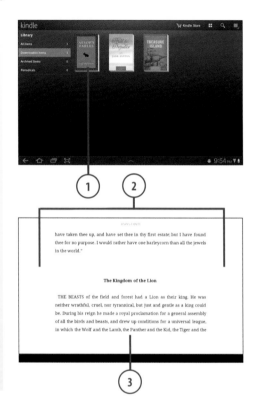

1. Tap the book you want to read from your Amazon Kindle app home screen. If a Reading Tips dialog opens, you can tap Dismiss.

2. Tap the right side of the book page to progress to the next page. Tap the page on the left side to revisit the previous page. You can also flick your finger on the screen left or right to turn pages.

3. Tap the screen to access reading aid controls.

ABOUT LOCATIONS

Go Further

The Kindle app does not use page numbers; instead, it uses what is referred to as locations, and for a very good reason. The Locations slider is located at the bottom of the screen when you touch the screen. Locations are independent of screen size or the size of the font you have chosen, which means you can read *The Great Gatsby* using Amazon Kindle on your Android phone or Galaxy Tab and use locations to jump to the same place within the book on either device. You can slide the location slider to jump to a new location within the book.

4. Tap to adjust screen brightness and background color.

5. Tap to adjust the font side by tapping a larger font.

6. Tap to perform a search within the book by entering text or speaking into your Tab.

7. Tap to access more menu options.

8. Tap to go to the Kindle Store to browse more books.

9. Tap to jump to the cover page, table of contents, the beginning of the book, or to a specified Location.

10. Tap to view any notes and marks you have made in the book. This option is grayed out if you have not left notes or marks in the book.

11. You can download a single book to multiple devices. Tap to sync the book on all devices to the furthest page read so you can pick up where you stopped.

12. Tap to bookmark a page.

13. Tap to share your progress in reading the book via Bluetooth, Email, Gmail, or another app. A message is generated including the name of the book, author, and what percentage of the book you have read.

14. Tap the Back icon to return to the Amazon Kindle app main screen.

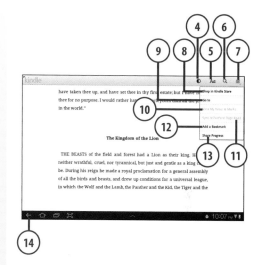

SYNCHRONIZING BETWEEN ANDROID DEVICES

You can access Kindle books located on your other Android devices from your Galaxy Tab. From the home screen of your Kindle app, tap the Menu key and choose Sync & Check for Items.

Adding Bookmarks, Highlights, and Notes (Galaxy Tab 7")

The Amazon Kindle app provides the convenience of placing a bookmark where you stopped reading, so you can begin at the right location at a later time. You also have the capability to highlight text in a book and to leave notes.

1. From any book page you are reading, press the Menu key.

2. Tap Bookmark to place a bookmark for that page. When you close the Amazon Kindle application and then open it again, the book opens to this bookmarked page.

3. You might want to specify a block of text in a block as a point of interest by highlighting it. Press your finger over the text you want to highlight onscreen. An overlay appears over the text and a menu appears.

4. Drag the handles of the overlay to specify the text you want to highlight.

5. Tap highlight in the menu. The text is highlighted in yellow after you make the selection.

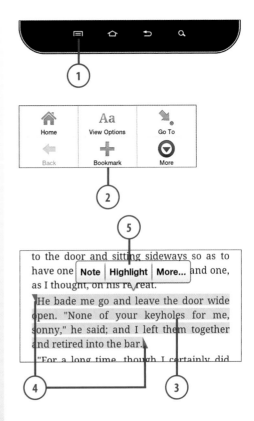

Removing Highlights from Text

You can remove the highlight from text by pressing your finger to the highlighted text, using the handles to specify the text, and then tapping Delete Highlight.

Go Further

PERFORMING A DICTIONARY SEARCH

When you come across a word in your readings for which you do not know the meaning, you can conduct a quick dictionary inquiry on your Galaxy Tab. Press your finger to the text, position the handles around the word, and then tap More in the menu. You can then choose Wikipedia or Dictionary.com to define the word.

6. You leave a note for an excerpt of text. To create notes in a book, press your finger over the text for which you want to leave a note onscreen. An overlay appears over the text and a menu appears.

7. Drag the handles of the overlay to specify the text for which you want to leave a comment.

8. Tap Note. A note field and the keyboard appear.

9. Type the note.

10. Tap Save. The note is marked with a number in the body of the text. Tap the number to view the note.

Deleting a Note

To modify or delete a note, you can tap the number associated with the note. Tap Edit in the menu that appears, and then you can either edit the note or choose to delete it.

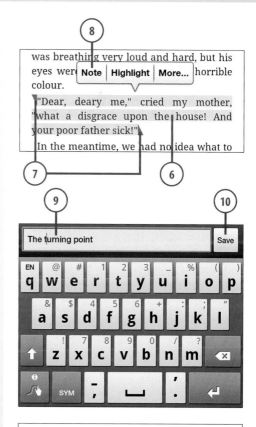

Go Further

VIEWING ALL NOTES AND MARKS

Your Galaxy Tab offers a quick and convenient way to view and jump to all notes, bookmarks, and highlights you have made within a book. You can tap the Menu key from any book page and choose Go To to access My Notes & Marks. The My Notes & Marks screen lists all bookmarks, highlighted text, and notes that you have made. You can tap anything in the list and be taken straight to that location within the book.

Adding Bookmarks, Highlights, and Notes (Galaxy Tab 10")

The Amazon Kindle app provides the convenience of placing a bookmark where you stopped reading, so you can begin at the right location later. You also have the capability to highlight text in a book and to leave notes.

1. Tap Bookmark to place a bookmark for that page. When you close the Amazon Kindle application and then open it again, the book opens to this bookmarked page.

2. You might want to specify a block of text in a block as a point of interest by highlighting it. Press your finger over the text you want to highlight onscreen. An overlay appears over the text and a menu appears.

3. Drag the handles of the overlay to specify the text you want to highlight.

4. Tap highlight in the menu. The text is highlighted in blue after you make the selection.

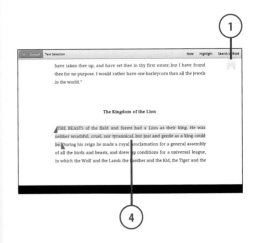

Removing Highlights from Text

You can remove the highlight from text by pressing your finger to the highlighted text, using the handles to specify the text, and then tapping Delete Highlight.

Go Further

PERFORMING A DICTIONARY SEARCH

When you come across a word in your readings for which you do not know the meaning, you can conduct a quick dictionary inquiry on your Galaxy Tab. Press your finger to the text, position the handles around the word, and then tap More in the menu. You can then choose Wikipedia or Dictionary.com to define the word.

5. You can leave a note for an excerpt of text. To create notes in a book, press your finger over the text for which you want to leave a note onscreen. An overlay appears over the text and a menu appears.

6. Drag the handles of the overlay to specify the text for which you want to leave a comment.

7. Tap Note. A note field and the keyboard appear.

8. Type the note.

9. Tap Save. The note is marked with a number in the body of the text. Tap the number to view the note.

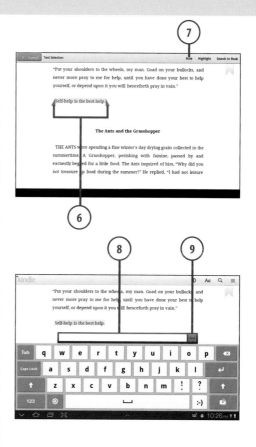

Deleting a Note

To modify or delete a note, you can tap the number associated with the note. Tap Delete in the menu that appears.

VIEWING ALL NOTES AND MARKS

Your Galaxy Tab offers a quick and convenient way to view and jump to all notes, bookmarks, and highlights you have made in a book. You can tap the Menu key from any book page and choose Go To to access My Notes & Marks. The My Notes & Marks screen lists all bookmarks, highlighted text, and notes that you have made. You can tap anything in the list and be taken straight to that location within the book.

Organizing Your Books

After you have accumulated many titles in your eBook library, you need a method to the madness of organizing your books. By default, your books are ordered by the most recently downloaded on the Amazon Kindle home page. You have a couple of other sorting options to choose from.

1. From your Amazon Kindle app's home page, press the Menu key on the Galaxy Tab.

2. Tap Sort By to choose from the sorting options.

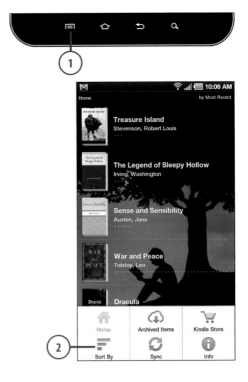

3. Tap Author to have all your titles listed in alphabetical order according to author. Your titles immediately rearrange after you make your selection.

REMOVING AND ARCHIVING BOOKS

You can access the option to remove books from your device by pressing your finger down on a book cover on your Amazon Kindle home page. A menu opens from which you can choose the Remove from Device option located at the bottom. The book is removed from the Amazon Kindle home page, but remains archived in your Amazon account. If you want to bring the archived item back to your Home page, you can tap the Menu key on your 7" Tab, choose Archived items, and then press and hold your finger to the archived book. Tap All Items if you are using the Galaxy Tab 10", and then tap Archived Items. A menu opens, enabling you to select Download to Home.

Capture a screenshot.

Capture photos.

Browse, manage, and share photos.

Capture a screenshot.

In this chapter, you learn how to capture photos and screenshots, share photos via email and slideshows, and view and manage photos with Gallery.

Capturing and Managing Photos

Along with transferring images from other sources, such as your computer, to your Galaxy Tab, your Tab is capable of taking high-quality photos and can house thousands of photos organized in categories. You also have the capability to take screenshots of the Tab's interface.

Your Galaxy Tab's high-resolution screen offers a great way to showcase photos to friends and family, but you don't have to stop there. You can also use Gallery to perform basic photo edits and even share pictures via AllShare, Bluetooth, Gmail, Messaging, Picasa, and more.

Using the Camera

Your Galaxy Tab uses a 3.0 megapixel rear-facing camera located on the back of the device to take photos, along with a 2.0 megapixel front-facing camera. Taking a photo can be as simple as choosing a subject, composing your shot, and pressing a button. The Galaxy Tab is also equipped with some helpful features commonly found on dedicated photo cameras, including shooting modes, scene modes, manual exposure, white balance, flash, manual exposure, and ISO settings.

Adjusting Settings and Taking Photos (Galaxy Tab 7")

Let's begin by taking a look at the Camera application's photo mode, before diving into sharing your images. The camera app's interface is simplistic, and deeper than you might expect at first glance.

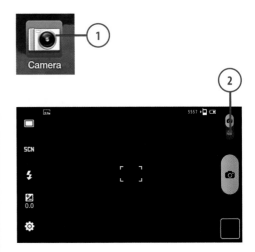

1. Depending on which cellular carrier or Galaxy Tab model you have, locate the Camera icon on a home screen or under Applications. Tap the Camera icon to access the camera feature.

2. Move the mode button into the still image position to capture photos. Your Galaxy Tab switches to Still Image mode. This is the default mode.

3. Tap the Shooting mode icon located in the upper-left corner of the viewer to select a shooting mode. The Galaxy Tab is set to Single shot by default. You can use these settings to determine how many images are shot and to apply effects.

>> Go Further

EXPLORING SHOOTING MODES

You can choose the Continuous shooting mode to take up to nine consecutive pictures. This feature has the capability to produce a particularly beautiful series of shots that can be showcased together, such as a heron taking flight from a lake.

The Panorama shooting mode enables you to take a picture and then use the onscreen guide to move the viewfinder and take seven more shots. This is a great mode for capturing wide vistas, such as landscapes and cityscapes.

Choose the Smile shot mode to focus the camera on the face of your subject. After the camera detects the person's smile, it takes the picture.

Use the Self-shot mode to use the front camera to take a picture of yourself.

4. Tap the Scene mode icon to select the appropriate Scene mode.

5. Tap the Flash icon to configure the built-in video light setting. By default, the flash is set to On and adds a little extra light to a dark scene. The flash is located next to the camera lens on the back of the device. You can tap Off to deactivate the flash if the subject you are capturing is well lit.

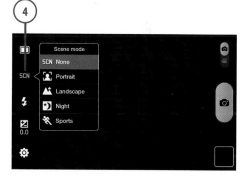

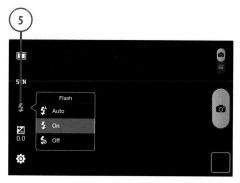

>>> Go Further

EXPLORING SCENE MODES

The scene mode options optimize your camera for special shooting situations. For example, if you are taking a picture of a person from her shoulders up, you can use the Portrait mode. The Portrait mode automatically optimizes your Galaxy Tab's camera to use the largest aperture setting, which shortens depth of field and slightly blurs the background, emphasizing your main subject.

The Landscape mode uses the smallest possible aperture setting for the greatest depth of field to help ensure that everything is in sharp focus.

The Night mode uses a flash in combination with a slow shutter speed to brighten dark backgrounds. The Sports mode uses a fast shutter speed to capture moving subjects without blurring.

6. An image that is too light or too dark degrades the appearance of your photos. To take full advantage of the camera feature of the Galaxy Tab, you need to adjust the exposure level for various bright or dark lighting conditions. Tap the Exposure Value icon.

7. Drag the exposure level up to achieve a proper exposure level in a low-light shooting environment or drag it down for a very bright shooting environment.

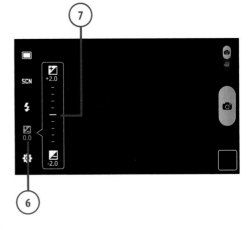

8. Tap the Settings icon in the lower-left corner of the viewer to customize more video settings.

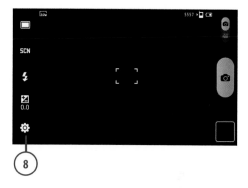

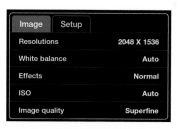

>> Go Further

MORE ABOUT IMAGE SETTINGS

The Image settings consist of two tabs: Image and Setup. You can use the Image settings to choose a size for the image, change the white balance setting, add effects, choose an ISO setting, and pick an image quality setting for photos. White balance helps to ensure color accuracy in your photos. You can tap the White Balance setting to choose the proper light source. The ISO settings enable you to adjust the camera sensor's sensitivity to light. You can use a higher ISO setting for low-light shots, but beware of increased noise in the image.

You can use the Setup menu to immediately display recently taken photos for review and to record GPS information into the picture. Embedded GPS information can come in handy if you use a photo editing and managing application such as iPhoto 9 and later, which enables you to use the location information to manage and showcase photos. You can also choose a different shutter sound for when you press the Camera button, and you can choose whether images are saved to the device or to a memory card. If you ever get to the point where you want to return your camera's settings to the factory defaults, tap Reset.

9. Compose the subject in the Viewer. You can tap the Exposure icon if you need to adjust the exposure.

10. Press the Camera button to focus on the subject. You hear a chime when the focus is set.

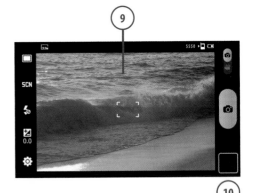

11. Remove your finger from the Camera button to capture the image. A thumbnail of the image appears in the Image Viewer.

12. Tap the Image Viewer to review the image you just captured. You can also access your photos by tapping the Gallery icon under Applications from any home screen.

ADDING CAMERA EFFECTS

Keep in mind when you use any of the photo effects, such as Negative, Black and White, and Sepia, they become a permanent part of your pictures. To give yourself more choices in the future as to how you use your images, consider purchasing a photo-editing program that enables you to perform such effects but still maintain your original photo.

Adjusting Settings and Taking Photos (Galaxy Tab 10")

The newly designed Camera application for the Galaxy Tab 10" is chock full of features that can help you capture high-quality images. Just like its predecessor, the interface is simplistic and intuitive.

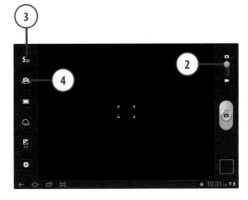

1. Tap the Camera icon to access the camera feature.

2. Move the mode button into the still image position to capture photos. Your Galaxy Tab switches to Still Image mode, which is the default mode.

3. Tap to enable or disable the flash.

4. Tap to switch between rear-facing and front-facing cameras.

5. Tap the Shooting mode icon to select a shooting mode. The Galaxy Tab is set to Single shot by default.

EXPLORING SHOOTING MODES

Go Further

Choose the Smile shot mode to focus the camera on the face of your subject. After the camera detects the person's smile, it takes the picture.

The Panorama shooting mode enables you to take a picture and then use the onscreen guide to move the viewfinder and take seven more shots. This is a great mode for capturing wide vistas, such as landscapes and cityscapes.

Use the Action shot setting to enable the camera to detect movement within a framed scene, and then create a panorama of the moving object.

EXPLORING SCENE MODES

>>> Go Further

The scene mode options optimize your camera for special shooting situations. For example, if you are taking a picture of a person from her shoulders up, you can use the Portrait mode. Portrait mode automatically optimizes your Galaxy Tab's camera to use the largest aperture setting, which shortens depth of field and slightly blurs the background, emphasizing your main subject.

The Landscape mode uses the smallest possible aperture setting for the greatest depth of field to help ensure that everything is in sharp focus.

The Night mode uses a flash in combination with a slow shutter speed to brighten dark backgrounds. The Sports mode uses a fast shutter speed to capture moving subjects without blurring.

6. Tap the Timer icon to designate a time for how long to wait before the camera takes a picture. This is great for allowing you time to set up the shot and then place yourself in the frame.

7. An image that is too light or too dark degrades the appearance of your photos. To take full advantage of the camera feature of the Galaxy Tab, you must adjust the exposure level for various bright or dark lighting conditions. Tap the Exposure Value icon.

8. Drag the exposure level up to achieve a proper exposure level in a low-light shooting environment, or drag it down for a very bright shooting environment.

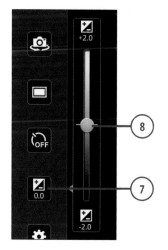

9. Tap the Settings icon to customize more settings.

10. Tap to change the focus mode from Auto focus to Macro. Macro focus enables you to pull a sharp focus on close-up subjects, such as flowers. This setting can help you showcase the fine detail in a close subject.

11. Tap to choose an automatic scene mode. Automatic scene modes offer quick and easy ways to adapt to various lighting conditions when taking photos.

12. Tap to adjust the white balance for the camera. The white balance features help accurately reproduce colors when you are shooting in various lighting situations, so that neutral colors such as white and gray are truly neutral, and all colors are rendered without undesired color casts.

13. Tap to add camera effects to your photos as you capture them. Your choices are Grayscale (Black and White), Sepia, and Negative.

14. Tap to set a size for the images you captures. Your choices are 3.2M (2048×1536) or 0.3M (640×480).

15. Tap to set how the camera measures or meters the light source. This setting determines how the camera factors light in a scene to achieve the proper exposure.

16. Tap to enable or disable GPS tagging of the photos you capture. Embedded GPS information can come in handy if you use a photo-editing and managing application such as iPhoto 9 and later, which enables you to use the location information to manage and showcase photos.

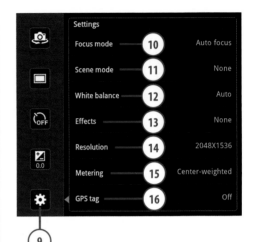

ADDING CAMERA EFFECTS

Go Further

Keep in mind that when you use any of the photo effects, such as Negative, Black and White, and Sepia, they become a permanent part of your pictures. To give yourself more choices in the future as to how you use your images, consider purchasing a photo-editing program that enables you to perform such effects but still maintain your original photo.

TALKING ABOUT CENTRE-WEIGHTED AND SPOT METERING

Go Further

The default Metering setting is Centre-weighted. Your other choices are Matrix, which measures light intensity in several points to achieve the best exposure, and Spot, where only a small area in the scene is measured. Matrix metering is usually considered the most accurate form of metering because it measures the entire scene and then sets the exposure according to an average. Spot measuring is generally used to capture very high contrast scenes, such as when a subject's back is to the sun.

17. Compose the subject in the Viewer.

18. By default, the camera automatically focuses on what is in the center of the Viewer. You can tap any area on the viewer and Camera automatically focuses and adjusts the exposure for that particular area.

19. Press the Camera button to focus on the subject. You hear a chime when the focus is set; remove your finger from the Camera button to capture the image. A thumbnail of the image appears in the Image Viewer.

20. Tap the Image Viewer to review the image you just captured. You can also access your photos by tapping the Gallery icon under Applications from any home screen.

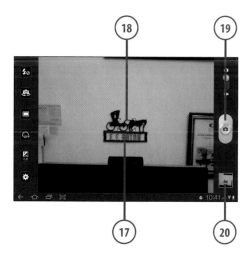

Navigating Image Viewer

Image Viewer provides a quick and easy way to review the photos that you have just taken. It also enables you to quickly share your pictures as soon as you capture them and even set images as a contact icon or wallpaper. You can also delete unwanted photos in Image Viewer.

Adjusting Settings and Taking Photos (Galaxy Tab 7")

As soon as you take a picture, a thumbnail of that photo appears next to the camera button. You can tap that thumbnail to review the picture you have taken and browse other photos.

1. Tap the Image Viewer to review the image.

2. The image opens full screen, the controls appear, and then they fade away. Tap the middle of the screen to access the controls again.

3. Tap the forward arrow to progress to the next image in Image Viewer.

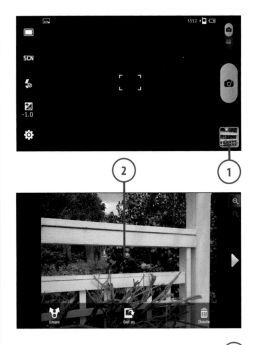

4. Tap the Share icon to share a picture via AllShare, Bluetooth, Gmail, Messaging, and Picasa.

5. Tap Set As to set the picture as a Contact icon or as Wallpaper.

6. Tap the Delete icon to delete any picture onscreen.

7. Tap Magnify to enlarge the image.

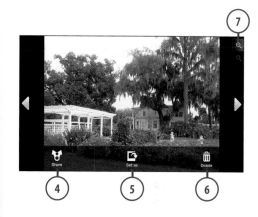

Adjusting Settings and Taking Photos (Galaxy Tab 10")

As soon as you take a picture, a thumbnail of that photo appears next to the camera button. You can tap that thumbnail to review the picture you have taken and browse other photos.

1. Tap the Image Viewer to review the image.

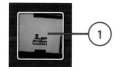

2. The image opens full screen, the controls appear, and then they fade away. Tap the middle of the screen to access the controls again.

3. Tap Slideshow to begin a slideshow of your photos. After the slideshow begins, you can tap anywhere onscreen to end the slideshow.

4. Tap the Share icon to share a picture via Picasa, Bluetooth, Gmail, Email, and by way of other installed apps you have downloaded to your Tab.

5. Tap to delete the photo that is being displayed.

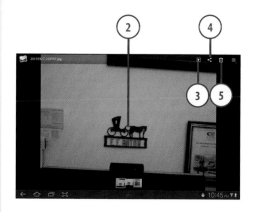

6. Tap to access the menu for more options.

7. Tap to view details about the photo, including the time it was taken, aperture, and exposure settings upon capture.

8. Tap to rotate the photo to the left.

9. Tap to rotate the photo to the right.

10. Tap Set Picture As to set the picture as a Contact icon or as Wallpaper for the Lock screen or home screen.

11. Tap to crop the photo that is being displayed.

12. Tap to print the photo, such as to a Bluetooth printer.

13. Tap to copy the photo to the Clipboard.

14. Tap to set motion activation settings, such as reducing or enlarging the screen when you tilt the Galaxy Tab back and forth.

15. With the menu closed, double-tap the image to enlarge it. You can double-tap it again to return it to its normal size.

16. Flick the image from left to right or right to left to navigate through all the photos you have captured.

17. Tap the Back arrow to return to Camera and take more pictures.

18. Tap Home to close Camera and return to the home screen.

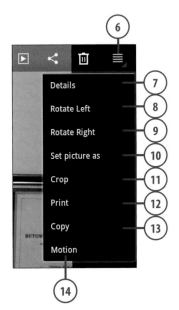

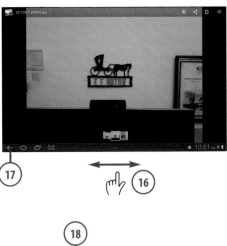

Tips for Capturing Photos

Shutter lag is the amount of time between pressing the shutter release button and the moment the picture is taken. A longer shutter lag is common among most compact cameras and also the Galaxy Tab. What this means for you is that is that you have to be particularly mindful of timing your shots when recording moving subjects. Shutter lag can cause you to miss out on a key action if you do not anticipate the shot.

One important thing to know about your Tab is that the shutter does not fire as you place your finger down on the Camera button; the shutter fires when you lift your finger off the button. Use this knowledge to your advantage by pressing your finger on the shutter button and holding while you frame the shot and focus on an object about the same distance as where the subject will pass, to anticipate the shot, and then lift your finger. This means you need to hold your Tab completely still for a little bit longer. Anticipating moving subjects to capture dynamic, moving shots can take some practice.

The Galaxy Tab's slow shutter makes it prone to producing blurry photos if you do not remain perfectly still during capture. Even the smallest movement can have an adverse effect on your photographs; this is especially true in low-light situations. A photo might appear to be fine when you review it on the Tab display, but when you download it and view it on a larger display, you can see the problem.

Gallery

Gallery offers a more robust photo and video management system than Image View, and it also enables you to view, capture, and perform basic edits on pictures. You can also share your photos from Gallery.

Managing Photos with Gallery (Galaxy Tab 7")

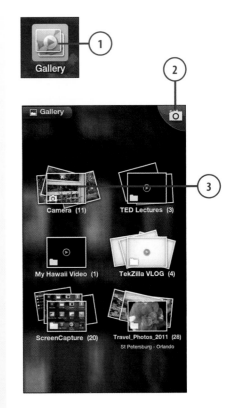

Depending on which cellular carrier or Galaxy Tab model you have, locate the Gallery icon on a home screen or under Applications.

1. Tap Gallery to access the features.

2. Content is arranged in categories/albums. If you have downloaded videos, such as video podcasts or recorded videos, with your Tab and transferred images from your computer, they are in here, too. Tap the camera icon to access the Camera feature from Gallery.

3. Tap the Camera category to access photos and videos taken with your Tab.

4. After you have captured many photos and videos, the thumbnail representation of images within this category becomes long. Tap the arrows at the bottom of the screen to progress through the thumbnails.

Follow the Bread Crumbs

If you look in the upper-left corner of the screen, you can see the path you have taken from the list of categories to the Camera folder. You can use this path to return to the previous screen by tapping the first icon in the path or by tapping the Back button on your Galaxy Tab.

A Change of View

By default, the content is arranged as individual thumbnails. You can tap a category icon to have Gallery arrange the thumbnails in albums according to the date in which they were acquired.

Deleting Multiple Images

You can mark multiple images for deletion on this screen by pressing the Menu button on your Galaxy Tab, selecting a check box in the corner of each thumbnail, and then tapping Delete.

5. Tap a photo in the album to open it. Videos are displayed with a Play button in the middle of the thumbnail.

Magnifying an Image

You can magnify a single image by tapping the Magnify icon. When you're viewing a photo, the Magnify icon is located in the upper-right corner when you hold your Tab in Portrait orientation or horizontally.

6. Tap Slideshow to view a slideshow of pictures. The first frame of any video that you have shot also plays in the slideshow. You can tap the screen again to stop the slideshow.

7. Tap Menu either at the bottom of the interface or press the Menu button located on your Tab to access more options. Both of these methods lead to the same options.

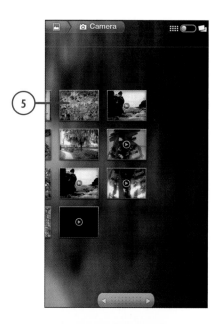

8. Tap Share to choose from a number of options in which you can share your images. Keep in mind that as you add an email account or Facebook account on your Tab, those options also display in this menu.

9. Tap Delete to receive the option to delete an individual photo.

10. Tap More to receive options to view image details, set a photo as wallpaper or a contact icon, crop an image, print an image, and rotate an image left or right.

Managing Photos with Gallery (Galaxy Tab 10")

By default, you can access the Gallery icon by flicking the main home screen from left to right, or you can access it from the Apps menu.

1. On the main home screen, scroll from left to right, and then tap Gallery to access the features.

2. Content is arranged in categories/albums. If you have downloaded videos, such as video podcasts or recorded videos, with your Tab and transferred images from your computer, they are in here, too. Tap the camera icon to access the Camera feature from Gallery.

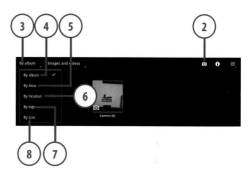

3. Tap the By Album menu to group your photos and videos in other ways.

4. Tap the By Album option to arrange photos based on the folder in which they are stored.

5. Tap By Time to arrange photos based on the time they were captured.

6. Tap By Location to arrange photos based on their GPS location.

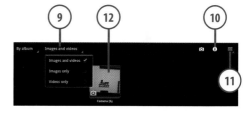

7. Tap By Tags to arrange photos based on the tags you have applied.

8. Tap By Size to arrange photos based on their file size. You can tap another area on screen to close the menu.

9. Tap Images and Videos to display photos only, video only, or both.

10. Tap the information icon, and then touch an album to display information about it.

11. Tap to make albums available when your Tab is not connected to the Internet.

12. Tap an album to view all photos in it.

13. After you have captured many photos and videos, the thumbnail representation of images in this category becomes long. Flick the screen right to left and left to right to view all thumbnails in the album.

14. Tap Slideshow to view a slideshow of pictures. The first frame of any video that you have shot also plays in the slideshow. You can tap the screen again to stop the slideshow.

15. Touch and hold your finger to a photo to reveal more Gallery options.

16. To delete images within an album, touch each image you want to delete. A green box appears around the image. You can touch Select All to select all the photos in the album.

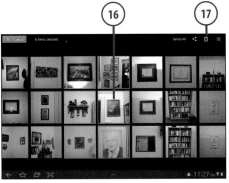

17. Tap the trash can to delete the selected photos.

18. Tap Confirm Deletion.

19. Select multiple images within an album, and then tap the menu icon to rotate each to the right or left at the same time.

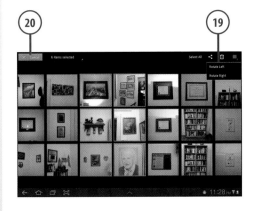

20. When finished, tap Cancel to exit the Gallery options.

21. Tap a photo in the album to open it full screen.

22. Touch the middle of the screen to reveal the controls, and then tap Delete to delete the displayed image.

23. Tap Share to view options for sharing the displayed image with friends and family.

24. Tap the Back button to return to the previous screen.

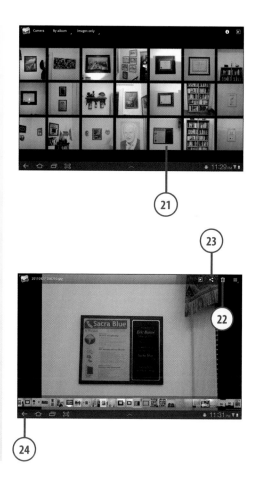

Sharing from Gallery

Your Galaxy Tab makes it easy for you to share your photos by streamlining the process within Gallery.

Emailing Photos from Gallery (Galaxy Tab 7")

Gallery

Emailing your photos to friends and family can be accomplished in just a few taps.

1. Depending on which cellular carrier or Galaxy Tab model you have, locate the Gallery icon on a home screen or under Applications. Tap Gallery to access the features.

2. Tap the Camera category to access photos and videos taken with your Tab.

3. Tap the arrows at the bottom of the screen to locate the thumbnail of the photo you want to email.

4. Tap a photo in the album to open it. Videos are displayed with a play button in the middle of the thumbnail.

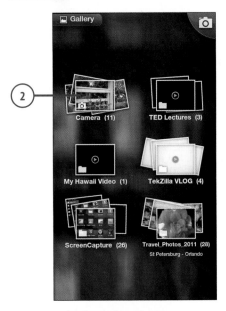

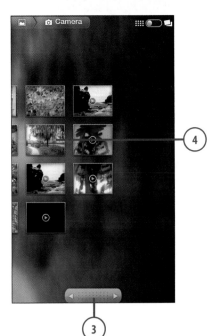

5. Tap Menu either at the bottom of the interface or press the Menu button located on your Tab to access more options. Both methods lead to the same options.

6. Tap Share to choose from a number of options in which you can share your images. Keep in mind that as you add an email account or Facebook account on your Tab, those options also display in this menu.

5

6

7. Tap Gmail or another email account that you have added to your Tab in the list. A new email message opens with the image attached. You could also tap the X located to the far right of the attachment field to remove the attachment. Keep in mind that you do not have the option to attach a new image at this stage if you choose to remove an attachment.

8. Tap in the To field to access the keyboard and type in the email address for the recipient.

9. Tap Next to jump to the Subject field.

10. Type the subject for the email.

11. Tap Next again to jump to the body of the email.

12. Compose a message to go with the photograph.

13. Tap Send to send the email.

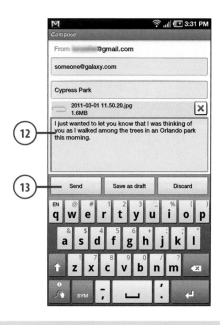

EMAILING FROM CAMERA

You can also email a photo from Camera within Image View. After you tap the Camera button to capture the image, a thumbnail of the image appears in the Image Viewer. Tap the Image Viewer to review the image and then choose Share to access your email. Email providers have varying file size limitations, so make sure you are aware of your provider's limitations before emailing photographs.

Go Further

Emailing Photos from Gallery (Galaxy Tab 10")

Emailing your photos to friends and family can be accomplished in just a few taps on your Galaxy Tab 10".

1. With the album open that has the photo you want to email, touch and hold your finger to that photo to access more Gallery options.

2. Touch more photos that you want to share. A green box appears around each photo, letting you know that it is selected. Email providers have varying file size limitations, so make sure you are aware of your provider's limitations before emailing photographs.

3. Tap the share icon to access the options. You can access these same Share options even if you are viewing a single photo, full screen. Keep in mind that as you add an email account or Facebook account on your Tab, those options also display in this menu.

4. Tap Gmail or any other mail account you have added to your Tab. The mail application opens with the images you selected attached. Tap the X located to the far right of each attachment field to remove the attachment. Keep in mind that you do not have the option to attach a new image at this stage, if you choose to remove an attachment.

5. Type the recipients email into the To field.

6. Tap in the next field, and then type a subject for the email.

7. Tap in the body of the email to compose a message.

8. Tap Send to send the email.

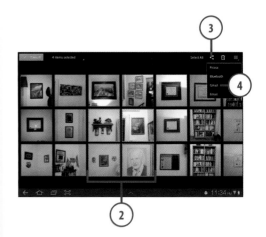

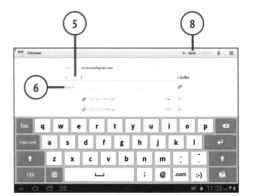

Go Further

EMAILING FROM CAMERA

You can also email a photo from Camera within Image View. After you tap the Camera button to capture the image, a thumbnail of the image appears in the Image Viewer. Tap the Image Viewer to review the image, and then tap the Share icon to access your email. Email providers have varying file size limitations, so make sure you are aware of your provider's limitations before emailing photographs.

Screen Captures

The 7" Galaxy Tab running Android 2.2 has a very helpful feature that enables you to take screen captures of its interface. The Galaxy Tab 10" requires a little outside help before you can take screenshots, but you can do it. The ability to take screenshots can come in handy for educational purposes, especially if you want to post a few Galaxy Tab tips online. Taking a screenshot is as simple as pressing two buttons simultaneously on your Tab.

Taking Screen Captures (Galaxy Tab 7")

On the 7" Galaxy Tab running Android 2.2, you can take screenshots simply by pressing the Back button and the sleep button on the device simultaneously.

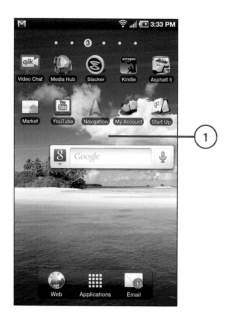

1. Open the screen that you want to take the screenshot of and position the Tab into the orientation in which you want to grab the screen capture: vertical or horizontal.

2. Press one finger down on the Back button located on the Galaxy Tab.

3. Continue holding your finger down on the Back button and press the Power/Lock key located on the Tab. You hear the shutter sound effect as it takes the screen capture.

4. Depending on which cellular carrier or Galaxy Tab model you have, locate the Gallery icon on a home screen or under Applications. Tap Gallery to view the screen capture.

5. The screen capture is located in the album named ScreenCapture. Tap the ScreenCapture category to access the image.

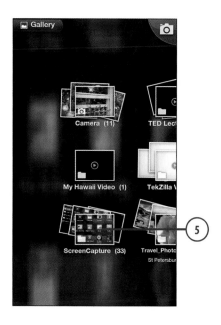

DIFFICULTIES TAKING SCREEN CAPTURES

Some screen captures of the Tab's interface or third-party apps can be difficult to acquire. The Back button is very sensitive. Occasionally, you come across a screen where you continue to hold the Back button down on the Tab, and you jump to the previous screen. When you hold the Back button, sometimes it executes more than once. To see this difficulty for yourself, try taking a screen capture of your Tab's Camera interface. When you encounter this problem, try holding down the Back button as you enter into a screen, such as the Camera interface. For example, hold your finger on the Back button, tap Camera to open it, and then press the Power/Lock key. This could take you a few attempts to grab the image.

Taking Screen Captures (Galaxy Tab 10")

The Galaxy Tab 10" requires a little help from the Android Software Developer's Kit (SDK) for you to take screenshots on your device. The Dalvik Debug Monitor Server (DDMS), which is part of the Android SDK, enables you to stage the screenshot and then capture the shot from your computer.

A number of options are available for taking screenshots on your Tab. Some methods void your warranty, so make sure you do your research. The DDMS is free and does not void your warranty. You can download the Android SDK and access more information here: http://developer.android.com/sdk/index.html.

After you download and install the SDK on your computer, you must place your Tab into debug mode.

1. Tap the Apps icon on the home screen.

2. Tap Settings.

3. Tap Applications.

4. Tap Development.

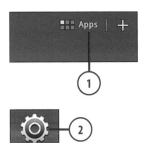

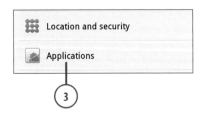

5. Tap USB Debugging. A warning
   pops up. Tap OK. A green check
   mark indicates that the USB
   Debugging setting has been
   enabled.

6. After you have downloaded the
   Android SDK, double-click the
   android-sdk folder, and then open
   the Tools folder.

7. Double-click the ddms file. The
   application opens.

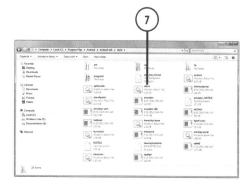

8. Connect your Tab to the computer.

9. The device name should appear
   in the monitor. Select the device.

10. Click Device in the main menu.

11. Click Screen capture in the menu.

12. Stage the screenshot on your
    Galaxy Tab.

13. Click Refresh in the application.
    The staged Galaxy Tab screen
    appears. In this example the
    screenshot has been rotated.

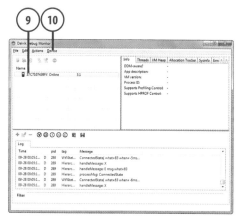

14. Click Save to capture the screen-
    shot and save the image. Take
    note that you can rotate images if
    needed, before capturing the
    image.

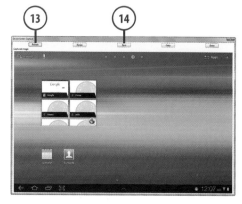

Editing Images

Your Galaxy Tab allows for some basic photo edits without having to use a third-party photo-editing application. You can improve some photos by performing simple edits such as cropping.

Cropping Images (Galaxy Tab 7")

The simple reframing of the composition of a shot to remove unwanted areas can perform wonders for some images.

Fortunately, Gallery makes it easy for you to crop your Galaxy Tab photos. Cropping is a great way to correct shot composition and can help focus and emphasize the main subject of a shot.

1. Depending on which cellular carrier or Galaxy Tab model you have, locate the Gallery icon on a home screen or under Applications. Tap Gallery to access the features.

2. Tap the Camera category to access photos taken with your Tab.

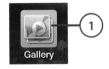

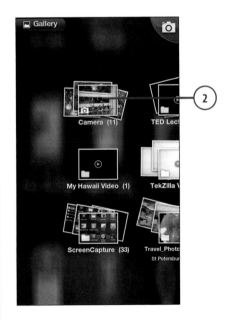

3. Tap a photo in the category to open it. Videos are displayed with a play button in the middle of the thumbnail.

4. Tap Menu either at the bottom of the interface or press the Menu button located on your Tab to access more options. Both methods lead to the same options.

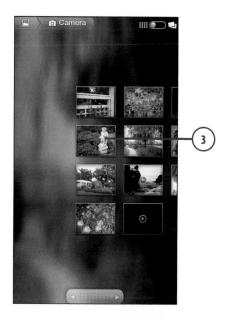

5. Tap More to access the Crop tool.

6. Tap Crop. The image opens with overlays.

7. Drag each side of the orange overlay to designate which parts of the image you want to keep.

8. Tap Save to crop the image.

Cropping Images (Galaxy Tab 10")

The Galaxy Tab 10" makes it easy for you to further define your photographic subject by performing a simple crop right from the device. You can crop a photo in no time and make huge improvements to photos that were less than perfectly framed.

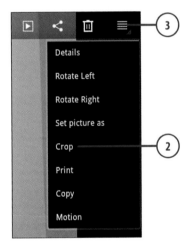

This section presumes you have already opened the Gallery from the Apps screen.

1. Tap an album that contains a picture that you want to crop, and then tap the picture.

2. Tap the screen to reveal more Gallery options.

3. Tap the menu icon.

4. Tap Crop. A blue overlay appears in the center of the picture.

5. Drag each side of the blue overlay to designate which parts of the image you want to keep.

6. Tap OK to save the newly cropped image.

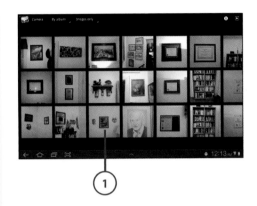

Non-Destructive Edit

When you crop an image, a new copy is made reflecting the edits you have made. The original captured image is untouched.

7. Tap X to cancel the edit.

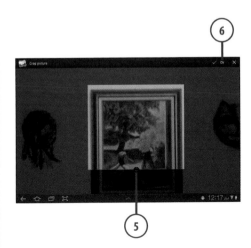

Receive turn-by-turn,
voice-guided, GPS navigation.

Search for
locations
and get
directions.

Locate
businesses
and quickly
receive more
information
about them.

Share locations
with friends.

In this chapter, you learn to use the Maps, Navigation, Latitude, and Places apps to find locations, get directions, and connect with friends.

→ Enabling GPS

→ Finding a Location with Maps

→ Getting Directions with Maps

→ Specifying Locations with Maps

→ Getting Voice Command Directions

→ Browsing Places

→ Adding New Places

→ Enabling Wireless Networks

→ Using Latitude

Using Maps, Navigation, Places, and Latitude

Your Galaxy Tab is equipped with four apps that can help you get where you need to go: Maps, Navigation, Latitude, and Places. If Verizon is your cellular carrier, you also have a fifth paid option in VZ Navigator. Each app helps you accomplish a unique task, yet most of their collective feature base is accessible within each app. Maps can supply detailed destination directions for a specific address. Navigation can provide voice-guided turn-by-turn directions to a location. Latitude enables you to share your location with friends and view their locations on a map. You can use Places to quickly locate local businesses and access contact information, coupons, and customer reviews.

Enabling GPS

Before you can begin to use the many features of your Galaxy Tab that utilize GPS, you must first enable your Tab's GPS capabilities. Activating your Tab's GPS capabilities is a very easy process.

Galaxy Tab 7"

1. Press your finger against the status bar at the top of your Tab's screen.

2. Pull down with your finger to access the Notifications panel.

3. Tap GPS to enable the feature.

4. Drag or flick the bottom of the Notifications panel upward to close it. GPS has now been enabled for your device.

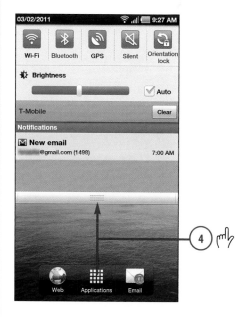

Galaxy Tab 10"

1. Tap Apps.

2. Tap Settings.

3. Tap Location and Security.

4. Tap Use GPS Satellites.

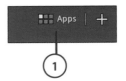

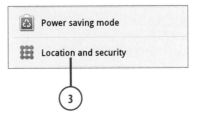

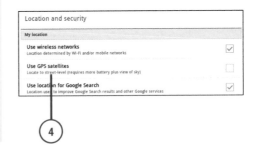

Getting Around with Maps (Galaxy Tab 7")

Maps is great for planning a trip across town or the nation. You can change your map view by adding layers that include traffic, terrain, satellite imagery, transit lines, and more. You do not even have to have an address for Maps to help you get where you need to go. Just specify the general area on a map and let the Maps app generate directions on how to get you there.

Finding a Location with Maps

The Maps app on your Galaxy Tab gives you the capability to find locations, get directions, and pinpoint locations. It also gives you access to features found in other apps, such as Navigation, Places, and Latitude. The Maps app can help you pinpoint your exact location if you should ever find yourself in an unfamiliar place. As soon as you launch Maps, your Tab uses GPS to pinpoint your current location. Maps does not cover every country or city, and you must have an active 3G data plan and connection before you can use the application. It is very easy for you to find a location by entering an address into Maps.

1. Depending on which cellular carrier or Galaxy Tab model you have, locate the Maps shortcut on a home screen or under Applications. Tap the Maps icon to access the Map features.

2. The first time you use Maps, a Location Consent dialog appears. Read the consent and then tap Agree, if you consent.

3. A street map opens displaying your current location. Press the Menu button located on your Galaxy Tab.

Go Further

FINDING PLACES IN YOUR AREA

Wherever you are, Maps makes it easy for you to find your favorite chain restaurant, coffee shop, ATM, or gas stations. Just tap the round Locator button in the top-right corner of the interface to pinpoint your current location. Tap the Places icon to receive information regarding the location of places and access contact information.

4. Tap Search to find a location.

5. Enter the address of the location you want to find. As you type, a list of possible locations displays.

6. Tap the correct address in the list. Your Tab displays the location on the map. If you cannot find the address you need in the list, Maps might not have complete data for that area or the information might be outdated.

7. Tap the location overlay.

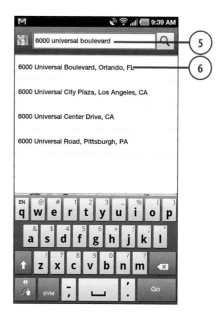

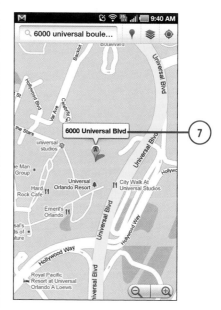

It's Not All Good

Inaccurate or Incomplete Data

The Maps application is not always correct. Some of the directions and navigation data that it presents might be inaccurate or incomplete due to change and time. Complete information might not be available for some locations. Always use your best personal judgment and pay attention to road signs, landmarks, traffic conditions, and closures when following directions generated on your Tab.

8. Tap the star to the right of the address to save this location for future searches.

9. Tap the Back button on your Tab to return to the previous screen.

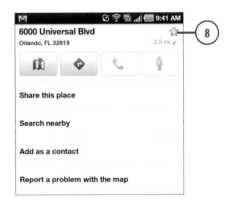

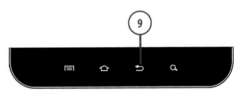

10. To add additional layers of information to the current map, tap the Layers icon. A list of layers displays.

11. Tap the layer of information that you want to add to the map. The information is added to the map, changing the map view.

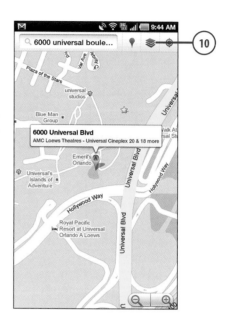

Go Further

SWITCHING MAP VIEWS

You can add multiple layers of information to a map by tapping the Layers icon again and choosing another layer. A green check mark is placed next to the layer you have chosen in the list. Tap Clear Map to clear the new layers from the map or tap More Layers to receive even more map views. You can also view map locations as a Satellite image or in Terrain view.

12. Tap the Magnify button to enlarge the map. You can also double-tap your finger in a specific location on the map to enlarge the area. As you move in closer on the map, you start to notice that new information appears in the map, such as the name of banks and restaurants.

13. Use your finger to physically move the map and pinpoint locations.

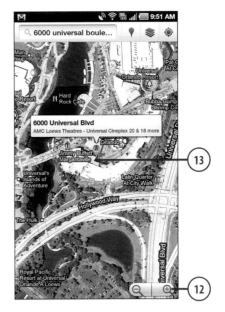

Getting Directions with Maps

Maps can help you get from point A to point B by providing detailed directions. You can get step-by-step driving, public transportation, biking, and walking directions to a specified destination by designating addresses for a starting location and a desired destination.

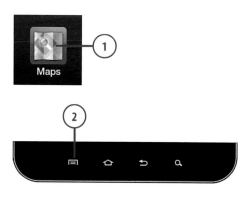

1. Depending on which cellular carrier or Galaxy Tab model you have, locate the Maps shortcut on a home screen or under Applications. Tap the Maps icon to access the map features. A street map opens, displaying your last location searched.

2. Press the Menu button located on your Galaxy Tab.

3. Tap Directions.

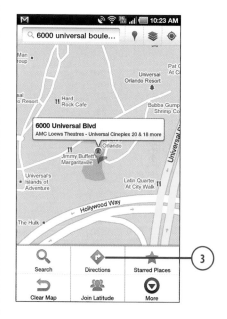

4. By default, Maps saves you a step by using GPS to pinpoint your current location, which Maps places into the Start Point field as My Location. If you need to enter a different starting point, tap in the first field and type a new address.

5. Type the destination address into the End Point field. As you type, a list of possible locations displays.

6. Tap the correct address in the list. If the address cannot be found in the list, Maps might not have complete data for that area, or the information might be outdated.

7. By default, Maps is set to display driving directions. Select the type of directions you want to receive.

8. Tap Go to receive directions. A screen of detailed directions appears as a list. The estimated travel time is displayed at the top of the page.

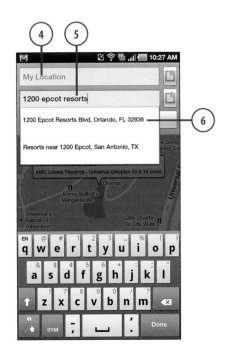

Go Further

USING CONTACT INFORMATION AS LOCATIONS

If you want to use the address information you have for a contact as a start or end point, tap the icon that looks like an address book located at the end of each field. You can then choose Contacts from the menu.

Go Further

BOOKMARKING LOCATIONS

Each time you generate directions within maps, they are bookmarked under the Layers menu. To use these bookmarked directions, tap the Layers icon and then tap the directions you want to use to display them again.

9. Tap Show on Map to have the directions represented on a map. You can also tap the Menu button on your Tab and choose See Map. When in Map view, you can use the forward and backward arrows at the bottom of the screen to move through each step in the directions.

10. Tap Navigate to receive step-by-step voice commands to the destination. This is a great hands-free driving option when coupled with a vehicle mount.

11. Tap any step in the directions to review it on the map.

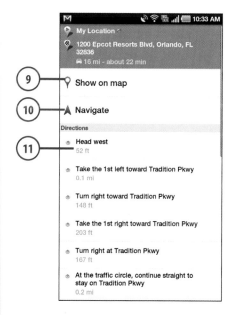

Go Further

UPDATING/MODIFYING DIRECTIONS

After Maps generates the directions, you can instruct Maps to generate new directions that avoid highways and toll roads. Tap the Menu button on your Tab, and then choose Options to designate which options you want. Tap Update for updated directions.

12. After you have found the destination, you can find your way back by reversing the directions. Press the Menu button on your Tab.

13. Tap Reverse in the menu to reverse the directions.

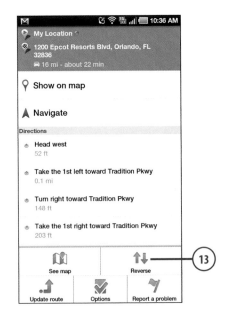

Specifying Locations with Maps

Maps can also help you find locations for which you do not have an address. For example, you might know that a café that you would like to visit is located downtown, but you do not know how to get downtown from your hotel. Maps enables you to specify a vicinity on a map where you want to go and generates directions from your current location.

1. Depending on which cellular carrier or Galaxy Tab model you have, locate the Maps shortcut on a home screen or under Applications. Tap the Maps icon to access the map features.

2. Your last location searched displays within Maps. Press the Menu button located on your Galaxy Tab. The Menu button on your Tab is a contextual menu. You need to be in a Map view to receive the proper menu options for the next step. If you previously received directions in the form of a list, you can tap Show on Map to access a Map view before you tap the Menu button on your Tab.

3. Tap Directions.

4. If My Location is not currently selected in the Start Point field, tap the Address Book icon located at the end of the Start Point field.

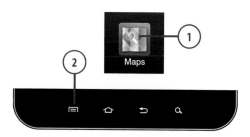
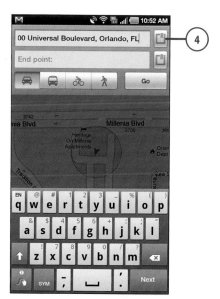

5. Select My Current Location so that Maps uses GPS to pinpoint your current location.

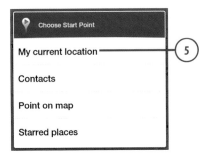

It's Not All Good

Current Location Unavailable

Occasionally, your Tab might not be able to pinpoint your current location because of lack of area coverage or a temporary disruption in the system. If for some reason Maps warn you that Your Current Location Is Temporarily Unavailable, you might have to enter it by hand.

6. Tap the Address Book icon located at the end of the End Point field.

7. Select Point on Map so that you can specify a location on the map for which you do not have an address. You are taken to the map.

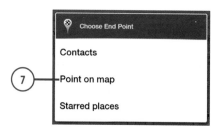

8. Navigate to the area on the map for where you want to specify a location, and Tap an area on the map. An overlay instructs you to Tap to Select This Point.

9. Tap the overlay to designate an End Point. You are taken back to the previous screen. The point on the map appears in the End Point field.

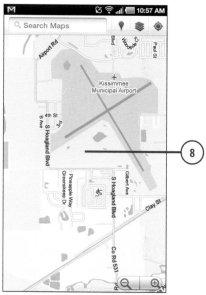

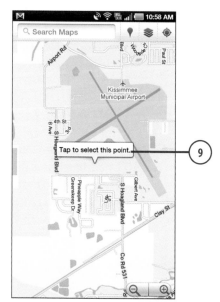

10. Driving directions are specified by default. Select the type of direction you need.

11. Tap Go to receive the directions.

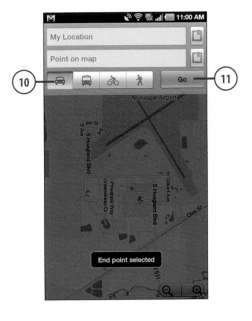

ANOTHER WAY TO SPECIFY AN UNKNOWN LOCATION

Go Further

You can navigate to a location in a map view and then hold your finger down on the area and let Maps generate the address for you. After Maps provides the information for that specified area, tap the information overlay to receive directions, search the nearby area, or share that place via messaging, email, Bluetooth, and more.

Getting Around with Maps (Galaxy Tab 10")

Maps is great for planning a trip across town or the nation. You can change your map view by adding layers that include traffic, terrain, satellite imagery, transit lines, and more. You do not even have to have an address for Maps to help you get where you need to go. Just specify the general area on a map and let the Maps app generate directions on how to get you there.

Finding a Location with Maps

The Maps app on your Galaxy Tab gives you the capability to find locations, get directions, and pinpoint locations. It also gives you access to features found in other apps, such as Navigation, Places, and Latitude. The Maps app can help you pinpoint your exact location if you should ever find yourself in an unfamiliar place. As soon as you launch Maps, your Tab uses GPS to pinpoint your current location.

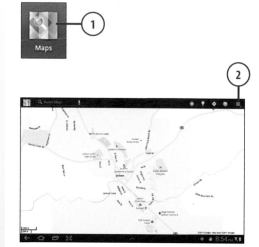

1. Tap Maps on the home screen.

2. A street map opens displaying your current location. Tap Menu.

3. Tap Search Maps to find a location.

Go Further

FINDING PLACES IN YOUR AREA

Wherever you are, Maps makes it easy for you to find your favorite chain restaurant, coffee shop, ATM, or gas stations. Just tap the round Locator button in the top-right corner of the interface to pinpoint your current location. Tap the Places icon to receive information about the location of places and access contact information.

4. Type the address of the location you want to find. As you type, a list of possible locations displays.

5. Tap the correct address in the list. Your Tab displays the location on the map. If you cannot find the address you need in the list, Maps might not have complete data for that area or the information might be outdated.

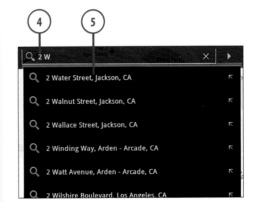

It's Not All Good

Inaccurate or Incomplete Data

The Maps application is not always correct. Some of the directions and navigation data that it presents might be inaccurate or incomplete due to change and time. Complete information might not be available for some locations. Always use your best personal judgment and pay attention to road signs, landmarks, traffic conditions, and closures when following directions generated on your Tab.

6. Tap the location overlay.

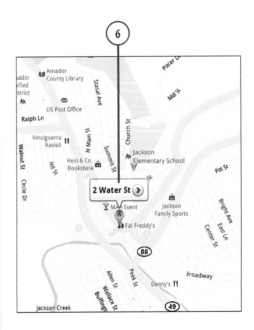

7. Tap the star to the right of the address to save this location for future searches.

8. Tap Back to return to the previous screen.

9. To add additional layers of information to the current map, tap the Layers icon.

10. Tap the layer of information that you want to add to the map. The information is added to the map, changing the map view.

Go Further

SWITCHING MAP VIEWS

You can add multiple layers of information to a map by tapping the Layers icon again and choosing another layer. A green check mark is placed next to the layer you have chosen in the list. Tap Clear Map to clear the new layers from the map, or tap More Layers to receive even more map views. You can also view map locations as a satellite image or in Terrain view.

11. Pinch inward to enlarge the map. You can also double-tap your finger in a specific location on the map to enlarge the area. As you move in closer on the map, you start to notice that new information appears in the map, such as the name of banks and restaurants.

12. Use your finger to physically move the map and pinpoint locations.

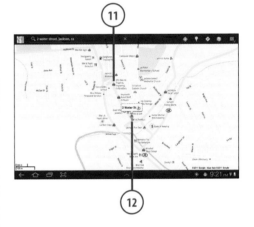

Getting Directions with Maps

Maps can help you get from point A to point B by providing detailed directions. You can get step-by-step driving, public transportation, biking, and walking directions to a specified destination by designating addresses for a starting location and a desired destination.

1. Tap Maps on the home screen.

2. A street map opens, displaying your last location searched. Tap the Directions icon at the top-right corner of the screen.

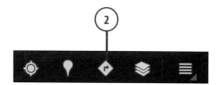

3. Type your starting address in the My Location box. Type at least your city and state (or province), but if you have a street address you should add that as well so Maps can give you more precise directions. As you type, suggested addresses appear in a list below the box; tap an address in the list to place that address in the box.

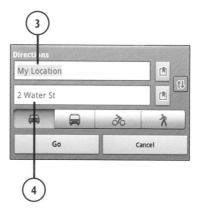

4. By default, the address you searched for appears in the End Point box. You can change the address by tapping in the box and typing a new address. As you type, suggested addresses appear in a list below the box; tap an address in the list to place that address in the box.

Go Further

USING CONTACT INFORMATION AS LOCATIONS

If you want to use the address information you have for a contact as a Start or End Point, tap the icon that looks like a bookmark located at the end of each field. You can then choose Contacts from the menu.

Go Further

BOOKMARKING LOCATIONS

Each time you generate directions within maps, they are bookmarked under the Layers menu. To use these bookmarked directions, tap the Layers icon, and then tap the directions you want to use to display them again.

5. By default, the car button is selected so you can determine how long your trip will take by car. You can also select how long the trip will take by bus, bicycle, or walking.

6. Tap Go to receive directions. A screen of detailed directions appears as a list. The estimated travel time is displayed at the top of the page.

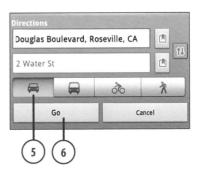

7. You can scroll up and down the Directions list to move through each step in the directions.

8. Tap Navigate to receive step-by-step voice commands to the destination. This is a great hands-free driving option when coupled with a vehicle mount. (You'll learn how to use Navigate later in this chapter.)

9. Tap any step in the directions to review it on the map.

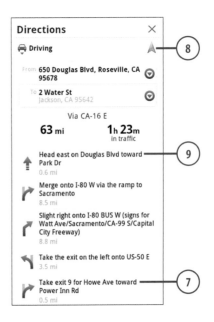

Go Further

UPDATING/MODIFYING DIRECTIONS

After Maps generates the directions, you can instruct Maps to generate new directions that avoid highways and toll roads. Tap the Menu button on your Tab, and then choose Options to designate which options you want. Tap Update for updated directions.

Specifying Locations with Maps

Maps can also help you find locations for which you do not have an address. For example, you might know that a café that you would like to visit is located downtown, but you do not know how to get downtown from your hotel. Maps enables you to specify a vicinity on a map where you want to go and generates directions from your current location.

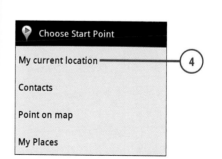

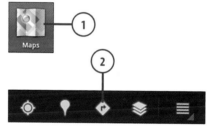

1. Tap Maps on the home screen.

2. Tap the Directions icon.

3. If My Location is not currently selected in the My Location box, tap the Bookmark icon located to the right of the box.

4. Tap My Current Location so that Maps uses GPS to pinpoint your current location.

It's Not All Good

Current Location Unavailable

Occasionally, your Tab might not be able to pinpoint your current location because of lack of area coverage or a temporary disruption in the system. If for some reason Maps warns you that Your Current Location Is Temporarily Unavailable, you might have to enter it by hand.

5. Tap the Bookmark icon located to the right of the End Point field.

6. Tap Point on Map so that you can specify a location on the map for which you do not have an address. You are taken to the map.

7. Navigate to the area on the map for where you want to specify a location, and tap an area on the map. An overlay instructs you to Tap to Select This Point.

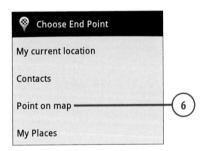

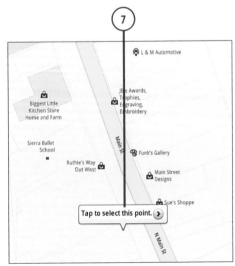

8. The point on map appears in the End point box. If you want, cut this text and replace it with a new address.

9. Driving directions are specified by default. Select the type of direction you need.

10. Tap Go to receive the directions.

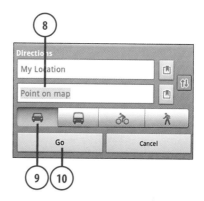

ANOTHER WAY TO SPECIFY AN UNKNOWN LOCATION

Go Further

You can navigate to a location in a map view and then hold your finger down on the area and let Maps generate the address for you. After Maps provides the information for that specified area, tap the information overlay to receive directions, search the nearby area, or share that place via messaging, email, Bluetooth, and more.

Getting Voice-Command Directions

The Navigation app enables you to turn your Galaxy Tab into a turn-by-turn voice-command GPS device. You can take full advantage of your Tab's GPS capabilities by investing in a Galaxy Tab Vehicle Power Adapter and Vehicle Mount from Samsung. The vehicle mount enables you to attach your Tab to the windshield or dashboard. Using the Navigation app for voice-command directions is quite easy.

Galaxy Tab 7"

1. If you have purchased a vehicle adapter, use it to power the device.

2. Depending on which cellular carrier or Galaxy Tab model you have, locate the Navigation shortcut on a home screen or under Applications. Tap Navigation to access the features.

3. Read the important message in the Navigation dialog box. If you want this message to show the next time you open the Navigation app, tap the check box area to select Show This Message Next Time.

4. Tap Accept. Behind the scenes, Navigation searches for your current location. The Navigation home screen displays.

5. Driving directions are selected by default. Tap Driving to change to walking directions, if needed.

6. Tap Speak Destination to speak the destination into your Galaxy Tab.

7. Tap Contacts to pick an address associated with a contact as a destination.

8. Tap Starred Places to choose a previous destination you have starred.

9. Tap Type Destination to type the name of the destination for which you need directions. The Destination field appears at the top of the screen.

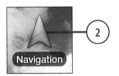

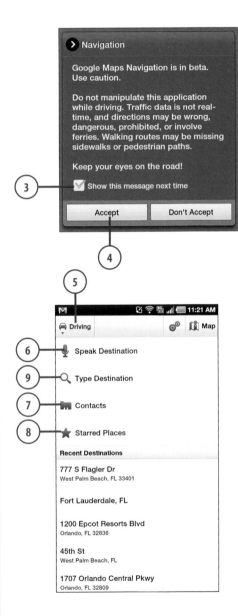

10. Type in the destination for which you want to receive directions. As you type, possible destinations appear as a list below.

11. Tap the correct destination in the list.

12. Read the important message in the Navigation dialog box and then tap Accept. This message might not appear again if you did not select Show This Message Next Time. Your Galaxy Tab searches for a GPS signal. After a connection is made, a street map appears with a highlighted route and the Navigation app speaks the first set of directions.

13. Attach your Galaxy Tab to the vehicle mount in your car.

14. Drive the route. Much like a dedicated GPS, your Tab senses where you are on the route and proceeds to give you instructions, verbally and graphically.

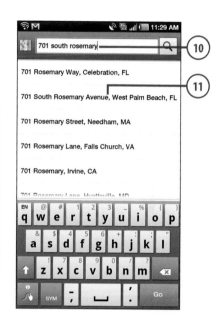

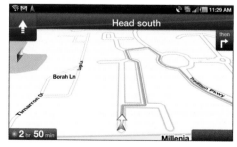

Go Further

VIEWING THE MAP

You can find the current step in the directions at the very top of the screen. In the top-left corner, you can view the direction for which you are to travel in the current step, as well as the estimated traveling distance for completing the step. Directions take the form of a left turn arrow, straight arrow, right arrow, or a U turn. In the upper-right corner, you find the direction for your next move. In the lower-left corner of the screen, you find the estimated travel time to your destination.

15. Press the Menu button on your Tab to access more navigation options.

16. Tap Search to speak or type a new destination.

17. Tap Route Info to view the starting and ending points, as well as the distance in miles and approximate arrival time in minutes.

18. Tap Layers to add information to the map, such as Traffic view, Satellite view, Parking, Gas Stations, ATMs & Banks, and Restaurants.

19. Tap Mute to mute or unmute all Navigation tones.

20. Tap Exit Navigation to end your session. If you don't exit navigation, you might still hear Navigation tones after you close the Navigation app and begin a new task.

21. Tap More for more options, including the Directions list, which displays the most recent destination.

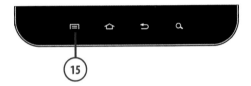

Exploring Route Options

You can access alternative routes from the Route Info screen. You can compare different route options by reviewing their distances in miles as well as overall travel times and highlighted map routes.

Galaxy Tab 10"

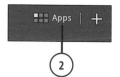

1. If you have purchased a vehicle adapter, use it to power the device.

2. On the home screen, tap Apps.

3. Tap Navigation.

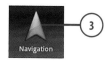

4. Read the important message in the Navigation dialog box. If you want this message to show the next time you open the Navigation app, you can tap in the check box area to tap the Show This Message Next Time check box.

5. Tap Accept. Behind the scenes, Navigation searches for your current location. The Navigation home screen displays.

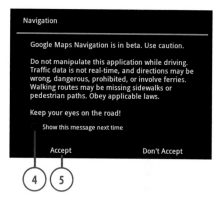

6. Driving directions are selected by default. Tap Driving to change to walking directions, if needed.

7. Tap Speak Destination to speak the destination into your Galaxy Tab.

8. Tap Contacts to pick an address associated with a contact as a destination.

9. Tap Starred Places to choose a previous destination you have starred.

10. Tap Type Destination to type the name of the destination for which you need directions. The Destination field appears at the top of the screen.

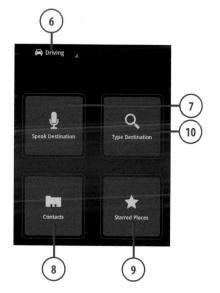

11. Type in the destination for which you want to receive directions. As you type, possible destinations appear as a list below.

12. Tap the correct destination in the list.

13. Read the important message in the Navigation dialog box, and then tap Accept. This message might not appear again if you did not select Show This Message Next Time. Your Galaxy Tab searches for a GPS signal. After a connection is made, a street map appears with a highlighted route and the Navigation app speaks the first set of directions.

14. Attach your Galaxy Tab to the vehicle mount in your car.

15. Drive the route. Much like a dedicated GPS, your Tab senses where you are on the route and proceeds to give you instructions, verbally and graphically.

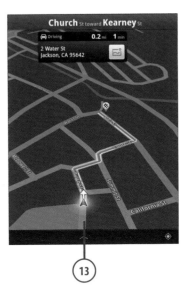

VIEWING THE MAP

You can find the current step in the directions at the very top of the screen. In the top-left corner, you can view the direction for which you are to travel in the current step, as well as the estimated traveling distance for completing the step. Directions take the form of a left turn arrow, straight arrow, right arrow, or a U turn. In the upper-right corner, you find the direction for your next move. In the lower-left corner of the screen, you find the estimated travel time to your destination.

16. Tap Route Info to view the starting and ending points, as well as the distance in miles and approximate arrival time in minutes.

17. Tap Layers to add information to the map, such as Traffic view, Satellite view, Parking, Gas Stations, ATMs & Banks, and Restaurants.

18. Tap Directions for the Directions list, which displays the most recent destination.

19. Tap the Menu button on your Tab to access more navigation options.

Exploring Route Options

You can access alternative routes from the Route Info screen. You can compare different route options by reviewing their distances in miles as well as overall travel times and highlighted map routes.

20. Tap Search to speak or type a new destination.

21. Tap Mute to mute or unmute all Navigation tones.

22. Tap Exit Navigation to end your session. If you don't exit navigation, you might still hear Navigation tones after you close the Navigation app and begin a new task.

23. Tap Set Destination to set a new destination.

24. Tap Help to get help for the Navigation app.

25. Tap Terms, Privacy & Notices to get information about the terms and conditions of use, the app's privacy policy, and legal notices.

Getting to Know Places (Galaxy Tab 7")

Places is a preinstalled app on your Galaxy Tab that enables you to locate places of interest with Google Maps and retrieve information, such as addresses, hours of operation, and phone numbers for those places. You can use Places to pinpoint the exact locations of restaurants, bars, ATMs, gas stations, and more, or you can create a new location, such as pharmacies or hospitals. Places offers a great way to explore nearby areas with which you might not be familiar.

Browsing Places

If you happen to stop in an unfamiliar town, Places is a great app that can help you quickly locate an ATM, a gas station, a hotel, or a place of business. Places uses GPS to pinpoint the nearest specified places and supplies you with directions, telephone numbers, customer reviews, and more.

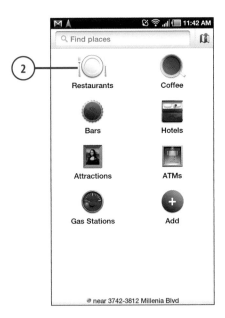

1. Depending on which cellular carrier or Galaxy Tab model you have, locate the Places shortcut on a home screen or under Applications. Tap Places to launch the app.

2. Places pinpoints your current location and displays it at the bottom of the screen. A screen of place categories appears. Tap a category for a place you would like to find in your area. A list of places displays.

3. Tap Distance to filter the list by one-half mile, 1 mile, 2 miles, 5 miles, or 10 miles.

4. Some places, such as restaurants and coffee houses, have been reviewed by customers. Tap Rating to filter the list by 1 star and up, 2 stars and up, and so on.

5. Tap Open Now to filter the list by places that are currently open.

6. Tap a star next to any of the places in the list to add it to your Starred Places.

7. Tap a place in the list to receive more information.

8. The information page for a place provides you with even more options. Tap the See Map icon to view the location on a map.

9. Tap the Navigation button to select navigation options, such as choosing Driving Navigation and Walking Navigation and Get Directions.

10. If you purchased your Tab outside the United States and have a cellular carrier outside the United States, you can tap the Phone icon to place a call to the place. (U.S. cellular providers do not allow the Galaxy Tab to place calls.)

11. Tap the More Options icon to receive options including Share This Place, Search Nearby, Buzz About This Place, Add as a Contact, and More Info. Buzz About This Place enables you to post public messages and photos at a location for others to access. The More Info options provide more Internet links to web pages for that place and more photos.

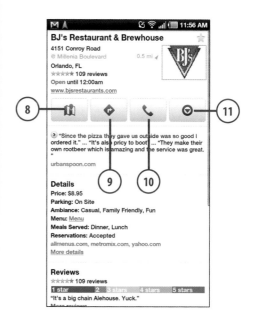

Adding New Places

Can you think of a place that should have been added as a category? Places gives you the capability to add other search categories, such as for pharmacies or hospitals. Adding a new place is very easy.

1. Depending on which cellular carrier or Galaxy Tab model you have, locate the Places shortcut on a home screen or under Applications. Tap Places to launch the app.

2. Places determines your current location and displays it at the bottom of the screen. A screen of place categories appears. Tap Add to add a category. The Add a Search box displays.

3. Type in a new place category.

4. Tap Add after you have finished. A new category is added on the Places home screen. You can now tap the category to bring up a list of places.

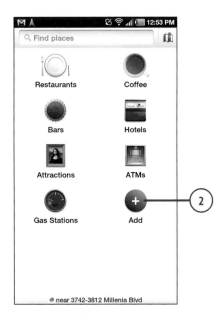

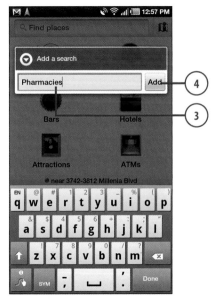

5. To remove a Search, hold your finger on the search until the pop-up menu appears.

6. Tap OK to remove the search.

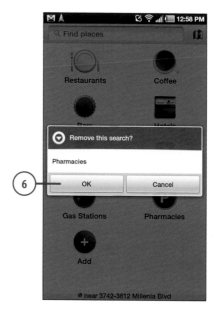

Getting to Know Places (Galaxy Tab 10")

Places is a preinstalled app on your Galaxy Tab that enables you to locate places of interest with Google Maps and retrieve information, such as addresses, hours of operation, and phone numbers for those places. You can use Places to pinpoint the exact locations of restaurants, bars, ATMs, gas stations, and more, or you can create a new location, such as pharmacies or hospitals. Places offers a great way to explore nearby areas with which you might not be familiar.

Browsing Places

If you happen to stop in an unfamiliar town, Places is a great app that can help you quickly locate an ATM, a gas station, a hotel, or a place of business. Places uses GPS to pinpoint the nearest specified places and supplies you with directions, telephone numbers, customer reviews, and more.

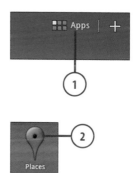

1. Tap Apps on the home screen.

2. Tap Places.

3. Places pinpoints your current location and displays it at the bottom of the screen. A screen of place categories appears. Tap a category for a place you would like to find in your area. A list of places displays.

4. Tap Distance to filter the list by one-half mile, 1 mile, 2 miles, 5 miles, or 10 miles.

5. Some places, such as restaurants and coffee houses, have been reviewed by customers. Tap Rating to filter the list by 1 star and up, 2 stars and up, and so on.

6. Tap Price to filter the list by the average price of products or services, such as restaurant food.

7. Tap a star next to any of the places in the list to add it to your Starred Places.

8. Tap a place in the list to receive more information.

9. The information page for a place provides you with even more options. Tap the Map icon to view the location on a map.

10. Tap the Directions icon to get directions.

11. Tap the Street View icon to view a photo of the business from the street.

12. Tap the More icon to view more options including Check In Here, Street View, Share This Place, Search Nearby, Add as a Contact, Report a Problem, and More Info.

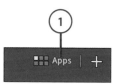

Adding New Places

Can you think of a place that should have been added as a category? Places gives you the capability to add other search categories, such as for pharmacies or hospitals. Adding a new place is easy.

1. Tap Apps on the home screen.

2. Tap Places.

3. Places determines your current location and displays it at the bottom of the screen. A screen of place categories appears. Tap Add to add a category. The Add a Search box displays.

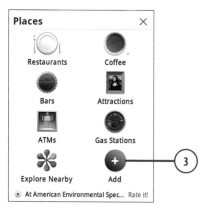

4. Type a new place in the Add a search box.

5. Tap Add.

6. The new category appears in the Places window. You can tap the category to bring up a list of places within it.

7. To remove a place category, tap and hold your finger on the category icon until the pop-up menu appears.

8. Tap Remove.

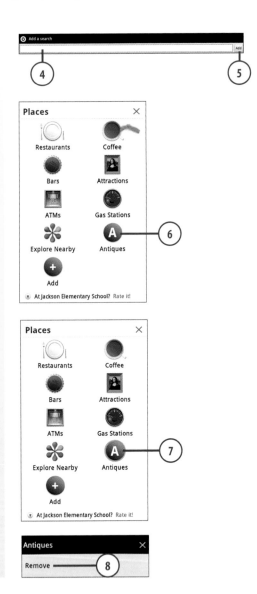

Enabling Wireless Networks

The Google Latitude app enables you to see the location of friends on a map or as a list. You can choose to share your location with others, or hide your location. Before you can use Latitude, you must first configure your Tab to use wireless networks and enable Wi-Fi.

Galaxy Tab 7"

1. Tap Applications from any home screen.

2. Tap Settings.

3. Tap Location and Security.

4. Tap Use Wireless Networks to enable the setting. A Location Consent dialog appears.

5. Read the Location consent and then tap Agree, if you consent.

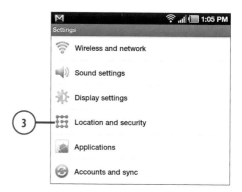

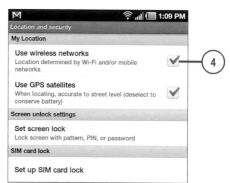

6. Press your finger on the status bar at the top of your Tab's screen.

7. Pull down with your finger to access the Notifications panel.

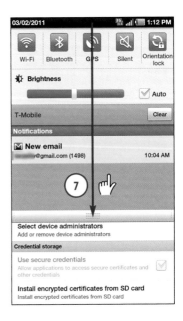

8. Tap Wi-Fi to enable the feature.

9. Drag the bottom of the Notifications panel upward to close it. Wi-Fi is now enabled for your device. You can also enable Wi-Fi in the Settings menu under the Wireless and Network option.

Galaxy Tab 10"

1. Tap Apps on the home screen.

2. Tap Settings.

3. Tap Location and Security.

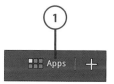

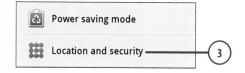

4. Tap Use Wireless Networks to enable the setting. A Location Consent dialog appears.

5. Read the Location consent, and then tap Agree if you consent.

6. Tap Wireless and Networks.

7. Tap Wi-Fi. Wi-Fi is now enabled for your device.

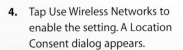

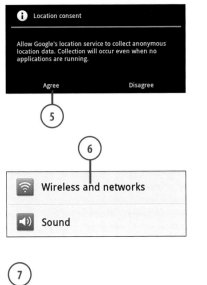

Using Latitude

Adding friends and sharing your locations with others is easy to accomplish after you have enabled your Tab to use wireless networks and Wi-Fi. Your friends need either a GPS-enabled mobile device or computer with Latitude installed in order to participate. Latitude is offered as a feature in Google Maps and can be found on many mobile devices. If a friend decides to use Latitude on a computer, he too is able to share his location automatically if he is connected to a Wi-Fi network and using a supported Internet browser such as Google Chrome.

Galaxy Tab 7"

1. Tap Applications from any home screen.

2. Tap the Latitude shortcut. A dialog box opens.

3. Read the consent and then tap Allow & Share if you agree. Latitude accesses your current location. The Latitude home screen opens, enabling you to manage your Friends list and security settings.

4. At first, you are the only friend in the list, but Latitude makes suggestions for friends you can add. Tap the red X to remove anyone from the suggested friends list.

5. Tap the plus sign to send a sharing request to someone in the list. The request is sent via email. You can refresh your Friends list by tapping the Menu button on your Tab and selecting Refresh Friends. After an individual accepts, he or she shows in the list.

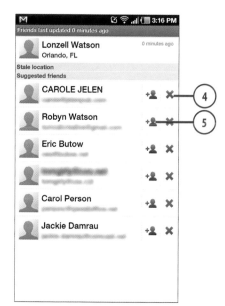

6. Tap the Menu button on your Galaxy Tab.

7. Tap Add Friends to add friends not found in the suggested Friends list.

8. Now you need to choose how you want to contact them. Tap Select from Contacts to send a request to someone in your contacts.

9. Tap Add via Email Address to enter an email address of a prospective friend.

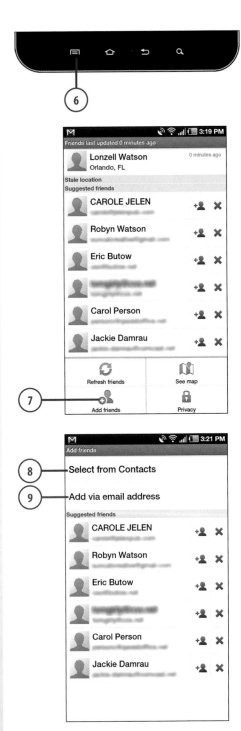

10. Press the Back button on your Tab to return to the previous screen.

11. Press the Menu button on your Tab.

12. Tap Privacy to configure your privacy settings. By default, Latitude is set to Detect your location. You can choose to manually select a location on the map, hide your location, and turn off Latitude altogether.

13. Tap See Map. You can now see your location on the map.

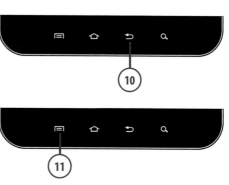

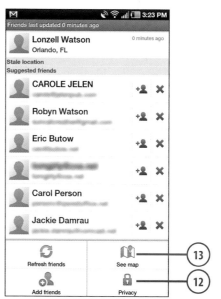

14. This map screen's options are identical to the options available in Maps when finding a location. Enter a location in the Search Maps field to find it on the map.

15. Tap the Places icon to receive location information for restaurants, coffee bars, hotels, attractions, ATMs, and gas stations.

16. Tap the Layers button to change the map view and add additional layers of information to the map.

17. Tap the Locator icon to view your own current position on the map.

18. Tap the Magnify icon to enlarge the map.

19. Press the Menu button located on your Tab.

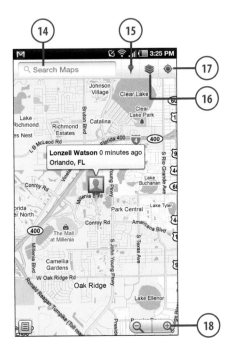

20. Tap Search to enter a new location to find on the map.

21. Tap Directions to enter a Start and End Point and receive directions.

22. Tap Starred Places to access a previous location you have starred.

23. Tap Clear Map to reset the map after you have finished viewing directions.

Return to Friends List

You can return to your friends list by tapping Latitude in the Menu.

24. Tap More to select additional options. Under this setting you'll find Google Mobile Help, Terms, Privacy & Policy Notices, General Information about Google Maps, and Labs. You can tap the Menu button on your Tab again to close it.

Experimenting with Labs

One option you might want to try is Labs. Labs is a list of experimental map features that are still being perfected. The content under Labs can change at any time.

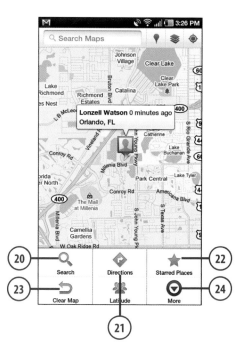

Galaxy Tab 10"

1. Tap Apps on the home screen.

2. Tap Latitude.

3. The Maps app opens and the Latitude window appears. At first, you are the only friend in the list, but Latitude makes suggestions for friends you can add if any.

4. Tap the Check In icon to tell your friends where you are.

5. Type the location you want to search for in the Search Nearby box. The search criteria should include the street address, city, and state or province so Latitude can find your location easily. If you find your location in the list, tap the location in the list.

6. Tap the Search icon.

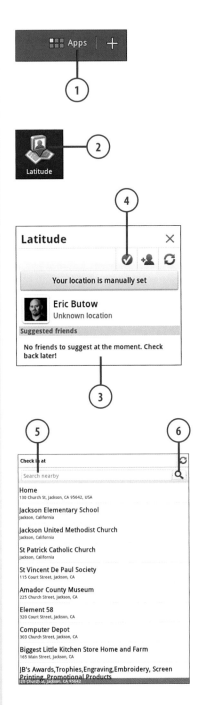

7. Tap the location in the list.

8. Type a comment to your check in.

9. Alert your friends on Latitude by tapping Friends on Latitude and any other Google services, such as friends on the Google+ social networking website.

10. Automatically check in to this location the next time you log into Latitude by tapping the Automatically Check in Here check box.

11. Tap Check in Here.

12. Your location appears as a pin on the map.

13. View information in the window. (Because this location is permanently closed, I'm obviously standing outside the building.)

14. Bookmark the location by tapping the star outline to the right of the address.

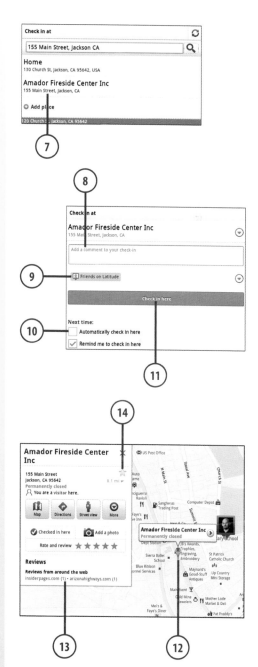

15. Tap the Add Friends icon to add friends from other sources than Latitude's suggestions.

16. Tap Select from Contacts to select a Contact.

17. Tap Add via Email Address to add a new friend by typing an email address. The Latitude app will send a sharing request to your recipient.

18. Tap the Close icon.

19. Refresh your Friends list by tapping Refresh.

20. Close the Latitude window by tapping the Close icon.

21. Tap the Menu button.

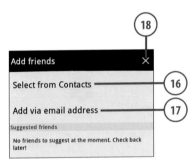

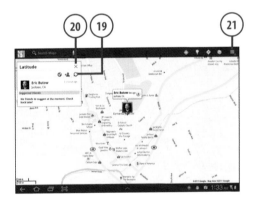

22. The first three options in the list allow you to refresh friends, check in, and add friends as you did in the Latitude window.

23. Tap Settings to change your location reporting, location history, and check-in information.

24. Tap My Places to access a previous location you have starred.

25. Tap Clear Map to reset the map after you have finished viewing directions.

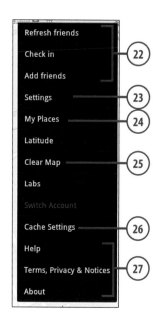

Return to Friends List

You can return to your friends list by tapping Latitude in the Menu.

26. Tap Cache Settings to clear the map tile cache.

27. View Maps help, view terms, privacy, and notices, and information about the Maps app.

Experimenting with Labs

One option you might want to try is Labs. Labs is a list of experimental map features that are still being perfected. The content under Labs can change at any time.

Search Android Market for
thousands of useful, educational,
and entertaining apps.

In this chapter, you learn how to expand the capabilities of the Galaxy Tab by installing new apps. You also learn how to browse and make purchases in the Android Market and organize application icons on your Galaxy Tab.

→ Searching for Android Applications
→ Purchasing Android Applications
→ Rating Applications
→ Getting Help with Apps
→ Arranging Application Icons on Your Galaxy Tab
→ Adding and Removing Home Pages
→ Adding a Dictionary and Thesaurus
→ Adding an RSS Reader
→ Using Note Everything

Enhancing Your Galaxy Tab with Apps

The Galaxy Tab is not just about superior hardware craftsmanship. Your Tab's true strength can be found in the incredible software that is developed for it. The Galaxy Tab comes with some truly amazing, preinstalled apps right out of the box, but you can expand its capabilities even further by downloading new apps from the Android Market. You can choose from thousands of innovative apps, ranging from games to productivity apps. The number of apps optimized for use on your Tab is growing rapidly.

Getting Apps Through Android Market (Galaxy Tab 7")

Android Market makes it easy for you to browse apps and games that you can download to your Galaxy Tab. If this is your first time shopping Android Market, you will find the interface quite intuitive. A great way to become acquainted with Market is just to start browsing. Many reviews of apps and games are available, so you can make an intelligence choice before downloading. A Google, Bing, or Yahoo! search for "Best Android apps for Galaxy Tab" can help you identify the most popular apps. Galaxy Tab users from around the world are writing articles telling about their experiences with apps that you might find useful. After you download and try out an app, consider giving your feedback so that new Galaxy Tab users can learn from you.

Searching for Android Applications

To access the Android Market for the first time, you need to use your Google account to sign in to the Android Market. After you launch Android Market, there are several ways for you to search apps from the home page. The home page search options change position on the page, depending on which orientation you hold your Tab: vertical or horizontal.

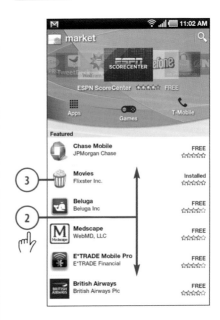

1. Tap the Market widget to access Android Market. After you read the terms of service you can tap Accept.

2. Featured applications are listed on the home page. Scroll up and down the page to review apps.

3. Tap an app to access a description page and read more about the product. You can purchase or download the app for free on the description page.

More About Product Descriptions

The description page for an app is chock full of useful information so that you can make an educated decision on whether you want to purchase the app. Sample screenshots of the app are featured on this page along with customer reviews and information about the developer.

4. The Market home page also makes it possible to browse apps by categories: Apps, Games, and your cellular carrier. Tap a category to browse the list of results.

5. Use your finger to flick through the list of popular apps featured horizontally at the top of the page. Tap an app to go to the product description page.

6. If you know the name of the app you want, tap the Search icon on the home page to specify a search term.

7. Type a search term into the field. As you type, results appear in the list below.

8. Tap a search result to access the results page for that product. For example, if you tap a search result for Angry Birds, you go to a results page that features all versions of that product.

9. Tap a result to access the product description page.

More Ways to Search for Apps

If your cellular carrier is Verizon, you also have the preinstalled widget V CAST Apps that enables you to browse and download applications and games. The V CAST icon is located on the Main home screen. The Multimedia Sync application by doubleTwist, discussed in Chapter 7, "Playing Music and Video," offers another portal to the Android Market from your PC or Mac desktop. Just click Apps Market located in the sidebar of the interface under doubleTwist.

Finding Great Apps

There are thousands of apps that you can download to your Galaxy Tab, so use your storage space wisely by finding the great ones. Finding the best apps might be the biggest challenge of all as you wade through your many options. Here are some tips on how to locate the highest performing apps.

1. Look at the featured apps on the Market home page. When you access a category such as Apps or Games, review the Top Free and Top Paid categories. Keep in mind that large companies, usually with well-established names, tend to dominate the featured list. Lesser-known developers are also producing outstanding apps, so look deeper.

2. Some apps have trial versions you can test drive before purchasing. Look for Lite or Free versions of applications to test before you buy.

3. After you locate an app that you might want to purchase, scroll down to the bottom of the page and take a look at the Related Apps. You see apps that are similar along with their ratings next to them. You might find a higher-rated app that you want to look into.

4. Check out customer reviews for products, but don't trust everything you read. Some reviews might not be in-depth or unbiased, and therefore they are less helpful.

USING OTHER RESOURCES TO FIND APPS

You can use other solid resources outside of the Android Market for finding great apps.

Perform a Google search—For example, if you are looking for an app suited for taking dictation, type "Galaxy Tab App Dictation."

Search for sites that feature and post reviews for apps—Be aware that some of these sites are sponsored by the developers and might not convey completely objective views.

Find a Galaxy Tab forum—There are many of these popping up every day. In a forum, you can post questions to other Galaxy Tab owners regarding apps. Be aware that experienced Tab users may not moderate all of these forums, and the advice you receive can be questionable.

>>> Go Further

Purchasing Android Applications

Software developers from around the world have developed thousands of apps for you to take advantage of with your Galaxy Tab. You can choose from many free apps in the Android Market as well as from a variety of more sophisticated apps for a fee. The process for downloading free apps and paid apps is similar, but you need to designate a payment method to make purchases.

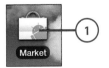

1. Tap the Market widget to access the Android Market.

2. Locate and then tap the app that you want to purchase. The product description page opens.

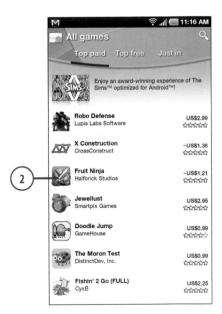

More About Product Descriptions

The description page for an app is chock full of useful information so that you can make an educated decision on whether you want to purchase the app. Sample screenshots of the app are featured on this page along with customer reviews and information about the developer. Be sure to tap More on the description page so that you review the complete description.

3. Tap the price of the app to see the permissions for this app. If this app is free, you would tap the Free button.

4. Review the permissions, and then tap OK to accept permissions. If this app is free, the downloading process would begin.

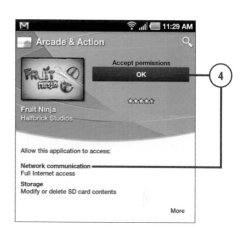

Accepting Permissions

If the application you have selected requires control of your Tab or access to data, Market displays the information in this area. The list of permissions changes from app to app. When you accept permissions, you are essentially allowing the application you are purchasing to access your Galaxy Tab, including Internet access.

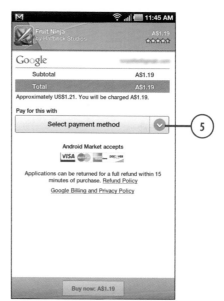

5. After you have accepted permissions, you must designate a payment method. Tap Select Payment Method to review your options.

6. Tap the option button next to a payment option.

More About Payment Options

Typically, there are two payment options: Add a Credit Card or Bill My *(cellular carrier)* Account. If you are purchasing an app from a seller in a different country, the Bill My *(cellular carrier)* Account option might not be offered.

7. Tap OK after you have chosen an option. If you choose the Bill My *(cellular carrier)* Account, you have to read a Carrier Billing consent form and then tap Accept.

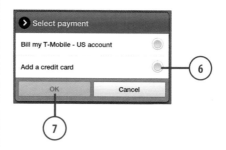

8. If you choose Add a Credit Card, enter your credit card information and contact information into the fields.

Removing a Credit Card

As of this writing, you cannot remove a credit card from your Tab as a payment option after you enter it as a payment option. You can sign in to your account at Google Checkout, https://check-out.google.com/, and edit your payment methods to remove the credit card.

9. Tap Save to make the purchase and begin downloading the app. The app is downloaded and a shortcut is placed in your menu of apps.

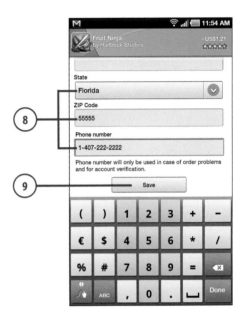

UPDATING APPS

Market periodically searches for updates for apps that have been downloaded to your Galaxy Tab. If an update has been found, a notification appears in the status bar, located in the top-left corner of your Tab. You can drag the notification menu downward to reveal the updates. Tap an item in the list to be taken to Android Market so you can begin the update.

Go Further

Go Further

DISABLING UPDATE NOTIFICATIONS

If you prefer to manually check for updates, you can configure Market to stop notifying you about updates. Just launch the Market app and press the Menu button on your Galaxy Tab. Select My Apps in the menu and then tap Settings to choose Do Not Notify Me. You have to periodically enter Market and choose My Apps from the Menu options to see if there are any updates. You can also set installed apps to update automatically by tapping one of the installed apps in the list, and then selecting Allow Automatic Updating.

Rating Applications

Rating content you have purchased in Android Market helps others to make educated decisions about their purchases. Android Market uses a five-star rating system to rate all content. Much of the content in Android Market features reviews that you can read to see how others like the product. You can easily write reviews of your own to make your feelings known about the content you have purchased.

1. Tap the Market widget to access the market.

2. Press the Menu button on the Galaxy Tab.

3. Tap My Apps to view the list of apps you have purchased in Android Market.

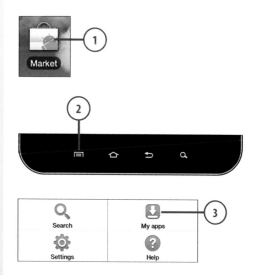

4. Tap the app in the list that you want to review.

5. Tap in the Stars field to access the Rate It pop-up menu.

6. Tap the number of stars you give this product.

7. Tap OK.

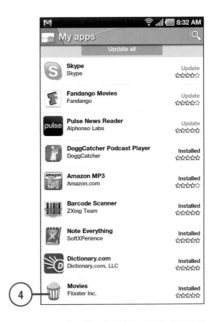

8. Tap the Post a Comment field to access the pop-up Post Comment box.

9. Tap in the comment field to reveal the keyboard and type your comment.

10. Tap OK. Your rating and comment are posted for everyone to see.

Getting Help with Apps

New applications are being developed for the Galaxy Tab every day. Many new apps are being added to the Android Market daily from well-known companies, small companies, and individual developers. Bugs and other problems are likely to arise in such a fast-moving market. There are ways for you to contact developers so that you can ask questions.

1. Check within an app for developer contact information. Many developers make it easy for you to find them by making their contact information readily available within their apps.

2. Tap the Market widget to launch Android Market.

3. Tap the Menu button on the Galaxy Tab.

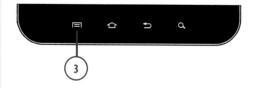

4. Tap My Apps in the menu. A list of the apps installed on your Tab appears.

5. Tap an app in the list. The product description page opens.

6. Scroll to the bottom of the page.

7. Tap Send Email to Developer to compose an email message asking your question(s).

8. Tap Visit the Developer's Web Page to visit the developer's site and search for information.

9. Tap Market Content to provide feedback to Android Market regarding the product.

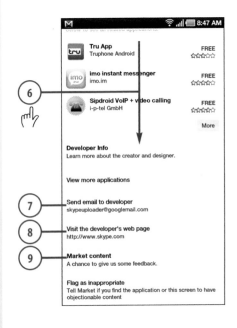

Getting Apps Through Android Market (Galaxy Tab 10")

Android Market makes it easy for you to browse apps and games that you can download to your Galaxy Tab. If this is your first time shopping Android Market, you will find the interface quite intuitive. A great way to become acquainted with Market is just to start browsing. Many reviews of apps and games are available, so you can make an intelligent choice before download-ing. A Google, Bing, or Yahoo! search for "Best Android apps for Galaxy Tab" can help you identify the most popular apps. Galaxy Tab users from around the world are writing articles telling about their experiences with apps that you might find useful. After you download and try out an app, consider giv-ing your feedback so that new Galaxy Tab users can learn from you.

Searching for Android Applications

To access the Android Market for the first time, you must use your Google account to sign in to the Android Market. After you launch Android Market, there are several ways for you to search apps from the home page. The home page search options change position on the page, depending on which orientation you hold your Tab: vertical or horizontal.

1. Tap Market on the Home screen.

2. Featured applications are listed on the home page. Scroll up and down the page to review apps.

3. Tap an app to access a description page and read more about the product. You can purchase or download the app for free on the description page.

More About Product Descriptions

The description page for an app is chock full of useful information so you can make an educated decision on whether you want to purchase the app. Sample screenshots of the app are featured on this page along with customer reviews and information about the developer.

4. The Market home page also makes it possible to browse apps by categories: Apps, Books, and Movies. Tap a category to browse the list of results.

5. Use your finger to flick through the list of popular apps featured horizontally at the top of the page. Tap an app to go to the product description page.

6. If you know the name of the app, book, or movie you want, tap Search Market to specify a search term.

7. Type a search term into the field.

8. Tap Search.

9. The Apps screen shows all results for that app search. For example, the Angry Birds results page features all versions of that app as well as related apps.

10. Tap a result to access the product description page.

More Ways to Search for Apps

If your cellular carrier is Verizon, you also have the preinstalled widget V CAST Apps that enables you to browse and download applications and games. The V CAST icon is located on the Main home screen. The Multimedia Sync application by doubleTwist, discussed in Chapter 7, "Playing Music and Video," offers another portal to the Android Market from your PC or Mac desktop. Just click Apps Market located in the sidebar of the interface under doubleTwist.

Finding Great Apps

There are thousands of apps you can download to your Galaxy Tab, so use your storage space wisely by finding the great ones. Finding the best apps might be the biggest challenge of all as you wade through your many options. Here are some tips on how to locate the highest-performing apps.

1. Tap Market on the home screen.

2. Take a look at the featured apps on the Market home page. When you access a category, such as Apps or Books, review the Top Free and Top Paid categories. Keep in mind that large companies, usually with well-established names, tend to dominate the featured list. Lesser-known developers are also producing outstanding apps, so look deeper.

3. Some apps have trial versions you can test drive before purchasing. Look for Lite or Free versions of applications to test before you buy.

4. Tap an app in the Apps list that you want to learn more about.

5. Scroll down to check out customer reviews for products, but don't trust everything you read. Some reviews might not be in-depth or unbiased, and therefore they are less helpful.

6. Scroll down to the bottom of the page and take a look at the Related Apps. You see apps that are similar along with their ratings next to them. You might find a higher-rated app that you want to look into.

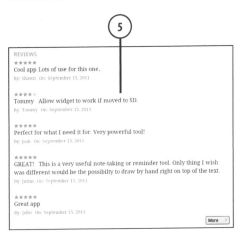

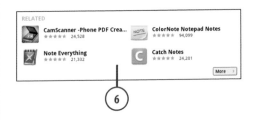

USING OTHER RESOURCES TO FIND APPS

You can use other solid resources outside the Android Market for finding great apps.

Perform a Google search—For example, if you are looking for an app suited for taking dictation, type "Galaxy Tab App Dictation."

Search for sites that feature and post reviews for apps—Be aware that some of these sites are sponsored by the developers and might not convey completely objective views.

Find a Galaxy Tab forum—There are many of these popping up every day. In a forum, you can post questions to other Galaxy Tab owners regarding apps. Be aware that experienced Tab users might not moderate all of these forums, and the advice you receive can be questionable.

Downloading Android Applications

Software developers from around the world have developed thousands of apps for you to take advantage of with your Galaxy Tab. You can choose from many free apps in the Android Market as well as from a variety of more sophisticated apps for a fee. The process for downloading free apps and paid apps is similar, but you need to designate a payment method to make purchases.

How to Purchase an App

Refer to "Purchasing an Application" earlier in this chapter for information about purchasing an app from the Market.

1. Tap Market on the home screen.

2. Locate and then tap the app that you want to download. The product description page opens.

More About Product Descriptions

The description page for an app is chock full of useful information so that you can make an educated decision on whether you want to purchase the app. Sample screenshots of the app are featured on this page along with customer reviews and information about the developer. Be sure to tap More on the description page so that you review the complete description.

3. Tap the price of the app to see the permissions for this app. If this app is free, as in this example, tap the Download button.

4. Review the download and allow access information, and then tap OK.

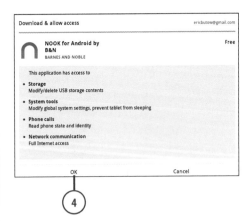

Accepting Permissions

If the application you have selected requires control of your Tab or access to data, Market displays the information in this area. The list of permissions changes from app to app. When you accept permissions, you are essentially allowing the application you are purchasing to access your Galaxy Tab, including Internet access.

5. Tap Open to open the application.

UPDATING APPS

Go Further

Market periodically searches for updates for apps that have been down-loaded to your Galaxy Tab. If an update has been found, a notification appears in the status bar, located in the lower-right corner of your Tab. You can drag the notification menu downward to reveal the updates. Tap an item in the list to be taken to Android Market so you can begin the update.

DISABLING UPDATE NOTIFICATIONS

Go Further

If you prefer to manually check for updates, you can configure Market to stop notifying you about updates. Just launch the Market app and press the Menu button on your Galaxy Tab. Select My Apps in the menu, and then tap Settings to choose Do Not Notify Me. You must periodically enter Market and choose My Apps from the Menu options to see whether there are any updates. You can also set installed apps to update automatically by tapping one of the installed apps in the list, and then selecting Allow Automatic Updating.

Rating Applications

Unlike Android 2.2 on the Galaxy Tab 7", you can't leave reviews in the Android Market in Android 3.1. You can, however, rate content on the Android Market website. You must sign in on the Market website to leave a review.

Rating content you have purchased in Android Market helps others make educated decisions about their purchases. Android Market uses a five-star rating system to rate all content. Much of the content in Android Market features reviews that you can read to see how others like the product. You can easily write reviews of your own to make your feelings known about the content you have purchased.

1. Tap Browser on the home screen.

2. Begin to type the web address market.android.com in the address box. When you see the site in the list below the box, tap it.

3. Tap Featured Tablet Apps.

4. Tap the app in the list for which you want to submit a review.

5. Tap Browser to view the app page in the Browser app.

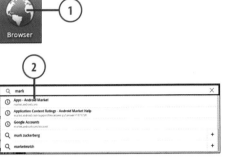

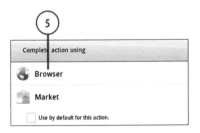

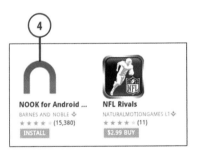

6. Scroll down and tap User Reviews.

7. Tap Write a Review. If you need to sign in, scroll to the top of the Market page and tap Sign In.

8. Tap a rating star on a scale from one to five. For example, if you tap the second star from the right the first four stars from left to right are highlighted in blue, which signifies that you give the app a four out of five-star rating.

9. Type a title in the Title box. You can type as many as 50 characters into the box.

10. Type the comment in the Comment box. You can type as many as 512 characters into the box.

11. Tap Submit Review. Your rating and comment are posted for everyone to see.

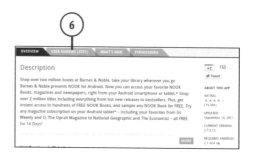

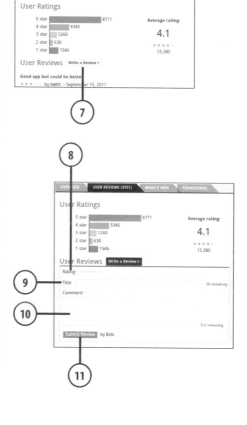

Getting Help with Apps

New applications are being developed for the Galaxy Tab every day. Many new apps are being added to the Android Market daily from well-known companies, small companies, and individual developers. Bugs and other problems are likely to arise in such a fast-moving market. There are ways for you to contact developers so that you can ask questions.

1. Tap Market on the home screen.

2. Tap My Apps. A list of the apps installed on your Tab appears.

3. Tap an app in the list. The product description page opens.

4. Tap See Details.

5. Scroll to the bottom of the page.

6. Tap Send Email to Developer to compose an email message asking your question(s).

7. Tap Visit Developer's Web Page to visit the developer's site and search for information.

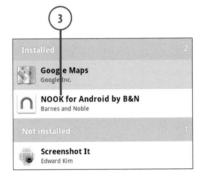

Managing Apps Through Your Home Pages (Galaxy Tab 7")

You begin many of your activities on the home screen of the Galaxy Tab. As you purchase new apps, the number of icons in your Applications menu multiplies, which might prompt you to rearrange them according to the ones you use the most. You can manage your apps through your home pages by creating new home pages, deleting existing home pages, and grouping and arranging apps as you see fit on respective pages.

Arranging Application Icons on Your Galaxy Tab

By default, when you download an application from the Android Market, a shortcut is placed in the Applications menu, which is accessible from any home screen. You can easily move shortcuts from the Applications menu to a home screen and then rearrange them.

1. Tap the Applications icon from any home screen.

2. Locate the application shortcut that you want to move and then press and hold your finger on it. The shortcut automatically appears on a home screen.

3. Move the icon to the location that you want and then release your finger.

4. Repeat steps 2 and 3 to move more widget icons from the Applications menu to a home screen page.

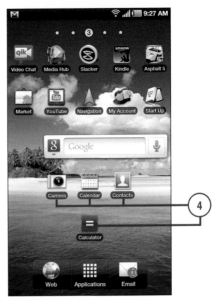

ADD TO HOME SCREEN

A quick way to add widgets, shortcuts, folders, and wallpapers is to use the Add to Home feature. Press your finger on an empty space on a home screen and hold until the Add to Home screen pop-up menu displays. Tap the option that you want, and then follow the prompts to complete the task.

5. When you have the apps you want on a home screen, press and hold your finger on an icon; after it pulsates once, move it to a new location on the home screen.

6. By default, your Galaxy Tab has five home screen panels. Press your finger on a shortcut that you would like to move to another panel, and let it pulsate once.

7. Drag the icon with your finger to the edge of the panel to progress to another panel.

8. Remove your finger from the shortcut when you reach the panel where you want to leave the shortcut.

9. When you hold your finger on a shortcut and after it pulsates once, the Applications icon turns into the Remove icon (trash can). Drag a shortcut to the Remove icon to remove it from a home screen.

Removing Shortcuts and Widgets

When you remove a shortcut or widget icon, it does not delete or uninstall the app from your Galaxy Tab; it simply removes it from that panel. If you want to create a shortcut for that application again, it is still located in the Applications menu, or you can use the Add to Home screen function.

Go Further

CUSTOMIZING HOME SCREENS

Each Galaxy Tab can be customized as unique as its individual owner. You can arrange your icons on any home screen for shortcuts or widgets that you frequently use. For example, you can arrange all your games on one home screen panel and all your productivity apps on another. You can even create new panels by tapping the Menu button located on your Galaxy Tab, from any home screen, and tapping Edit.

Go Further

UNINSTALLING APPS FROM YOUR TAB

After you purchase an app from on the Android Market, you own it forever. You can uninstall a paid app from your Galaxy Tab, and then choose to reinstall it later for free in the future. To uninstall an app, press the Menu button on your Galaxy Tab, and then tap Settings. Tap Applications, and choose Manage Applications from the menu to view a list of applications. At the top of the Manage Applications window you can choose which group of applications you want to manage: Third-party, Running, All, and On SD Card. Tap the app in the list that you want to uninstall. Tap Uninstall at the top of the screen to uninstall the app. You can also uninstall apps by using the Uninstall option for the application in Android Market.

Adding and Removing Home Pages

Your Galaxy Tab comes with five home screens by default. As you download more apps to your device, you can add extra home screens to accommodate your shortcuts. You can also remove unneeded home screens.

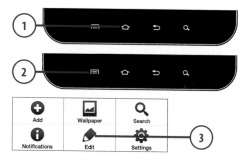

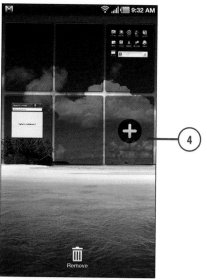

1. Press the Home button on the Galaxy Tab to return to the default home page from any screen.

2. Press the Menu button on your Galaxy Tab to reveal the menu options.

3. Tap Edit in the menu. Five panel icons representing your five default home screens appear, along with a sixth with a plus sign in the middle of it.

4. Tap the panel with the plus sign to add a new home screen. The panel with the plus symbol moves to the last panel position.

5. Press the Home button on the Galaxy Tab to return to the home screen. If you view the Panel Counters at the top of the screen, you can see that a sixth has been added.

6. Press the Menu button again to reveal menu options.

7. Tap Edit.

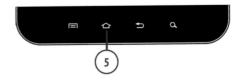

Panel counters

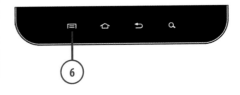

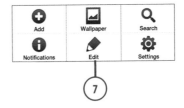

8. Press your finger against the last panel you added and then wait for it to darken.

9. Drag the panel to the Remove icon (trash can) and wait for it to turn red; then release it to remove that home screen.

Removing Home Screens

Removing a screen that includes widgets or shortcuts does not delete those programs from your device. You can always go to the Applications menu and place those icons back on a home screen, and add an extra home screen when needed.

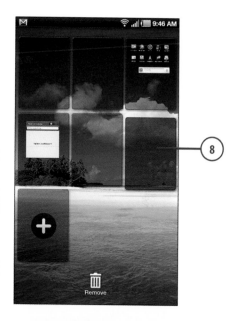

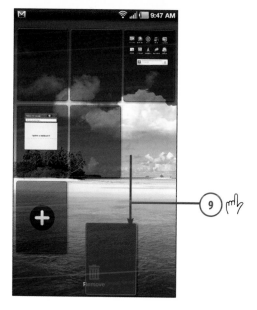

Managing Apps Through Your Home Pages (Galaxy Tab 10")

You begin many of your activities on the home screen of the Galaxy Tab. As you purchase new apps, the number of icons in your Applications menu multiplies, which might prompt you to rearrange them according to the ones you use the most. You can manage your apps through your home pages by creating new home pages, deleting existing home pages, and grouping and arranging apps as you see fit on respective pages.

Arranging Application Icons on Your Galaxy Tab

By default, when you download an application from the Android Market, a shortcut is placed in the Applications menu, which is accessible from any home screen. You can easily move shortcuts from the Applications menu to a home screen and then rearrange them.

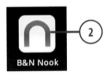

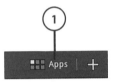

1. Tap Apps on the Home screen.

2. Locate the application shortcut that you want to move, and then press and hold your finger on it. The five Home screens (with the main Home screen in the center) appear at the bottom of the screen.

3. Move the icon to your desired Home screen, and then release your finger.

4. Repeat Steps 2 and 3 to move more widget icons from the Applications menu to a Home screen.

5. Tap Home in the status bar.

Go Further

ADD TO HOME SCREEN

A quick way to add widgets, shortcuts, folders, and wallpapers is to use the Add to Home feature. Press your finger on an empty space on a home screen and hold until the Add to Home screen pop-up menu displays. Tap the option that you want, and then follow the prompts to complete the task.

6. By default, your Galaxy Tab has five Home screens. Press your finger on a shortcut on the main home screen (Home screen 3) that you would like to move to another home screen, and let it pulsate once.

7. Drag the icon with your finger to the edge of the screen to move to another home screen (in this example, home screen 2).

8. Remove your finger from the shortcut when you reach the home screen where you would like to leave the shortcut.

Go Further

CUSTOMIZING HOME SCREENS

Each Galaxy Tab can be customized as unique as its individual owner. You can arrange your icons on any home screen for shortcuts or widgets that you frequently use. For example, you can arrange all your games on one home screen panel and all your productivity apps on another. You can even create new panels by tapping the Menu button located on your Galaxy Tab, from any home screen, and tapping Edit.

10. When you hold your finger on a shortcut and after it pulsates once, the Applications icon turns into the Remove icon (trash can). Drag a shortcut to the Remove icon to remove it from a home screen.

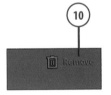

Removing Shortcuts and Widgets

When you remove a shortcut or widget icon, it does not delete or uninstall the app from your Galaxy Tab; it simply removes it from that panel. If you want to create a shortcut for that application again, it is still located in the Applications menu, or you can use the Add to Home screen function.

>>> Go Further

UNINSTALLING APPS FROM YOUR TAB

After you purchase an app from the Android Market, you own it forever. You can uninstall a paid app from your Galaxy Tab, and then choose to reinstall it later for free in the future. To uninstall an app, press the Menu button on your Galaxy Tab, and then tap Settings. Tap Applications, and choose Manage Applications from the menu to view a list of applications. At the top of the Manage Applications window you can choose which group of applications you want to manage: Third-party, Running, All, and On SD Card. Tap the app in the list that you want to uninstall. Tap Uninstall at the top of the screen to uninstall the app. You can also uninstall apps by using the Uninstall option for the application in Android Market.

Managing Home Screens with the Action Bar

Your Galaxy Tab comes with five home screens by default. As you download more apps to your device, keeping track of all that stuff can become cumbersome. The Action Bar makes it easy for you to see all home screens and the apps and widgets on your system on one screen.

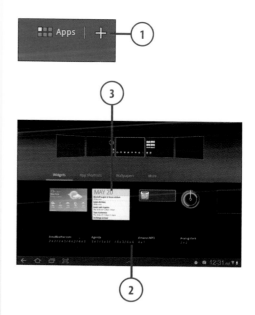

1. Tap the plus icon to open the Action Bar. The Action Bar shows the five home screen thumbnails from left to right with the main home screen in the middle.

2. Scroll left and right through the list of widgets.

3. Tap and hold your finger on a widget that you want to add to a home screen.

4. Drag the widget to the home screen you want. The home screen outline enlarges so you can place the widget in your desired area on the screen.

5. The widget appears in the home screen, and the screen is outlined in blue. Tap the screen thumbnail to view the home screen in full-screen mode.

6. Tap App shortcuts.

7. Scroll left and right through the list of app shortcuts you can add to one or more home screens.

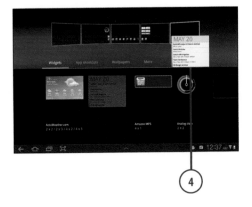

8. Tap and hold your finger on the app shortcut in the list.

9. Drag the app shortcut to the home screen you want. The home screen outline enlarges so you can place the shortcut in your desired area on the screen.

10. The app shortcut appears in the home screen and the screen is outlined in blue. Tap the screen thumbnail to view the home screen in full-screen mode.

11. Tap Wallpapers to view wallpapers you can apply to your home screens and your lock screens.

12. Tap the wallpaper type to select wallpaper.

13. Tap More to view more shortcuts you can add to your home screens, including a contact and your music playlist.

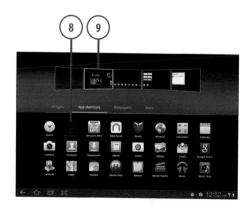

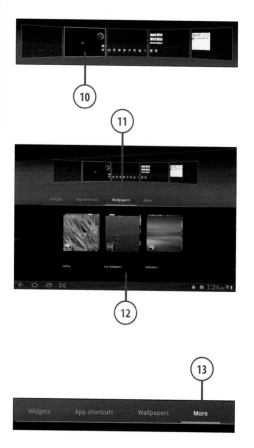

Adding Useful Apps (Galaxy Tab 7")

The true power of the tablet revolution lies not only in the simplification of computing, but also in personalization. Apps enable you to optimize your Galaxy Tab for your own unique lifestyle. Your Galaxy tab can be a virtual dictionary or thesaurus. Add an RSS reader and transform your Tab into a news-gathering device so that you are always up to date on current news and events. There are many practical apps on the market that enhance the capabilities of your Galaxy Tab, freeing you from having to purchase and carry a second device such as a digital audio recorder or scanner. There are too many options to list them all here, but let's explore a few practical apps that you might want to consider.

Adding a Dictionary and Thesaurus

Adding a dictionary and thesaurus app to your Galaxy Tab is a very handy and practical solution for having to lug around an actual paper reference book. The Dictionary.com app is free in the Android Market and delivers content from the trusted references Dictionary.com and Thesaurus.com.

1. After you have downloaded the app from Android Market, tap the Dictionary.com widget.

Use Any Dictionary App

There are many other free options for dictionary and thesaurus reference apps out there. If you prefer another, don't hesitate to use it. This is just a recommendation for the usefulness of such a reference to exist on your Galaxy Tab. As of this publication, the Dictionary.com app has not been optimized for the Galaxy Tab, but it gets the job done.

2. Tap in the Search box and enter a word to look up.

3. Tap Search on the keyboard. The definition(s) for the entry appear.

4. You can tap the speaker icon to hear the pronunciation of the word.

5. Tap the Thesaurus icon that looks like three book spines at the top of the screen to switch to using the thesaurus.

6. Type a new word into the Thesaurus search box.

7. Tap Search on the keyboard to view synonyms for the word.

Adding an RSS Reader

If part of your daily routine includes reading news websites and blogs, adding an RSS reader can help you manage your news sources from one app in the form of feeds instead of visiting multiple websites. Pulse is a free RSS feed reader that enables you to acquire and manage multiple news feeds as an interactive mosaic.

1. After downloading the Pulse app from Android Market, tap the Pulse icon on the home page. If this is your first time launching Pulse, handwritten instructions on how to use the app appear onscreen. You can tap anywhere to hide the instructions.

2. Pulse is loaded with predefined news feeds to get you started. Each row represents individual news feed with its name appearing in a gray tab. Flick to the left in a news feed to view the rest of the news items for the feed.

3. Tap a news story to open it. The news story opens in the window and the other stories in the feed appear at the bottom.

4. Share the story with others by way of Facebook, Twitter, messaging, or email.

5. Tap the Mosaic icon to view all feeds again.

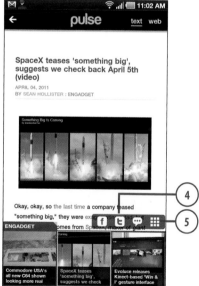

Go Further

CHANGING DISPLAY SETTINGS

You can change the font size for articles and also the tile size for news feeds by accessing the Display options. You can access the Display options by tapping the Menu button on your Tab and then choosing Settings.

6. Tap the Refresh button located at the top of the interface to refresh all news stories. You can also tap the Refresh button within each news feed to refresh that feed only.

7. Tap the Settings icon located in the top-left corner of the interface to manage your news resources.

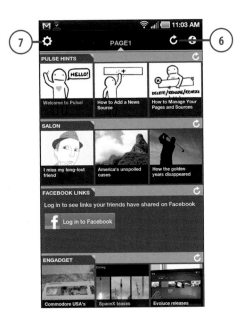

Go Further

REFRESHING AUTOMATICALLY

You can choose an automatic refresh option by tapping the Menu button on your Galaxy Tab, and then selecting Settings to access the Data Sync menu.

8. The predefined news feed appears in a list. To rearrange the order in which news feeds appear within the mosaic, place your finger on a feed tab in the list, and then drag that feed to a new location within the list.

9. Tap an X next to a list item to delete that feed.

10. Tap the blue Add button at the bottom to add a new news feed. You can also flick the page from right to left to populate a new page with feeds by tapping the blue Add button. A list of featured feeds appears. You can also tap the Menu key on your Tab to add a new feed.

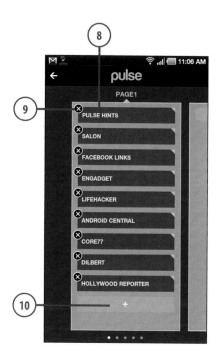

Multiple Pages of News Feeds

You can add five pages of news feeds within Pulse. If you choose to populate a new page with feeds you can access the new pages by tapping Page 1 at the top of the Pulse home screen. After you tap Page 1, links for the other four pages appear that you can tap and go to the new page.

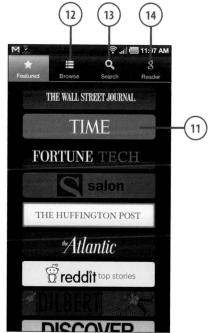

11. Tap a featured feed to add it to your list.

12. Tap Browse to browse feeds by categories.

13. Tap Search to look for a specific feed.

14. Tap Reader to use Google Reader.

Adding Useful Apps (Galaxy Tab 10")

The true power of the tablet revolution lies not only in the simplification of computing, but also in personalization. Apps enable you to optimize your Galaxy Tab for your own unique lifestyle. Your Galaxy tab can be a virtual dictionary or thesaurus. Add an RSS reader and transform your Tab into a news-gathering device so that you are always up to date on current news and events. Many practical apps on the market enhance the capabilities of your Galaxy Tab, freeing you from having to purchase and carry a second device such as a digital audio recorder or scanner. There are too many options to list them all here, but let's explore a few practical apps that you might want to consider.

Adding a Dictionary and Thesaurus

Adding a dictionary and thesaurus app to your Galaxy Tab is a very handy and practical solution for having to lug around an actual paper reference book.

The Dictionary.com app is free in the Android Market and delivers content from the trusted references Dictionary.com and Thesaurus.com. The following steps presume you have already downloaded the Dictionary.com app from the Market.

1. Tap Dictionary on the Home screen.

Dictionary

Use Any Dictionary App
There are many other free options for dictionary and thesaurus reference apps out there. If you prefer another, don't hesitate to use it. This is just a recommendation for the usefulness of such a reference to exist on your Galaxy Tab. As of this publication, the Dictionary.com app has not been optimized for the Galaxy Tab, but it gets the job done.

2. Tap in the Search box and enter a word to look up.

3. Tap Search. The definition(s) for the entry appear.

4. You can tap the speaker icon to hear the pronunciation of the word.

5. Tap the Thesaurus icon to switch to using the thesaurus.

6. Delete the old search term in the Search box, and then type a new search word.

7. Tap Search to view synonyms for the word.

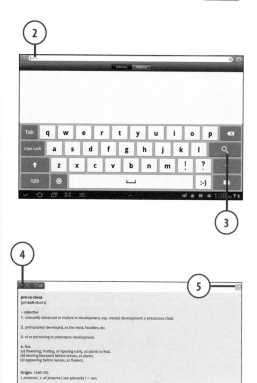

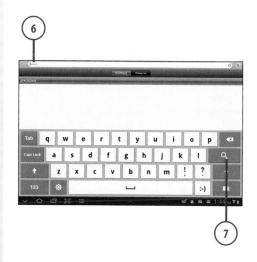

Adding an RSS Reader

If part of your daily routine includes reading news websites and blogs, adding an RSS reader can help you manage your news sources from one app in the form of feeds instead of visiting multiple websites. Pulse is a free RSS feed reader that's prein-stalled on your Tab; it enables you to acquire and manage multiple news feeds as an interactive mosaic.

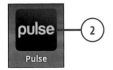

1. Tap Apps.

2. Tap Pulse.

3. Pulse is loaded with predefined news feeds to get you started. Each row represents individual news feed with its name appear-ing in a gray tab. Flick to the left in a news feed to view the rest of the news items for the feed.

4. Tap a news story to open it.

5. The news story opens in the win-dow and the other stories in the feed appear to the left.

6. Share the story with others by way of Facebook, Twitter, or Messaging.

7. Tap the Mosaic icon to view all feeds again.

CHANGING DISPLAY SETTINGS

You can change the font size for articles and the tile size for news feeds by accessing the Display options. You can access the Display options by tapping the Menu button on your Tab and then choosing Settings.

8. Tap the Refresh button located at the top of the interface to refresh all news stories. You can also tap the Refresh button within each news feed to refresh that feed only.

9. Tap the Settings icon located in the top-left corner of the interface to manage your news resources.

REFRESHING AUTOMATICALLY

You can choose an automatic refresh option by tapping the Menu button on your Galaxy Tab, and then selecting Settings to access the Data Sync menu.

10. The predefined news feed appears in a list. To rearrange the order in which news feeds appear within the mosaic, place your finger on a feed tab in the list, and then drag that feed to a new location within the list.

11. Tap an X next to a list item to delete that feed.

12. Tap the blue Add button at the bottom to add a new news feed. You can also flick the page from right to left to populate a new page with feeds by tapping the blue Add button. A list of featured feeds appears.

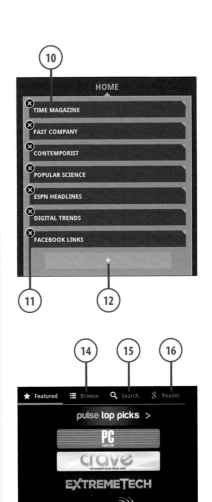

Multiple Pages of News Feeds

You can add five pages of news feeds within Pulse. If you choose to populate a new page with feeds you can access the new pages by tapping Page 1 at the top of the Pulse home screen. After you tap Page 1, links for the other four pages appear that you can tap and go to the new page.

13. Tap a featured feed to add it to your list.

14. Tap Browse to browse feeds by categories.

15. Tap Search to look for a specific feed.

16. Tap Reader to use Google Reader.

Using Note Everything (Galaxy Tab 7")

A digital voice recorder can be a priceless tool if you ever need to record some notes for yourself. Or have you ever wished you had the capability to scan barcodes on a product so that you could store the information? Note Everything is a free app that can do all of this and more, including taking handwritten notes and tucking information away neatly in folders.

1. After downloading the Note Everything app from Android Market, tap the Note Everything icon on the Home page. You can tap Close on the Welcome screen.

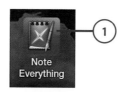

Receiving Help

When you first use certain functions, a help screen appears and provides you with tips.

2. Press the Menu button on the Galaxy Tab.

3. Tap New Note.

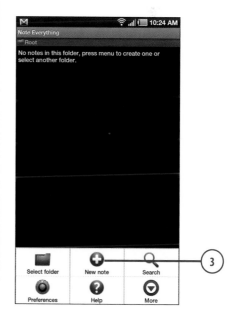

4. Tap Textnote to leave a note using the keyboard. This is very similar to how the preinstalled Memo widget works on your Tab, but you might find it more beneficial to have all your notes in one location.

5. Tap Paintnote to leave a note using your finger as a pen. You can tap the Menu button on your Galaxy Tab and change the color of ink, erase marks, change stroke width, clear colors, work full screen, and more. This is a great option for jotting down a quick visual note.

6. Tap Voicenote to record voice memos. Each Recording is stored as an individual file that you can play back on your Galaxy Tab.

7. Tap Note from Barcode to use your Galaxy Tab camera to read barcodes and note the barcode for later reference. This option requires that you install another free app named Barcode Scanner in order for it to work. The installation process is streamlined within the Note Everything app and only takes a few moments.

8. Tap Note from Google Docs to import and export text notes from Google Docs. This option requires that you install another free app named Note Everything (NE) GDocs. These two apps can work seamlessly together or independently.

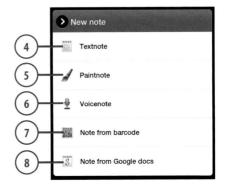

Recording Voice Notes

After each recording, you can choose whether to use or discard the recording. If you choose to keep the recording, you are taken to a page with a notepad where you can play back the voice memo and take text notes at the same time.

It's Not All Good

Not Always Accurate

Be advised that not all barcode scanners on your Galaxy Tab are 100% accurate. That goes for any product, not just the one featured here. Sometimes these scanners might not recognize the product, or the price they provide for the product might be way off the mark. Use all these apps with caution. If you don't like this app, you can choose from many other free options.

9. After you create a note, it is placed in the main (root) menu. Hold your finger on any note that you would like to move to a different folder, and a pop-up menu appears.

10. Tap the Move to Folder option. Tap Close after you read the help screen. Help screens appear when you access a function for the first time.

11. Press the Menu button on your Galaxy Tab.

12. Tap Create Folder.

13. Tap in the Folder Name field to access the keyboard and then enter a name for the folder.

14. Tap OK to move the note to the new folder.

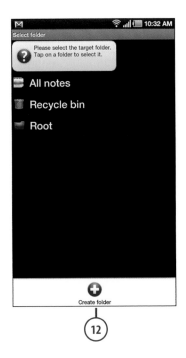

Using Note Everything (Galaxy Tab 10")

A digital voice recorder can be a priceless tool if you ever need to record some notes for yourself. Or have you ever wished you had the capability to scan barcodes on a product so that you could store the information?

Note Everything is a free app that can do all of this and more, including taking handwritten notes and tucking information away neatly in folders. This section presumes you have already downloaded the Note Everything app from the Market.

1. Tap the Note Everything icon on the Home screen.

Receiving Help
When you first use certain functions, a help screen appears and provides you with tips.

2. Tap Close in the What's New screen.

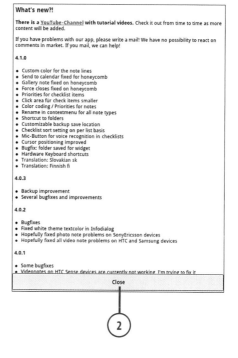

What's new?!

There is a YouTube-Channel with tutorial videos. Check it out from time to time as more content will be added.

If you have problems with our app, please write a mail! We have no possibility to react on comments in market. If you mail, we can help!

4.1.0

- Custom color for the note lines
- Send to calendar fixed for honeycomb
- Gallery note fixed on honeycomb
- Force closes fixed on honeycomb
- Priorities for checklist items
- Click area für check items smaller
- Color coding / Priorities for notes
- Rename in contextmenu for all note types
- Shortcut to folders
- Customizable backup save location
- Checklist sort setting on per list basis
- Mic-Button for voice recognition in checklists
- Cursor positioning improved
- Bugfix: folder saved for widget
- Hardware Keyboard shortcuts
- Translation: Slovakian sk
- Translation: Finnish fi

4.0.3

- Backup improvement
- Several bugfixes and improvements

4.0.2

- Bugfixes
- Fixed white theme textcolor in Infodialog
- Hopefully fixed photo note problems on SonyEricsson devices
- Hopefully fixed all video note problems on HTC and Samsung devices

4.0.1

- Some bugfixes
- Videonotes on HTC Sense devices are currently not working. I'm trying to fix it

Close

3. Tap the Menu button in the status bar.

4. Tap New Note.

5. Tap Textnote to leave a note using the keyboard. This is similar to how the preinstalled Memo widget works on your Tab, but you might find it more beneficial to have all your notes in one location.

6. Tap Paintnote to leave a note using your finger as a pen. You can tap the Menu button on your Galaxy Tab and change the color of ink, erase marks, change stroke width, clear colors, work full screen, and more. This is a great option for jotting down a quick visual note.

7. Tap Voicenote to record voice memos. Each recording is stored as an individual file that you can play back on your Galaxy Tab.

8. Tap Note from Barcode to use your Galaxy Tab camera to read barcodes and note the barcode for later reference. This option requires you to install another free app named Barcode Scanner for it to work. The installation process is streamlined within the Note Everything app and takes only a few moments.

9. Tap Note from Google Docs to import and export text notes from Google Docs. This option requires you to install another free app named Note Everything (NE) GDocs. These two apps can work seamlessly together or independently.

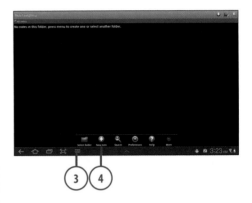

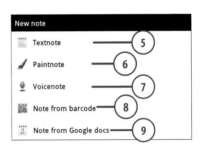

Recording Voice Notes

After each recording, you can choose whether to use or discard the recording. If you choose to keep it, you are taken to a page with a notepad where you can play back the voice memo and take text notes at the same time.

It's Not All Good

Not Always Accurate

Be advised that not all barcode scanners on your Galaxy Tab are 100% accurate. That goes for any product, not just the one featured here. Sometimes these scanners might not recognize the product, or the price they provide for the product might be way off the mark. Use all these apps with caution. If you don't like this app, you can choose from many other free options.

10. After you create a note, it is placed in the main (root) menu. Tap and hold your finger on any note that you would like to move to a different folder, and a pop-up menu appears.

11. Tap Move to Folder.

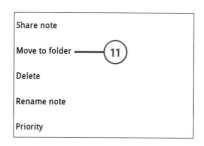

12. Tap Close after you read the help screen. Help screens appear when you access a function for the first time.

13. Tap the Menu button in the status bar.

14. Tap Create Folder.

15. Tap in the Folder Name box to access the keyboard and then enter a name for the folder.

16. Tap OK to move the note to the new folder.

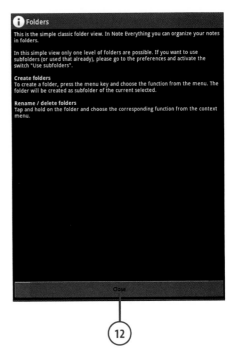

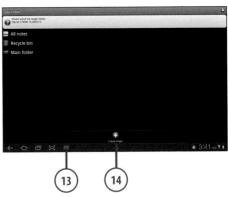

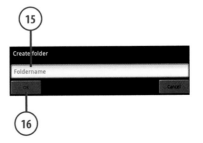

Extend your Galaxy Tab
with accessories.

This chapter covers how to get the most from your Galaxy Tab by exploring hardware accessories such as the optional Multimedia Desk Dock, the Keyboard Dock, and memory card options.

→ Samsung HDMI Multimedia Desk Dock
→ Samsung Keyboard Dock
→ Using Wireless Devices
→ MicroSD Cards

Adding New Hardware

Your Galaxy Tab is fully capable of providing an amazing multimedia experience right out of the box, but whether you are viewing movies, capturing photos and video, or composing a long email, you want your Galaxy Tab to be versatile. Accessories such as the Samsung Multimedia Desk Dock, Keyboard Dock, and extra memory cards can offer some much needed practical support for your Tab use.

You can find accessories for the 7" and 10" Galaxy Tabs in electronics stores such as Best Buy or at your local Verizon cellular store. As of this publication, Verizon, T-Mobile, AT&T, Sprint, and U.S Cellular carry only the 7" Tab and accessories. Online stores, such as Samsung.com and Amazon.com, are also great places to find hardware accessories for both Galaxy Tabs. Always make sure that you pick the right accessory for your Galaxy Tab model.

Samsung HDMI Multimedia Desk Dock

Samsung has created two docks for both the 7" and 10" Galaxy Tabs. The Samsung HDMI Multimedia Desk Dock is a handy accessory that enables you to situate your Galaxy Tab in an upright position while you're using it or while it's powered down. An important thing to keep in mind when considering the Multimedia Desk Dock is that if you normally keep your Tab in a case, you have to remove it from the case to mount it on the dock. You can use the dock to charge your Galaxy Tab while you check mail, listen to music, and browse photos. You can also put your Tab into digital frame mode to show-case your favorite photographs as the Tab charges on your desk. You can con-nect the Multimedia Desk Dock to your computer, which enables you to sync music, video, contacts, calendar, and photographs between your PC or Mac and your Tab.

The Samsung Multimedia Desk Dock is equipped with HDMI output so that you can view HD content on an HDTV up to 1080p. You can conveniently use your HDTV as a giant Galaxy Tab display screen to accommodate a large viewing audience. The 3.5mm stereo line-out port on the dock enables you to plug in powered speakers or a home stereo for higher quality sound. When shopping online, make sure you read product descriptions carefully so you get the right dock for your Galaxy Tab model.

HDMI Cable Not Included

The Samsung Multimedia Desk Docks does not come with an HDMI cable. You need to buy an HDMI cable to take full advantage of this dock's features.

Media Hub Content Blocked

As of this publication, all protected DRM content cannot be displayed using this dock, which means you cannot watch media you have purchased through Media Hub on an HDTV via the Samsung HDMI Multimedia Dock.

Samsung Keyboard Docks

Both the 7" and 10" Galaxy Tabs have available keyboard docks that enable you to connect your Tab and enjoy the typing comforts of a full-size key-board. Your Galaxy Tab also comes with Bluetooth 3.1 technology, which enables you to use devices such as wireless headphones and wireless keyboards. These keyboard accessories provide the convenience of typing with a physical keyboard while you're charging the Galaxy Tab. The keyboard dock provides a typing experience similar to using a computer keyboard, so inputting information is easier than using the onscreen keyboard. Users who perform extensive writing tasks might find the more ergonomically pleasing Samsung Keyboard Dock a better alternative to the onscreen keyboard. You can also use the keyboard dock to sync content between your PC or Mac to your Tab. The Samsung keyboard dock offers an audio jack so you can connect the Galaxy Tab to a stereo for higher-quality sound for media playback.

Remove From Protective Case

If you have your Galaxy Tab in a protective case, you must remove the Tab from the case to properly mount the tablet to the keyboard dock.

Some amazing products are being developed for the Galaxy Tab by third-party manufacturers. One such product is the Bluetooth Keyboard Case that gives the tactile benefits of a physical keyboard with no physical connection required. A Bluetooth Keyboard Case not only protects your Galaxy Tab, but it is also more travel-friendly than the Keyboard Dock. Another benefit the Bluetooth keyboard case has over the keyboard dock is that it allows you to type while your Tab is in the landscape orientation, providing you more screen real estate.

Using Wireless Devices

Along with the many other comfort features and conveniences found with the Galaxy Tab, your Tab gives you the capability to connect some external hardware devices wirelessly. The Galaxy Tab is equipped with Bluetooth 3.1 technology, enabling you to connect cable-free with Bluetooth-capable keyboards and headphones. By default, Bluetooth is disabled on your Tab. If you have already played with this setting, you can tell if Bluetooth is turned on by verifying that the Bluetooth symbol is visible in the status bar at the top of the screen.

Pairing Bluetooth Devices (Galaxy Tab 7")

You can easily connect your Tab to a Bluetooth device in two phases: discovering and pairing.

1. Turn on the wireless device that you want to pair with your Galaxy Tab, and make it discoverable.

Discoverability

Bluetooth devices broadcast their availability only after you instruct them to do so. If necessary, refer to your device's manual to learn how to make it discoverable.

2. From a home screen, press the Menu button on your Galaxy Tab.

3. Tap Settings in the menu.

4. Choose Wireless and Network in the menu.

5. Tap Bluetooth Settings.

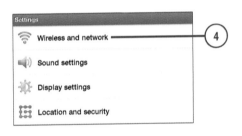

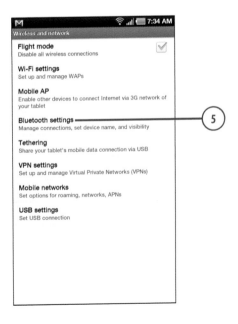

6. Tap Bluetooth to turn on Bluetooth. A green check mark appears at the right.

7. Tap Scan Devices. Your Galaxy Tab searches for discoverable Bluetooth devices. Found Bluetooth devices appear in the bottom half of the screen.

8. Choose the device that you want to pair with.

9. Enter the password for the device, if prompted. You might have to refer to your wireless device's manual to locate the password. The Connected message appears under the device name to tell you that you can now enjoy your wireless device with your Galaxy Tab.

Once Paired

Once a device is paired with your Galaxy Tab, you never have to configure the devices again.

Pairing Bluetooth Devices (Galaxy Tab 10")

You can easily connect your 10" Galaxy Tab to a Bluetooth device in two phases: discovering and pairing.

1. Turn on the wireless device that you want to pair with your Galaxy Tab, and make it discoverable.

Discoverability

Bluetooth devices broadcast their availability only after you instruct them to do so. If necessary, refer to your device's manual to learn how to make it discoverable.

2. From a home screen, tap the Apps icon in the upper-right corner of your Galaxy Tab.

3. Tap Settings.

4. Tap Bluetooth to access Bluetooth settings. A green check mark appears in the right of the field, and Bluetooth is activated.

5. Tap Bluetooth settings. The device appears in the Device Name row.

6. In the Paired devices field, tap Find Nearby Devices.

7. Tap the name of the device in the list.

8. The Connected message appears under the device name to tell you that you can now enjoy your wireless device with your Galaxy Tab.

Once Paired

Once a device is paired with your Galaxy Tab, you never have to configure the devices again.

MicroSD Cards

Not all Galaxy Tab models come equipped with a MicroSD card. If you have a 7" Tab from Verizon, Sprint, or a U.S. Cellular model Galaxy Tab, you already have a 16GB MicroSD card preinstalled that you can upgrade to 32GB. The 10" Galaxy Tab is not equipped with a card slot. If you are an AT&T or T-Mobile customer, you can purchase an optional MicroSD card as large as 32GB. Increasing the capacity of your existing memory card or adding an optional memory card is the best way to increase storage capacity on your Galaxy Tab.

Formatting MicroSD Cards (Galaxy Tab 7")

If you buy a new card, you need to format it for your Galaxy Tab. Whether you are upgrading your MicroSD card or adding a new card, follow these steps to format your new memory card:

1. From a Galaxy Tab home screen, press the Menu button.

2. Tap Settings.

3. Choose SD card and Tablet Storage.

4. If you already have a card installed, tap Unmount SD Card. If you are adding a card for the first time, skip to step 6.

5. Remove the old MicroSD card.

Unmount Before Removing

It is very important that you first unmount the MicroSD card before removing it from the slot. Failing to do so can result in damage to the MicroSD card.

6. Insert the new MicroSD card.

7. Tap Format SD Card. A warning displays.

8. Tap the Format SD Card button. Another warning appears.

9. Tap Erase Everything. The MicroSD card is formatted. The card becomes instantly available for use.

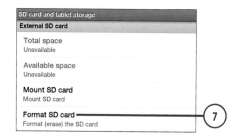

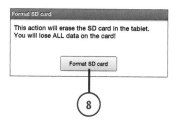

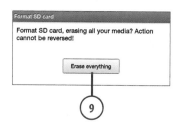

Extend your Galaxy
Tab with docks,
cases, connectors,
and keyboards.

This chapter offers options on how to accessorize your Galaxy Tab by exploring protective cases, screen protectors, chargers, and adapters. It also covers ways to maximize the longevity of your Galaxy Tab.

→ Protective Cases

→ Types of Screen Protectors

→ Chargers and Adapters

Finding Galaxy Tab Accessories

There are many accessories available for both the 7" and 10" Galaxy Tabs, ranging from those that increase its usability to those that protect your iPad or enhance its style. You can start on the Samsung website to explore which accessories are right for you, but don't stop there. Many other companies create high-quality accessories for the Galaxy Tab. Amazon.com is a great place to browse the many offerings for the Galaxy Tab and read product reviews from other buyers. Let's take a look at a variety of accessories to see how they can benefit you.

Protective Cases

Perhaps the most fundamental duty you have as a Galaxy Tab owner is to protect your Tab from becoming damaged. There are many cases on the market to choose from, all providing a varying range of protection for your Tab.

Skins are stylish and provide a thin layer of protection around your Galaxy Tab, which can be effective for protecting your

Tab against dust, nicks, and scratches. A skin by itself is less effective for absorbing shock, such as from a drop, than a padded case that remains on your Tab at all times.

Some padded cases, such as the Samsung Protective Leather Easel Case and Snugg Leather Case Cover and Flip Stand, also act as stands.

1. Fold the front cover of the Leather Easel Case underneath the Tab.

2. Set the tab down on a flat surface so the screen is in a landscape orientation.

3. Angle the Galaxy Tab display so that it is easy to view. This is a great orientation in which to watch videos or movies.

4. Set the Galaxy Tab up in portrait orientation by positioning the folded cover behind it.

>>> Go Further

Protective cases aren't the only way to keep your Galaxy Tab safe from the elements and damage. Here are some alternatives.

Galaxy Tab Protective Leather Pouch: Some Tab owners prefer a pouch, sleeve, or slip case that acts as a carrying case for their Tab. If you prefer the tactile experience of the Galaxy Tab body in your hands while you use it, you can use a pouch when you're carrying your Tab and then slip the device from the pouch when you're ready to use it. A Galaxy Tab Protective Leather Pouch can also act as an extra layer of protection for that stylish skin you have been eyeing for your Tab.

Galaxy Tab Snap on Protective Case, Leather: This snap-on case is custom molded into the shape of the Galaxy Tab and protects all corners and sides of your Tab while maintaining its original sleek style. All your Tab's ports and buttons remain visible while the Tab is in the case.

Screen Protectors

Some cases, skins, and pouches do not include a protective screen cover to keep your high-resolution screen from getting scratched, so you might have to purchase one separately. You can choose from a variety of protective screens; the most popular are privacy, mirrored, and antiglare.

A privacy screen prevents your Galaxy Tab screen from being viewed by others nearby. A privacy screen uses a polarized filter that allows light to pass only in certain directions. When someone looks at your screen from an angle other than straight into the display, the screen appears blurred.

A mirrored screen does exactly what it says. When your Galaxy Tab screen is off, the screen reflects as a mirror. When the Galaxy Tab screen is on, the mirror goes away. This option not only protects your screen but also adds a stylish aesthetic to your tab. One thing to keep in mind when choosing this option is the glare factor when using your Tab in the sun. A substantial glare can impede screen visibility.

Antiglare screen protectors make it easier for you to view your Galaxy Tab display indoors or outdoors in direct sunlight. While protecting your screen, they also help to reduce annoying surface glare caused by bright indoor lighting.

Chargers and Adapters

The Galaxy Tab was designed for a person who is on the go. Put your Tab in your back pocket and go. Many accessories are available to the power user, including additional power chargers and adapters. For example, you might want to charge your Galaxy Tab at the office as well as at home. Instead of remembering to transport a single cable, wall jack, or Dock, why not invest in two? You can also have the convenience of charging your Galaxy Tab while in a car.

Galaxy Tab USB Charging/Data Cable: You can use this data cable to connect your Tab to a PC, Mac, or Samsung charger. This offers a two-in-one solution for charging power and transferring data simultaneously via USB data sync cable. You can also use it to connect your Tab to your HDMI Multimedia Dock or Full Size Keyboard Dock.

Galaxy Tab 30-pin Vehicle Power Adapter with Detachable Cable: The Samsung Car Adapter, with data cable, enables you to charge your Galaxy Tab while in your car. You can plug it into your car's 12-volt cigarette lighter socket. If you have to transfer data from your Galaxy Tab to your laptop, or vice versa, this car charger provides a detachable USB cable that enables you to connect to your laptop and make the transfer. You can also simultaneously charge your Galaxy Tab through the same connection to your laptop.

MORE CAR ACCESSORIES

Go Further

Take advantage of your 7" Galaxy Tab's GPS capabilities and check out the Galaxy Tab Vehicle mount from Samsung. This mount makes it possible for you to use your Tab as a navigation device by enabling you to mount your Tab to the windshield or dashboard. Passengers can also use this mount to watch videos and movies, hands free. There is no vehicle mount made for the 10" Galaxy Tab. It's too big to sit on your dashboard.

Galaxy Tab 30-Pin Travel Adapter with Detachable Cable: Charge your Tab while on the go or at home with this adapter that plugs into any standard wall outlet. This adapter includes a USB port for universal charging and a 2A charger.

Go Further

OTHER CHARGERS AND ADAPTERS

When it comes to accessories, perhaps the biggest decision to make is choosing from the variety of available manufacturers' products. There are many options for the power user, such as worldwide travel plug adapters, mini surge protectors, and dual cigarette lighter sockets. Always make sure that the accessories you use are compatible with your Galaxy Tab. Not all manufacturers' accessories are of equal quality.

Troubleshoot Galaxy Tab software, hardware, and accessories.

In this chapter, we look at ways that you can properly maintain your Galaxy Tab and troubleshoot basic software or hardware problems.

14

Troubleshooting Your Galaxy Tab

Although problems concerning the Galaxy Tab software, hardware, and accessories are rare, on occasion, you might experience incidents where your Tab does not perform properly. There are a few fixes you can try if you experience the occasional glitch that can occur with any hardware device.

Although your Galaxy Tab is a sophisticated piece of hardware, it is less complex than an actual computer, making any issue that might arise more manageable.

Maintaining Your Galaxy Tab

Regular maintenance of your Galaxy Tab not only helps extend the life of your Tab, it also helps ensure peak performance. Making sure your Galaxy Tab software is up to date and understanding basic troubleshooting concepts is important.

Properly cleaning and protecting your Tab's body can be equally important. The Galaxy Tab was designed to be sturdy, but like any other electronic device, it can collect dust, and a simple drop on the sidewalk can prove disastrous. The first step in maintaining your Galaxy Tab is prevention. You can start by purchasing a protective case.

A sturdy case designed for the Galaxy Tab is important for the overall protection of your device. A number of companies have created a variety of cases for the Tab, so search the Internet or go to Amazon to see what's out there. The more padded the case, the better it can absorb a shock if you happen to drop your Tab. A case can also help protect your Tab from dust and keep it dry if you happen to get caught in the rain. Make sure that you keep the inside of your case clean. Dust and sand can find its way into even the most well constructed cases. Instead of using your sleeve to wipe off your Galaxy Tab's display, invest in a micro fiber cloth; you can find them in any office supply or computer store.

Your first instinct might be to wet a cloth to clean your Galaxy Tab touchscreen. Don't use liquids to clean the touchscreen, especially if they are alcohol and ammonia. These harsh chemicals can cause irreparable damage to the touchscreen, rendering it difficult to see. Consider purchasing a screen protector at your local Best Buy or cellular store to keep the touchscreen dust and scratch free. Some screen protectors also come with a micro fiber cleaning cloth.

Update Galaxy Tab Software

Every so often, Google releases software updates for your Galaxy Tab's Android operating system. To get the most from your Galaxy Tab, it is good practice to upgrade soon after an upgrade has been released. When an update is available, you receive a message that indicates that a system upgrade is available. At that point, you'll see the options to Install Now, Install Later, and More Info. You can also check for system updates manually by pressing the Settings button on your Galaxy Tab while on any home screen, tapping About Device, and then choosing System Updates. If your system is up to date, your Tab alerts you to this fact. If an update is available, follow the provided directions to upgrade your software.

The Android operating system is not the only software you need to update on your Galaxy Tab. Your Tab also uses software, called *firmware*, to run its internal functions,. Make sure that you accept all firmware updates so that your Tab continues to perform smoothly.

Backing Up and Restoring Your Galaxy Tab

Backing up the contents of your Galaxy Tab is a good practice for securing your important information and multimedia content. You can ensure that your contacts, photos, videos, and apps are copied to your PC or Mac in case something happens to your Tab.

Ensuring Automatic Google Account Backup (Galaxy Tab 7")

Your Google account information, such as your Gmail inbox, Contacts list, and Calendar app appointments, automatically sync with Google servers, so this information is already backed up for you. To ensure that your Google account information is being automatically backed up, follow these directions.

1. Press the Menu button on your Galaxy Tab from any home screen.

2. Tap Settings.

3. Tap Accounts and Sync. Your Google account(s) appear under Manage Accounts in the bottom half of the screen.

4. Choose a Google account.

5. Ensure that the Sync Contacts, Sync Gmail, and Sync Calendar fields all have a green check mark to the right. If not, tap the box to place a green check mark within the box.

Multiple Google Accounts
If you have multiple Google accounts, repeat steps 1 through 6 for each account.

6. Press the Back button twice on the Galaxy Tab to return to the Settings screen.

7. Tap Privacy.

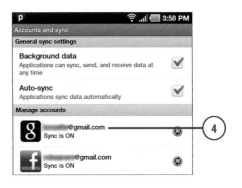

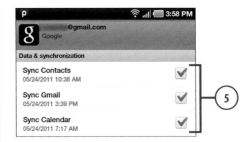

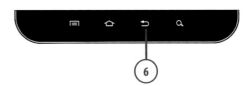

8. Ensure that a green check mark appears next to the Back Up My Settings and Automatic Restore fields. If not, tap the box to place a green check mark within the box. The information associated with your Google address will now be automatically backed up.

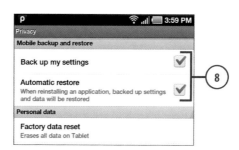

The Automatic Restore Option

When checked, the Automatic Restore option ensures that any data or settings placed on third-party apps are restored when you restore those apps to your Galaxy Tab.

Ensuring Automatic Google Account Backup (Galaxy Tab 10")

Your Google account information, such as your Gmail inbox, Contacts list, and Calendar app appointments, automatically sync with Google servers, so this information is already backed up for you. To ensure that your Google account information is being automatically backed up, follow these directions.

1. Tap the Apps icon from any home screen.

2. Tap Settings.

3. Tap Accounts & Sync. Your Google account(s) appear under Manage Accounts in the bottom half of the screen.

4. Choose a Google account, and then tap the account.

5. Ensure that the Sync Calendar, Sync Contacts, and Sync Gmail fields all have a green check mark to the right. If they don't, tap the box to place a green check mark within the box.

Multiple Google Accounts
If you have multiple Google accounts, repeat steps 1 through 6 for each account.

6. Tap the Privacy category.

7. Ensure that a green check mark appears in the Back Up My Data and Automatic Restore fields. If not, tap the box in each field to place a green check mark within the box. The information associated with your Google address is now automatically backed up.

Back up my data Back up application data, Wi-Fi passwords, and other settings to Google servers	☑
Backup account	›
Automatic restore When reinstalling an application, backed up settings and data will be restored	☑

The Automatic Restore Option
When checked, the Automatic Restore option ensures that any data or settings placed on third-party apps are restored when you restore those apps to your Galaxy Tab.

Syncing and Using Manual Backup

There are multiple ways for you to back up content that is outside of your Google account information on your Galaxy Tab, such as your apps and multimedia content, onto your computer. If you have a 7" tab with 3G service, your cellular provider may have proprietary software already loaded onto your Galaxy Tab that helps you sync content with your computer, such as Verizon's Backup Assistant program. You can also connect your Galaxy Tab to your PC or Mac by connecting as a mass storage device and manually dragging and dropping files.

Your internal storage and (or) MicroSD card includes all the data on your Galaxy Tab. If your Galaxy Tab came equipped with an internal SD card, most of the important information is on the card. If your Galaxy Tab model did not come with a MicroSD card, you can find your content in the internal storage. Regardless, there are some specific folders you need to copy. Be sure to copy the following folders: DCIM, Download, and Music. Also, copy all folders with the names of apps installed on your Galaxy Tab.

You can also use Multimedia Sync for PCs and Macs to sync your content. See Chapter 7, "Playing Music and Video," to learn how to exchange content between your Galaxy Tab and your computer by connecting as a mass storage device and by using Multimedia Sync by doubleTwist.

Extending Battery Life

Your Galaxy Tab is capable of up to 10 hours of battery life, but battery life can vary depending on how you use the Galaxy Tab. Strenuous tasks, such as playing HD video, dramatically lower your battery life more than surfing the Web does. You can monitor your battery power at the top of the screen in the Status area. The blue battery icon located in the right of the status bar lets you keep an eye on how much battery power you have left. When the battery gets low, a warning appears, informing you of the percentage of battery power you have left and instructing you to connect the charger. When the battery is too low, your Tab automatically shuts down. There are a few things you can do to extend the life of your Tab's battery.

Battery icon

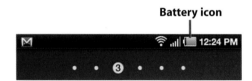

Monitoring Power Usage (Galaxy Tab 7")

Your Galaxy Tab has a very convenient screen that lets you review which activities have been consuming the most battery power. The types and number of items that appear in the list depend on the activities you have performed on your Tab between charges. These activities could include using the Maps app to get directions or battery power used by Bluetooth. Not every activity that you perform appears in the list. Use the information on this screen to help you manage the power consumption of your Tab.

1. Press the Menu button on your Galaxy Tab from any home screen.

2. Tap Settings.

3. Tap About Device (Tablet).

4. Tap Battery Use. The screen displays the items that are consuming the most battery power.

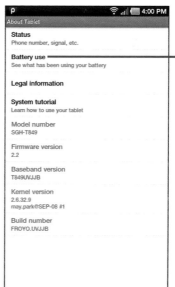

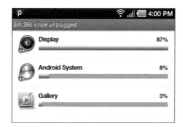

Monitoring Power Usage (Galaxy Tab 10")

On the Galaxy Tab 10", you can use the Battery Usage screen to see which of the apps you use consumes the most power, and then you can reduce the use of those apps. Your battery power savings are small, but if you're running low on power with no way to recharge, every little bit counts. Follow these directions to access the Battery Usage screen.

1. Tap the Apps icon on your Galaxy Tab from any home screen.

2. Tap Settings.

3. Tap About Tablet.

4. Tap Battery Use. The screen displays the items that are consuming the most battery power.

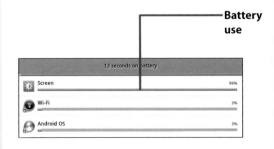

Battery use

Dim Screen Brightness

The high-quality touchscreen of the Galaxy Tab can consume plenty of battery power. The higher the brightness level set on your Galaxy Tab the more power the touchscreen uses. If you are viewing the screen in very bright conditions, you probably do not need a very high brightness setting. Consider dimming the screen to extend the battery life.

Adjust Screen Brightness (Galaxy Tab 7")

You can adjust the screen brightness for your 7" Tab by accessing the Settings menu. Follow these directions to dim the screen.

1. Press the Menu button on your Galaxy Tab from any home screen.

2. Tap Settings.

3. Tap Display Settings.

4. Tap Brightness to access the brightness controls.

5. Tap Automatic Brightness to deselect the settings. The brightness slider appears.

Automatic Brightness

When the Automatic Brightness setting is selected, your Tab uses sensors to determine your current light conditions and then adjusts the screen brightness automatically. In bright conditions, the screen is dimmed, and vice versa.

6. Slide the slider to the left to lower the brightness level.

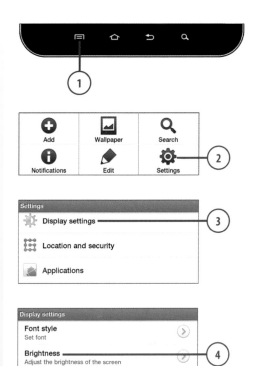

Adjust Screen Brightness (Galaxy Tab 10")

The Galaxy Tab 10" offers a quick way for you to access the brightness controls by providing quick settings in the notification panel. Follow these directions to dim the screen.

1. Tap in the far-right corner of the status bar.

2. Tap Auto in the Brightness field to deselect the Automatic Brightness setting. The brightness slider appears.

3. Slide the slider to the left to lower the brightness level. After you have made your adjustments, you can tap anywhere onscreen to hide the menus.

Automatic Brightness

When the Automatic Brightness setting is selected, your Tab uses sensors to determine your current light conditions and then adjusts the screen brightness automatically. In bright conditions, the screen is dimmed, and vice versa.

Utilize Sleep Mode

Your Galaxy Tab goes to sleep after a specified period of inactivity, but you don't have to wait for it to fall asleep, you can put it to sleep manually. When your Tab is awake, it consumes battery power. Press the sleep button on the side of your Tab when you have finished using the device to conserve battery power.

Conserve Power by Turning Off Wi-Fi

When the Wi-Fi antenna is activated on your Galaxy Tab, your device is incessantly looking for available Wi-Fi networks to join, which uses battery power. To see if Wi-Fi is turned on, check the status bar in the top-left corner of your Galaxy Tab for the Wi-Fi symbol. If you do not need a Wi-Fi connection, turn it off to conserve battery power. If you are not wandering and are using Wi-Fi in a single location, look for a power outlet and plug in.

Turn Off Wi-Fi (Galaxy Tab 7")

You can easily turn off Wi-Fi in the Notifications panel. Follow these directions.

1. Place your finger on the status bar and drag downward to reveal the Notifications panel.

2. If the Wi-Fi button at the top of the screen is green, Wi-Fi is turned on. Tap Wi-Fi to turn it off.

3. Place your finger at the bottom of the Notifications panel and drag upward to close the window.

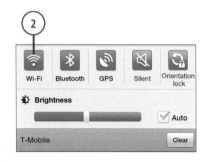

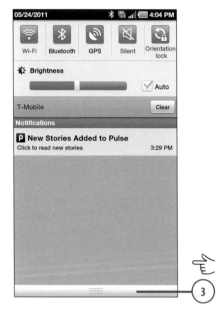

Turn Off Wi-Fi (Galaxy Tab 10")

Turn off Wi-Fi in the Settings options under Wireless Networks. Follow these directions to turn off Wi-Fi and help conserve some battery power.

1. Tap Apps from any home screen.

2. Tap Settings.

3. Tap Wi-Fi to turn off the setting.

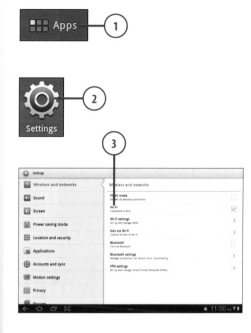

Conserve Power by Turning Off Bluetooth

When Bluetooth is activated on your Galaxy Tab, your device is constantly checking for other Bluetooth devices, which drains battery power. To see if Bluetooth is turned on, check the status bar in the top-left corner of your Galaxy Tab for the Bluetooth symbol. If you are not using a Bluetooth device, turn this function off. There are also security reasons why you should turn off Bluetooth when you are not using it, so get in the habit of turning Bluetooth off as soon as you finish using a wireless device with your Galaxy Tab. You can easily deactivate Bluetooth in the Notifications panel. Follow these directions.

Turn Off Bluetooth (Galaxy Tab 7")

You can quickly turn off Bluetooth in the Notifications panel located at the top of a home screen. Follow these directions to turn off Bluetooth.

1. Place your finger on the status bar and drag downward to reveal the Notifications panel.

2. If the Bluetooth button at the top of the screen is green, it is turned on. Tap Bluetooth to turn it off.

3. Place your finger at the bottom of the Notifications panel and drag upward to close the window.

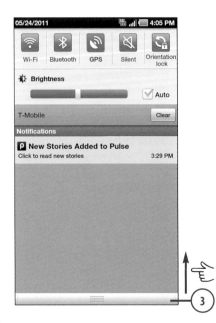

Turn Off Bluetooth (Galaxy Tab 10")

You can turn off Bluetooth in the Settings options under Wireless Networks. Follow these directions to turn off Bluetooth.

1. Tap Apps from any home screen.

2. Tap Settings.

3. Tap Bluetooth to turn off the setting.

Conserve Power by Turning Off Vibration Settings

As you have probably noticed, by default, your Galaxy Tab vibrates using a tiny motor whenever you tap a button. Deactivating this feature does not help you conserve a significant amount of battery power, but it saves you something, and that's better than nothing.

Turn Off Vibration Settings (Galaxy Tab 7")

You can set your Tab to not vibrate when you tap buttons from within the Settings options under the Sound category. Follow these directions to turn off the Vibrate setting.

1. Press the Menu button on your Galaxy Tab from any home screen.

2. Tap Settings.

3. Choose Sound settings.

4. Tap Vibrate.

5. Tap Never. The vibration setting
    has been deactivated.

Turn Off Vibration Settings (Galaxy Tab 10")

You can set your Tab's Vibrate setting
to Never from within the Settings
options under the Sound category.
Follow these directions to turn off
the Vibrate setting.

1. Tap Apps from any home screen.

2. Tap Settings.

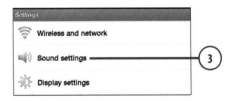

3. Tap the Sound category.

4. Tap Vibrate.

5. Tap Never.

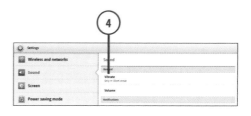

Solving Random Galaxy Tab Issues

The occasional hardware or software glitch happens to even the best of electronic devices. You might encounter an issue, although rare, where an app you are using freezes, a wireless device proves difficult to pair with your Galaxy Tab, the touchscreen becomes unresponsive, or landscape orientation is not available at all times. Fortunately, it is not very difficult to troubleshoot some of these issues. If you should happen to come across a problem that you can't solve yourself, there are plenty of channels for you to find technical support.

Difficulty Turning Your Tab On or Off

On rare occasions, you might find your Galaxy Tab stubborn when you try to turn it on or off. It might appear that the device has locked or become unresponsive. If this happens to you, hold the power button down for eight seconds to see if it responds. If this does not work, you might need to let your Tab sit for a few seconds before you again try holding the power button down for eight seconds.

Touchscreen Becomes Unresponsive

This tip assumes that your Galaxy Tab and any app you are using is responsive, but the touchscreen is not responding to your touch. If you attempt to use your Galaxy Tab touchscreen while wearing conventional gloves, it does not work. This can prove inconvenient on a very cold day, so you might want to consider a capacitive stylus for your Galaxy Tab.

Your Tab uses a capacitive touchscreen that holds an electrical charge. When you touch the screen with your bare finger, capacitive stylus, or special static-carrying gloves, it changes the amount of charge at the specific point of contact. In a nutshell, this is how the touchscreen interprets your taps, drags, and pinches.

The touchscreen might also be unresponsive to your touch if you happen to have a thin coat of film on your fingertips. So no sticky fingers, please.

Force Stop an App

Sometimes an app might get an attitude and become unruly. For example, an app might provide a warning screen saying that it is currently busy and is unresponsive, or it might give some other issue warning to convey that a problem exists. If an app is giving you problems, you can manually stop the app. After you stop the app, try launching it again to see if it works correctly. Follow these steps to force stop an unruly app.

Stop a Rogue App (Galaxy Tab 7")

You can force stop a problematic app from the Manage Applications option located under the Settings.

1. Tap Applications on a home screen.

2. Tap Settings.

3. Tap Applications.

4. Tap Manage Applications.

5. Tap Running at the top of the screen to view only the apps that are currently running.

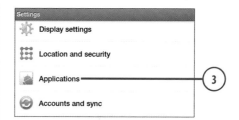

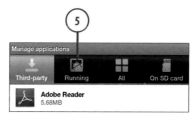

6. Tap the problem app.

7. Tap Force Stop. The app stops running.

Send an Email to the Developer

If you keep having problems with a particular app, perhaps it is an issue you should take up with the developer. Launch the Market app, and then press the Menu button on the Galaxy Tab. Choose My Apps. Tap the app in the list to access the developer's info and send an email alerting the developer to the problem(s) you are having.

Stop a Rogue App (Galaxy Tab 10")

You can stop a problematic app from running by accessing the Manage Applications option located under the settings. You can also report a problem regarding the app to the developer from the same Settings options. Follow these directions.

1. Tap Apps on a home screen.

2. Tap Settings.

3. Tap Applications.

4. Tap Manage Applications.

5. Tap Running at the top of the screen to view only the apps that are currently running.

6. Tap the problem app.

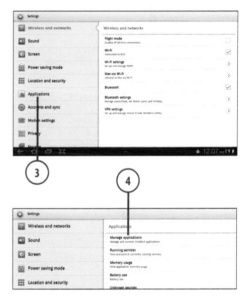

7. Tap Stop. The app stops running. Take note that you can tap the Report option to report a problem to the app's developer.

Battery Does Not Charge

If you find that your battery is not charging, first start with the power outlet. Is the outlet supplying power? Is the power strip turned on? Plug something else into the outlet to see if it works, or try another outlet.

Make sure that everything is connected properly. Is the adapter secure on both ends? If the outlet supplies power and the cables are connected properly, but the battery still does not charge, try another cable. If this does not solve the issue, your battery might be defective. Contact Samsung technical support. There is no way for you to remove the battery yourself.

Overheating

Overheating is rare, but if your Galaxy Tab becomes too hot and regularly turns itself off, you might need to replace the battery. You can tell if your Tab is getting too hot by holding it in your hands. Use caution.

Landscape Orientation Does Not Work

The orientation setting on your Galaxy Tab could be set so that your Tab stays in either portrait or landscape mode, regardless of how you hold the device. If your Tab no longer utilizes landscape orientation, first check the setting for screen orientation. For the 10" Tab, you need to go into the settings under Screen and ensure that the Auto-rotate screen option is enabled. A green check mark next to this setting means that it is enabled.

Check the Orientation Lock Button (Galaxy Tab 7")

The 7" Tab has an Orientation Lock button in the Notifications panel. The lock feature needs to be off for the screen to adjust to how you are holding your device. Follow these directions to confirm that the Orientation lock is turned off.

1. Place your finger on the status bar and drag down to reveal the Notifications panel.

2. If the Orientation lock button at the top of the screen is green, it is turned on. Tap Orientation lock to turn it off.

3. Place your finger at the bottom of the Notifications panel and drag up to close the window.

Landscape Orientation and Apps

Not every app on the Android Market was developed to take advantage of the landscape orientation of your Galaxy Tab. If you notice this issue while using an app, close the app, and then see whether your Tab can situate itself in landscape orientation.

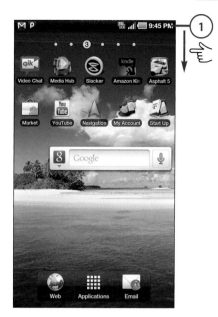

Check the Orientation Lock Button (Galaxy Tab 10")

The 10" Tab has an Autorotate setting that must be selected for the screen to adjust from portrait to landscape mode, depending on how you hold the device. You can easily confirm that the Autorotate setting is selected from the Settings menu.

1. Tap Apps on any home screen.

2. Tap Settings.

3. Tap Screen.

4. Locate the Autorotate Screen setting and confirm that there is a green check mark in the field. If a green check mark is not present, tap the field to activate the setting. Your Galaxy Tab screen should now adjust to the orientation in which you hold the device.

Troubleshooting Wi-Fi Accessibility Problems

Your Galaxy Tab provides you the convenience and flexibility of wireless Internet access via Wi-Fi connectivity. Along with this convenience and flexibility comes the potential for connectivity issues regarding wireless networks. If you are unable to access a Wi-Fi network, or if your connection is sporadic, there are some troubleshooting tips you can use to pinpoint basic accessibility options.

Make Sure Wi-Fi Is Activated

First and foremost, make sure that the Wi-Fi antennae is on. You can determine this by looking in the status bar at the bottom of your Galaxy Tab to see whether the Wi-Fi icon is visible. If it is not on, you can place your finger on the status bar on your 7" Galaxy Tab and drag down the Notifications panel, and then tap the Wi-Fi button at the top of the screen to activate Wi-Fi. If you have the 10" Tab, you can tap in the Notifications panel in the lower-right corner of the screen, and then tap the Settings icon. Tap the Wi-Fi option to activate the setting.

Wi-Fi Antennae, Galaxy Tab 7"

Wi-Fi Antennae, Galaxy Tab 10"

Check Your Range

If Wi-Fi is activated on your Galaxy Tab and you still cannot connect, take note of how far away you are from the Wi-Fi access point. You can be only 115 feet from a Wi-Fi access point before the signal becomes weak or drops altogether. Structures such as walls with lots of electronics can also impede a Wi-Fi signal. Make sure you are close to the access point or turn on the access point's range booster, if it has one, to improve your connection.

Reset Your Router
The issue might not be your distance from the Wi-Fi access point, a signal-impeding barrier, or your Galaxy Tab. As a last resort, you might need to reset the router. After you reset your router, you have to set up your network again from the ground up.

Reset the Galaxy Tab Software

If all else fails and your technical problems still persist, as a last ditch effort, you might need to reset the Galaxy Tab software. Resetting your Galaxy Tab software restores your Tab to the factory defaults, just like when you took it out of the box for the first time. Consider contacting support before you reset your Tab, but if you must, follow these directions to reset the device.

Reset Your Tab (Galaxy Tab 7")

You can reset your tab from the Privacy options located in the Settings. Consider resetting your Tab as a last effort for solving persistent performance issues.

1. Press the Menu button on your Galaxy Tab from any home screen.

2. Tap Settings.

3. Tap Privacy.

4. Choose Factory Data Reset.

5. Tap the Reset Tablet button.

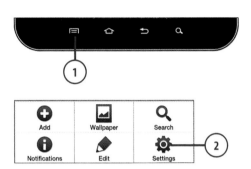

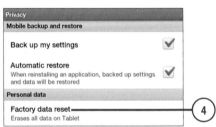

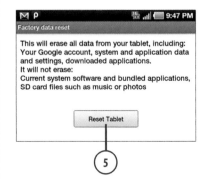

6. Tap the Erase Everything button to confirm. Your Tab is returned to its factory state.

Reset Your Tab (Galaxy Tab 10")

You can reset your tab from the Privacy options located in the settings. Consider resetting your Tab as a last effort for solving persistent performance issues.

1. Tap Apps from any home screen.

2. Tap Settings.

3. Tap Privacy.

4. Choose Factory Data Reset.

5. Tap the Reset Tablet button.

6. Tap the Erase Everything button to confirm. Your Tab is returned to its factory state.

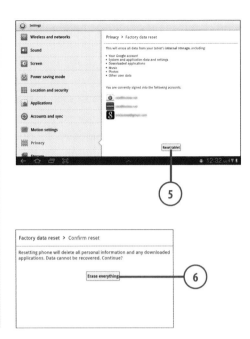

Getting Technical Help

There are many outlets available where you can find help if you run across a Galaxy Tab technical problem that you can't seem to beat. Although limited, the user's manual is a good place to start. You can download the correct manual for your Galaxy Tab model online, in the form of a PDF, and scan the table of contents or perform word searches in the document pertaining to your problem. In most user manual PDFs, topics in the Table of Contents are often linked to the section they pertain to within the document, so when you find what you are looking for, click the topic and jump to the page.

Websites and Galaxy Tab forums are also a great way for you to get support for your device. Type a search phrase, such as "Galaxy Tab Google Calendar sync problem," into Google. Chances are there are plenty of people who are experiencing the same issue. Doing some online research of your own could save you a few minutes on the telephone with technical support and help you solve your problem more quickly.

Contact Your Cellular Provider or Samsung

Your cellular provider and Samsung are great resources for getting help with technical issues with your Galaxy Tab. Before you call, you'll need to have your device's phone number and (or) model number so that you can give it to the technical support representative.

Locate Tab Phone Number and Model Number (Galaxy Tab 7")

Follow these directions to locate your Galaxy Tab's phone number and model number. It is important to note that Wi-Fi only Tabs do not have telephone numbers associated with them.

1. Press the Menu button from any home screen emulator.

2. Tap Settings.

3. Tap About Tablet.

4. Tap Status. Your Tab's number is located in the field named Phone Number.

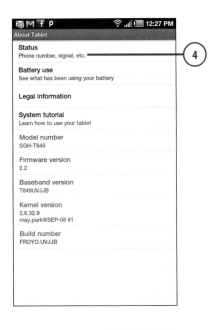

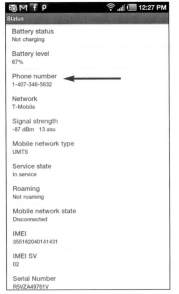

Locate Tab Model Number (Galaxy Tab 10")

No telephone number is associated with a Wi-Fi only Tab. Follow these directions to locate your Galaxy Tab's model number.

1. Tap Apps from any home screen.

2. Tap Settings.

3. Tap About Tablet. Your Galaxy Tab's information appears to the right of the screen.

Support Contact Information

Carrier	Phone	Website
AT&T	(800) 331-0500	http://www.wireless.att.com/support
Sprint	(800) 639-6111	http://support.sprint.com
T-Mobile	(800) 937-8997	http://support.t-mobile.com
US Cellular	(800) 944-9400	http://www.uscellular.com/support
Verizon	(800) 922-0204	http://support.vzw.com
Samsung	(800) 987-4357	http://www.samsung.com/us/support/

Index

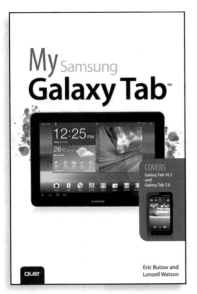

FREE Online Edition

Your purchase of **My Samsung Galaxy Tab** includes access to a free online edition for 45 days through the Safari Books Online subscription service. Nearly every Que book is available online through Safari Books Online, along with more than 5,000 other technical books and videos from publishers such as Addison-Wesley Professional, Cisco Press, Exam Cram, IBM Press, O'Reilly, Prentice Hall, and Sams.

SAFARI BOOKS ONLINE allows you to search for a specific answer, cut and paste code, download chapters, and stay current with emerging technologies.

Activate your FREE Online Edition at www.informit.com/safarifree

> **STEP 1:** Enter the coupon code: PAIJPXA.

> **STEP 2:** New Safari users, complete the brief registration form.
> Safari subscribers, just log in.

If you have difficulty registering on Safari or accessing the online edition, please e-mail customer-service@safaribooksonline.com